Technology Business Management:
The Four Value Conversations CIOs Must Have With Their Businesses

Todd Tucker

 TBM COUNCIL

What Others Are Saying About Technology Business Management

" Forget big data, social, mobile, and cloud. The real change in the past decade is that technology is no longer a business enabler; it _IS_ the business. When your business is on the line and your function is front and center, you need a method and system born in technology and designed for technology leaders. TBM is that method and system, and this book is the definitive manual for the management system of the modern technology-based enterprise."

> — Ralph Loura
> Global CTO
> Rodan + Fields

" Every CIO and finance leader is challenged to ensure their budget and resources are driving efficiency and creating value for the business. Increasingly, the oversight of those resources and governance of IT is both within and outside the traditional IT structure. TBM helps connect the supply and demand of IT, making transparent the consumption of IT."

> — Jim DuBois
> Corporate Vice President and CIO
> Microsoft Corporation

" Technology Business Management (TBM) provides forward-looking information to drive better decisions and root-cause analytics to improve performance. As revealed in this book, TBM is a discipline for economic added-value, while accounting is focused on financial reporting and classification. In a world where technology is essential to business success, TBM is similarly essential to shareholder value, market share gains, and business efficiency."

> — Carl Stumpf
> Former Managing Director and Technology Controller
> CME Group

Contents

Figures

Foreword

No matter how long you've been a technology leader, how many people you employ, or the industry you serve, you share common challenges with your peers: How do you balance the infinite demand for IT services and innovation with your finite supply of resources? How do you prioritize investments? How do you engage your business partners using a language they understand? How do you organize your team to deliver the most value? Technology Business Management — or TBM — provides the framework to overcome these challenges.

The four of us have been leading IT organizations for nearly 40 years combined. Until we discovered TBM, we were on our own in determining how to manage the *business of technology*. This situation had become unacceptable. Our role as IT leaders had fundamentally changed, requiring new skills and better business management systems. More than ever before, our businesses were looking to us to provide competitive advantage. Thus, we needed a best-practice approach to improving value. TBM would provide that approach.

TBM correlates data from finance, IT operations, and the lines of business. It reveals facts about the cost, consumption, and quality of what we deliver. By providing these facts along with a framework for decision-making and business outcomes, TBM helps us:

- enable better prioritization of our IT investments
- optimize the cost of running the business and free up capital for new capabilities
- accelerate decisions through the use of facts and analytics
- create more balanced discussions with our business partners around cost, performance, risk, and value

The last point above should not be underestimated. Too often business executives view the IT *department* as an obstacle to their mission. This problem does not rest entirely on the shoulders of IT. Many IT leaders and their business partners fail to *collaborate* effectively on tough decisions, resulting in a we-versus-they mentality and impeding value generation. The two groups don't *trust* one another, so collaboration is replaced by assumptions about cost (i.e., "IT costs too much"), capacity (i.e., "IT is the department of *NO*") and competence (i.e., "IT doesn't understand our business"). In our experience, four very solvable issues stand in the way of collaboration and trust: unclear value, perceived uncontrolled cost, disconnected planning, and lack of agility.

TBM directly addresses these issues. By putting costs into the context of the services and revealing how business consumption drives those costs, TBM helps show value for the money. By enabling IT leaders to benchmark costs and drive down unit costs, TBM helps demonstrate cost control. By connecting business demand to IT resource requirements, TBM helps IT leaders plan in lockstep with their business. And by providing more effective levers for managing IT supply and demand, TBM helps the business respond faster to new threats and opportunities.

TBM is both pragmatic and transformational. Its core elements, such as transparency, benchmarking, billing, and planning, have helped IT leaders optimize costs, rationalize application portfolios, accelerate service management, and execute cloud-first strategies. But most importantly, TBM has helped hundreds of CIOs, including the four of us, improve and communicate value to our business partners.

This book is the handbook for educating IT executives, finance leaders and other stakeholders on the essential components of the TBM framework. It provides insights into organizational considerations, how to create a performance-based culture, and most importantly business outcomes. By reading this book, you'll learn the lessons garnered from hundreds of interviews with CIOs, CTOs, CFOs and other business-savvy technology leaders, case studies in TBM from leading enterprises, plus the contributions of the TBM Council's founder, partners, and advisors.

Imagine a world where your business partners look to IT to drive competitive advantage and understand how to optimize value from their IT investments. That's the world TBM makes possible.

What makes TBM different from so many other approaches is that it was built from real-world experiences and hard work. It has not been an academic exercise. The executives who have used TBM have tackled big challenges around innovation, adopting the cloud, optimizing infrastructures, orienting to service delivery, rationalizing portfolios, and more. This book shares that knowledge.

Debra Bailey
CIO, Nationwide Building Society

Mike Brown
IT Vice President, ExxonMobil

Tom Murphy
University CIO, University of Pennsylvania

Jim Scholefield
Global CIO, Nike

TBM Council Board of Directors

The TBM Council is governed by a Board of mostly enterprise CIOs and other heads of technology. The current and emeritus board members are:

- Brian Adams, CIO, WorleyParsons

- Debra Bailey, CIO, Nationwide Building Society

- Mike Benson*, EVP & CIO, DIRECTV

- Mike Brady, Global CTO, AIG

- Mike Brown, IT Vice President, ExxonMobil

- John Bruno, CIO, Aon

- Tim Campos*, CIO, Facebook

- Anil Cheriyan, EVP & CIO, SunTrust Banks

- Jim DuBois, CIO, Microsoft

- Christopher Furst, EVP & CIO, Univision Communications

- Larry Godec, SVP & CIO, First American Financial

- Sunny Gupta, CEO, Apptio

- Guillermo Diaz, SVP & CIO, Cisco

- Rebecca Jacoby*, SVP Operations, Cisco

- Bill Krivoshik*, CTO, Kroll

- James LaPlaine, CIO, AOL

- Ralph Loura, Global CTO, Rodan + Fields

- Greg Morrison, SVP & CIO, Cox Enterprises

- Tom Murphy, University CIO, University of Pennsylvania

- Michael Neff, CIO, RWE

- Jim Scholefield, Global CIO, Nike

- Tony Scott*, U.S. CIO

- Phuong Tram, CIO, DuPont

- Robert Webb*, Chief Information and Technology Officer, Etihad Aviation Group

- George Westerman**, Research Scientist, MIT Initiative on the Digital Economy

- Erez Yarkoni*, CIO & Head of Cloud BU, Telstra

- Carol Zierhoffer*, Principal VP and CIO, Bechtel Corporation

 * *Emeritus Board Members*   ** *Academic Advisor*

To learn more about the TBM Council, find the current list of board members, or become a member, please go to www.TBMCouncil.org.

Acknowledgments

Many people gave their time and expertise to building this body of knowledge by sharing the lessons, disciplines, and best practices they have gained during their successful careers. With their support, this book was built upon real-world experiences and practice, not theory. I have stood on the shoulders of these giants.

I would like to thank first our board of directors and those emeritus directors who have paved the way by not only adopting Technology Business Management (TBM) within their enterprises but also guiding the Council and our work. I owe the following directors a particular debt of gratitude for spending extra time with me to share their points of view and, in some cases, detailed case studies: Rebecca Jacoby, Larry Godec, Sunny Gupta, Mike Brown, Ralph Loura, Tom Murphy, Debra Bailey, Mike Brady, Mike Benson, Guillermo Diaz, Greg Morrison, Mike Dreyer, Rob Webb, and James LaPlaine. Thank you, George Westerman, for your guidance, review, and feedback during the writing and editing process as well.

Other TBM leaders, some of whom have served as principal members of the TBM Council, have been especially generous with their time and expertise. They've given sweat, blood, and tears as the pioneers in this discipline. Thank you all: Arthur Borges, Dan Cavey, Jodi Hunter, John Jarvis, Pete Letizia, Chris Levitt, Mareida MacKenna, Chuck Niethold, Randall Pfeifer, Jon Sober, Lisa Stalter, Carl Stumpf, Lance Warner, Suzette Unger, Ulka Wilson, and Donna Woodruff.

Many more principal members helped shape the TBM framework and other ideas in the book through workshops, presentations, teleconference calls, and direct input: Drew Adam, Steve Adams, Caroline Arnold, Chris Beaudin, Tony Bishop, Susan Blew, Kevin Brown, Khalid Chaudhary, Monica Cirillo, Vincent DiGiovanni, John Donnarumma, Scott Duquette, Tony Farah, Julie Flaschenriem, Chris Gibbons, Kate Grasman, Jerry Hermes, Majid Iqbal, Matt Kellerhals, Cason Lee, Martin Lieberman, Joel Manfredo, Kim Manigault, Diana

McKenzie, Greg Panik, Joe Rafter, Mike Roberts, Clark Robinson, Kevin Salmon, Richard Spalding, Josh Sparaga, and Matt Temple.

To the chairpersons and leaders of our workgroups over the past couple of years — Shohreh Abedi, Mike Brady, Mike Dreyer, Jim Green, Bill Krivoshik, Dean Nelson, Alan Peacock, Colin Scott, Carl Stumpf, and Robert Webb — thank you for sharing your leadership and wisdom. You helped us come together to better understand how TBM works in a variety of vertical industries and disciplines.

A special thanks to our partners and sponsors over the years, especially the following professionals with whom my team has had the honor of collaborating: Steve Hall, Nigel Hughes, Korey Bernard, Alex-Paul Manders, and Scott Feuless at ISG; Steve Bates, Denis Berry, Demetrios Mahramas, Gary Plotkin, Mark Tackley-Goodman, and Jason Byrd of KPMG; Leandro Santos, Himanshu Agarwal, Giovanni Maglia, Dhruv Pilania, and Ritesh Agarwal of McKinsey & Company; Mitchell Bostelman, Kevin Corcoran, and Brian Toba with Deloitte; Kathleen Flynn and Doug Lane of Capgemini Government Solutions; Paul Webb and Tamara Alairys of EY; Mark Larsen, Dain Belyeu, Paul Gvoth, and Brian Wissinger of Cask LLC.

As a data-driven discipline, TBM would not be a reality without applied research and innovation. For that, I have mostly the people at Apptio to thank. In particular, the following current and former employees have significantly contributed to my understanding of the technology, taxonomy, data, metrics, reports, and use cases that are essential to TBM: Phil Alfano, Ben Allard, Rahul Auradkar, Jack Bischof, Suzanne Chartol, Andrew DeMaio, Michel Feaster, Genesa Garcia, Phil Gormley, Ken Haniu, Ed Hayman, Mark Jones, Venky Krishnan, Ted Kummert, Jesse Lee, Stuart Meredith, Joe Mitchell, Patchen Noelke, John Novak, Joe Plantenberg, Allen Stanley, Kevin Teets, and Khek Teh.

The TBM Council is, if nothing else, a virtual campfire for like-minded business, IT, and finance leaders to sit around and tell their stories. This book shares several such stories, but many more have been told through our conferences, summits, and our annual awards program.

The awards program elicited many of the success stories and lessons shared in this book and wouldn't have been possible without the hard work of Maria Galindo, Dave Wilt, Renee Boucher Ferguson, and Ronen Kadosh. The conference and summits are put on by a very talented team led by Josh Harbert, Michelle Speirs, Paula Darvell, and Eileen Wade. Thank you all.

Thank you to the following people who contributed directly to delivering this book. My contributing editor, Allen Bernard, worked tirelessly with me weekly and oftentimes daily for nearly ten months, helping me distill mountains of content and ideas into a cohesive story. Brenda Ziegler, Phil Gormley, Linda Kleinschmidt, Sarah Vreugdenhil, Jen Houston, and Chris Davidson reviewed and edited copy, helping correct the not-uncommon-enough grammar and spelling mistakes and suggesting more substantive improvements to content. Ron Rieneckert led the production of the book, while Chris Straehla provided many rounds of beautiful cover and graphic options.

To my good friend, creative genius, and mentor, Chris Pick, thank you for making the book a priority of the TBM Council and entrusting me to share these ideas and stories. You made the book possible through your vision for how it fits into our overall strategy for membership, standards, education, and certification. Furthermore, the Council and our members benefit from your unmatched ability to "enlarge the tent." Keep pushing the limits.

Last but certainly not the least, I thank those who make me the most happy. To Anna, Mary, Sela, and Noah — my young musicians, aspiring writers, gamers, martial artists, and students extraordinaire, and to Roxy, my clan chieftain who keeps everyone in order while I play road warrior or home-office recluse: I couldn't do this without your support.

With my sincere gratitude,

Todd

Introduction:
Be the CEO of Your Technology Business

Try to imagine your business running without its enterprise resource management system in place. Your CEO would lack a handle on the full state of the enterprise, an essential tool for making informed decisions. Line managers might have their own systems for managing their own teams and resources, but they would fail to see how their decisions impacted enterprise goals overall. It's not that work wouldn't get done; it's that the CEO would lack an important command and control capability; so value wouldn't be optimized.

As an IT leader, hopefully you've not let this scenario happen. Instead, you've given your business partners[1] a system for managing the business as a whole and not just its parts. Your CEO and CFO use that system to translate corporate goals into business unit objectives and incentivize their managers to meet them. This system, denominated in money, connects the top of your business with all its underlying parts. It is an indispensable management tool.

Now imagine you're the CEO of your own technology business. Your revenues come as operating funds from your business; you receive capital to buy or build assets; and you employ people, assets, and outside services to deliver value to your business partners. What you do is no small matter. If your budget is in the tens of millions of dollars, you command more resources than many Silicon Valley CEOs; if it's more than a hundred million dollars, your business is bigger than most B2B SaaS companies on the planet.[2]

---

[1] We use the term "business partners" to mean your internal customers and stakeholders. Alternatively, we use "customers" to mean the customers of your business that pay for its products and services.

[2] According to a report by PwC in 2014, only 35 of the largest 100 software companies had SaaS revenues of $100 million or more. (See http://www.pwc.com/globalsoftware100)

Now consider the systems you are using to manage enterprise value. As the CEO, are you able to connect the top of your business all the way down to your people, technologies, and vendor services? Can you show the corporate impact of the decisions you and your people make? Do you have a system of incentives that drives good business decisions (and not just good technology decisions)? If your technology department is like many others, probably you do not.

Instead, you have tools for managing the parts, but not the whole. Your financial information treats IT as an expense center. You know the overall cost of IT, but you can't easily connect that cost with the value that your department provides. You have few facts available to discuss value, consumption, and cost with your business partners. Worse still, you can't optimize your resources or shape business demand to create the most value for the money being spent. Does this scenario sound familiar?

In today's digitally-driven business world, this scenario is a dangerous situation. Your company needs so much from you, and yet your resources are very limited — your budget is tight, talent is scarce, and the time horizon you're given to effect change is constantly shrinking. To give your firm the power to compete, you have little room for error.

Consider this as well: the opportunity cost of an inefficient, misaligned technology department is much greater than its actual costs. Wasting precious resources comes at the expense of creating new revenue streams, accelerating a new business model, improving customer service, or reducing business costs. Mistakes in allocating your resources are compounded by both time and the operating leverage of IT. For a typical billion dollar company, misspending just 3 percent of its IT resources each year can reduce revenues in Year 5 by more than $117 million![3]

---

[3] Assuming a modest 15% return on investment over a five-year payback period, a 10% operating margin rate, and IT spending at 4% of total revenues. In addition to lower revenues, the loss in operating margin over the same five years would be greater than $27 million.

Optimizing value depends on making tradeoffs to achieve the right cost for performance, portfolio alignment, innovation, and agility. Should you increase capacity at an extra cost to reduce risk? Where can you shift resources from one service to another to accelerate corporate growth? How can you reduce portfolio complexity to create better economies of scale? How can you better fund an innovation program? Should you invest more in the cloud to improve agility? These are the kinds of tradeoffs you need to make, and just like tuning a modern car engine (e.g., more horsepower *or* higher fuel economy?), you need instrumentation and data to optimize value.

A great example of this optimization comes from eBay. Most people view eBay as an auction company, but in reality they are a technology-driven global commerce company with over 800 million listings at any given second. eBay competes in a diverse array of retail spaces, from electronics, fashion, and automotive to online tickets to classified ads. eBay's markets are highly competitive as both larger (e.g., Amazon, Alibaba, Walmart) and smaller (e.g., SeatGeek, Craigslist) competitors have entered the firm's core spaces. To maintain margins, customer engagement is essential and speed, agility, service, and trust are paramount.

Dean Nelson leads eBay's Global Foundation Services, the infrastructure driving the digital engine that connects over 25 million sellers with nearly 160 million active buyers across 190 markets.[4] In 2011, Nelson's team was struggling to articulate the value of eBay's infrastructure to their business leaders. It's not that they didn't know their digital engine was essential to their business; it's that they couldn't tell if they were spending too much, too little, or the right amount on it. Was their approach the right one? Could they get what they needed cheaper somewhere else? Most importantly, could infrastructure, which represents a large capital investment for eBay, be a competitive weapon?

---

[4] "Who We Are." eBay, Inc. n.d., n.pag., Web. 28 Feb. 2016. https://www.ebayinc.com/our-company/who-we-are/

To answer these questions, Nelson knew he had to shift from a technology discussion to a business discussion with his business partners: "We had this bottom-up approach and it never got us anywhere. You had so many engineering metrics, so many opinions… but nothing was digestible by an executive." In other words, his team spoke in bits, bytes, and watts, while the business spoke in listings, users, and revenue.

Nelson's team decided to change the language they used with the business. "We looked at what types of metrics our business execs cared about — performance, cost, environmental impact, and revenue," said Nelson. "We then set up a structure to connect those four dimensions to our infrastructure cost and performance. Now, if we want different business results, we can show what we are providing under the hood to deliver them."

Nelson says this approach provides a "miles per gallon" measurement for his digital engine. It makes an end-to-end connection between what eBay's customers do and the fundamental business metrics that his team influences, such as transactions per kilowatt hour, cost per transaction, and CO_2e[5] per transaction.

These metrics also provide several benefits:

- They communicate what value eBay's digital engine provides and how much that costs *in business terms.*

- They connect business demand to infrastructure cost and utilization, so eBay can plan better.

- They provide more useful measures of efficiency, focusing on per-unit measures, so eBay can understand the relationship between the volumes it processes and its costs and resources consumed.

---

[5] Equivalent carbon dioxide is a measure "for describing how much global warming a given type and amount of greenhouse gas may cause, using the functionally equivalent amount or concentration of carbon dioxide (CO2) as the reference." See: "Carbon Dioxide Equivalent." Wikipedia. Wikimedia Foundation, 30 Mar. 2016. Web. 10 Apr. 2016.

- They demonstrate environmental stewardship at a *business* level, going beyond simple data center efficiency metrics like power usage effectiveness (PUE) to show emission equivalents per transaction.

However, the simplicity of these metrics belies the power of the underlying model that makes them possible. Nelson's approach is data driven, relying on many of those underlying engineering metrics that weren't relevant to his business partners. With their data-driven model, Nelson's team, along with application owners and architects, are using business-connected metrics to tune their digital engine.

Figure Intro-1: eBay's dashboard shows performance, cost, environment, and revenue KPIs for its digital engine

For example, eBay's model provides transparency into the infrastructure consumption and cost of its different business units. The team can connect the infrastructure use of any group (e.g., search, analytics, cloud, development) or customer vertical (e.g., electronics, automotive, electronics, garden) to the revenue that is generated. They also see how new marketing programs drive increases in infrastructure consumption and cost. They then use these insights to refine their engine's cost for performance.

These capabilities are useful for managing changes, too. With transaction volumes like eBay's, simple changes to application code can lead to significant increases in infrastructure costs. When the team saw a mismatch in workloads to usage, they worked with the cloud team to do a simple code change that would save $750,000 in operating expenses, avoid $2.6 million in capital expenditures while giving back a megawatt of power.

eBay has an enterprise management system for their technology business, i.e., eBay's digital engine. This system makes tradeoffs clear and accelerates decisions. It provides a business-linked dashboard, so business and technology leaders can optimize the engine and create the best balance of cost, risk, and performance. Yet don't assume this system is unique to online Silicon Valley businesses like eBay: It has been implemented by hundreds of CIOs, CTOs, VPs, and GMs around the world at banks, insurance companies, hospitals, manufacturers, media companies, government agencies, not-for-profits, and many more.

All these executives have several things in common. They each spend tens of millions of dollars or more each year on information technology. They understand the power of data-driven decision-making. They recognize that both supply and demand must be managed. They focus on continuous improvement, and transformation of their teams and their businesses is paramount.

However, the similarities end there. Some of these executives come from technology backgrounds, and some don't. Some are responsible for infrastructure services, while others own the gamut of IT services and applications, and still others own shared services such as back-office operations. Some of these come from early adopter organizations; others from fast followers and yet others from highly cautious firms.

This system of people, data, tools, and processes that eBay has employed has a name — Technology Business Management — a name given to it by the Council of CIOs that were among its earliest adopters.

The name reflects what they know to be true, specifically, that each must manage (and be the CEO) of his or her technology business.

This book will show you how these technology business *chief executives* use Technology Business Management (TBM) to optimize the value they deliver. You'll learn how TBM exploits the power of transparency to inform better decisions (Chapter 1). You'll discover the tools of TBM (Chapter 2), including a framework of organizational principles, management disciplines, value conversations, and maturity hallmarks that take the mystery out of TBM.

We'll then walk through the TBM framework component by component (Chapters 3 through 10) to give you a better understanding of each component, including how they're applied at companies like AOL, Cisco, Cox Enterprises, First American, Nationwide Building Society, and, of course, eBay. Capping the discussion off (Chapter 11), we'll share a bit about where many enterprising executives are now going with TBM — *beyond* IT — before wrapping up with how you can get started (Chapter 12).

This book was written for IT leaders, especially CIOs and CTOs, based on the journeys that many other successful IT leaders have taken and shared over the past couple of years. Their stories involve IT finance, planning and strategy, architecture, portfolio management, service management, and TBM leaders; others acting in these roles will benefit from the lessons we share here.

Of all the lessons you'll learn, the most important was shared by First American Financial Corporation's CIO, Larry Godec. When asked how important TBM is for today's CIO, he replied, "If you don't do it, your successor will. The stakes are that high."

There has never been a better time to become the CEO of your technology business than today.

Chapter 1:
The Business Revolution in IT

Technology Business Management (TBM) is a value-management framework instituted by CIOs, CTOs, and other technology leaders. Founded on transparency of costs, consumption, and performance, TBM gives technology leaders and their business partners the facts they need to collaborate on business-aligned decisions. Those decisions span supply and demand to enable the financial and performance tradeoffs that are necessary to optimize run-the-business spending and accelerate business change. The framework is backed by a community of CIOs, CTOs, and other business leaders on the Technology Business Management Council.

While TBM applies common business management practices to IT — ones that have defined the modern, data-driven enterprise — it also represents nothing less than a *business revolution* in IT. As Brian Adams, CIO of WorleyParsons put it, "TBM represents the first real change to the way IT is managed that's occurred during my 25-year career. Everything else has been evolutionary; TBM is revolutionary." Adams's viewpoint and his passion for TBM have been shaped by his somewhat unique perspective. His career actually spans roles far beyond IT, including CFO, strategy and development, marketing, product quality, and customer satisfaction.

IT is not the first domain to undergo a similar revolution. In the 1970s and the 1980s, manufacturers implemented a data-driven approach to optimize their supply chains from procurement through production. For the first time, they used technology to connect supply to demand, in turn reducing inventories, cutting production times, and improving margins. Material requirements planning (MRP), as this method was known, led to new manufacturing techniques, such as just-in-time (JIT) inventories and total quality management (TQM). MRP was a game changer, and it gave birth to today's enterprise resource planning (ERP) software.

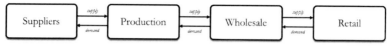

*Figure 1-1: Applying MRP and ERP, manufacturers use
technology and data to manage their supply chains*

More recently, marketing departments have made similar changes. Just a decade ago, they were led by brand-savvy, creative leaders who made only gut-check decisions based on a knowledge of their products, buyers, and competitors. Marketing was a battle of wits, not data. Now, many chief marketing officers (CMOs) apply data to every aspect of their discipline. Using marketing automation tools and analytics, CMOs are working hard to connect every part of the marketing supply chain from website inquiries to qualified leads to active opportunities to closed deals. Many CMOs understand the conversion rates and costs at each stage of this supply chain, which they call the revenue engine. They continuously optimize that engine using data. Marketing is today quickly becoming as much science as it is art.

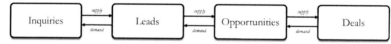

*Figure 1-2: With marketing automation and customer relationship management (CRM), CMOs use
data to manage and tune their revenue engines to improve corporate returns*

It works the other way around too. By measuring conversion rates, CMOs now understand the total cost of generating a single deal, what they call their customer acquisition cost. They use these facts to create a practical plan and a defensible budget. If the business needs 20 more transactions (deals) next year, it will need to fund a sufficient number of inquiries and leads at a known (historical) cost. The CMO's budget request is now formulated on facts and figures, not educated guesses or long-held assumptions.

Now it's your turn. IT must use facts to answer important questions about its own supply chain: How are your resources (money, people, and time) spent to deliver towers of infrastructure and other technologies? How are those resources used to deliver projects? How are your towers cobbled together into applications and services? How are those apps and services consumed by your business partners to generate revenue and manage costs? If you can make these connections, you can make decisions that improve efficiency, grow return on capital, and add business value. Further, you can change the conversations you have with your business partners.

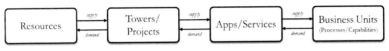

Figure 1-3: With TBM, CIOs manage the supply and demand of IT

As with the marketing supply chain, you can look at yours in reverse. You can see precisely how business demand drives the cost of your apps and services, and in turn, you can identify the consumption of infrastructure towers and resources. This is powerful information. Not only does it help you create a financial plan based on how resources are actually allocated and consumed, it connects everything your people do to business outcomes.[6]

It is no coincidence that the development of TBM was influenced by someone who understands firsthand the challenges of managing supply and demand. Rebecca Jacoby, SVP of Operations at Cisco, started her career in manufacturing and supply chain roles, and at one point she was responsible for the global consolidation of Cisco's supply chain. After becoming CIO in 2006, she advocated a management approach that addressed both the supply of and the demand for IT. For Jacoby, this went beyond the supply-chain management for only IT. Instead, it would fundamentally change the conversations that she and her team were having with their business partners.

"At Cisco, we recognized that in order to drive business value and innovation, we had to become a competitive provider of IT services. This meant, among other things, that we had to change the very conversations we were having internally and with our business partners. Our conversations

---

[6] Conversely, connecting IT supply with business demand lifts the veil on things you still deliver that no longer support any business outcome at all.

and our vocabulary needed to move beyond technologies, SLAs, and projects, to discussions about the tradeoffs needed to balance cost, quality, and value. Only in doing so could we free up resources for business growth and strategic execution. These tradeoffs are at the core of Technology Business Management." — Rebecca Jacoby[7]

Jacoby went so far as to define those value conversations by setting standards for them. They included strategy alignments, IT portfolio planning, architectural reviews, and quarterly value discussions with stakeholders. They centered on value considerations — scope, source, architecture, quality of service, time to capability, risk — all balanced by a new dimension: cost. The result allowed her to align business and IT plans more closely, shape the portfolio of applications and services to meet the business's needs better, tweak their technology stack to increase performance (even while reducing costs), and shape demand by putting a price tag on consumption. Now, as Chief Operating Officer, Jacoby is putting these practices to work beyond IT.[8]

Still, it's not just former CFOs and supply chain leaders who are shaping TBM. Many CIOs who have spent a majority of their careers in IT also are putting their mark on TBM. Larry Godec has spent the majority of his career working in various IT roles — much of it as the CIO of First American, a leading provider of title insurance, settlement services, and risk solutions for real estate transactions.

In 2012, with the housing market starting to recover, Godec needed to shift his IT department to respond to the demands of a growing business. Godec recalls in great detail precisely when his TBM journey began — a budget meeting with his CEO Dennis Gilmore. "Dennis said, 'We're going to focus on growth.' He told me I needed to know where

---

[7] Jacoby, Rebecca. Phone interview. 10 Apr. 2012.
[8] More on applying TBM practices beyond IT, including Cisco's experience, in chapter 11.

we should be investing in customer-facing technology, because that's what the business will need to compete."[9]

However, with a majority of his budget dedicated to supporting the existing IT estate, Godec needed to figure out how to shift resources quickly without putting the business at risk. He needed to see his resources in business terms, so he could collaborate with his CEO, CFO, and his line-of-business leaders on where to make the changes.

In a stroke of good timing, Godec heard what he needed to hear at a presentation by Tony Scott, then the CIO of Microsoft. "I was at Microsoft for a briefing by Tony when he showed this dashboard I had never seen. For the first time, I saw someone who put IT costs, resources, and investments into terms I could easily explain — by the applications and technologies that the business was using."

Godec now saw the way to put everything he did into business terms. Godec's first pass at TBM helped him create a simple portfolio view of the IT-business landscape, so he could have informed discussions about which apps and services were being consumed and by whom; how much he was spending on each of his major applications; and how much he needed to spend to support each line of business.

These facts led to several revelations about their portfolio. Many of the insights helped lead to cost reduction, while others led to the opposite conclusion. For example, by seeing for the first time the percentages of total spending on their app portfolio, they could justify increased investment in customer-facing technologies.

Other insights came in rapid succession, such as identifying end-of-life applications that were still consuming infrastructure and resources. In the end, these insights added up to significant budget savings and reallocations to more valuable purposes. Godec knew there were more, so he put his team on the hunt for new discoveries. His goal? Significantly reduce annual operating costs without reducing the quality

---

[9]   Godec, Larry. Personal interview. 13 Mar. 2012.

of service and support. His team of only two people, mostly in their spare time, exceeded this goal in just a few months.

This is an important lesson. TBM isn't necessary because IT is too expensive. Instead, it's needed because your resources are in short supply. IT budgets of course never satisfy everything your business wants; but the real problem is that skilled people are hard to find and your business's competitive clock is ticking faster and faster. You can't afford to waste people or time. IT may represent less than a tenth of your business cost structure, but it is inextricably linked to your ability to compete, serve your customers, and reduce those business costs. Your IT capital must thus be invested wisely to create the most *value*.

Value is what TBM — this business revolution in IT — is all about.

Transparency: The Key to Value

In describing this business revolution in IT, we talk a lot about facts and data. Sure, facts and data are part of IT's response to most business challenges: it's what you do for a living. But *fact-based* conversations and *data-driven* decision-making are the core elements of TBM. An interrelated principle called transparency is also the core for understanding, improving, and communicating value.

Anyone who has dined at a restaurant with an open kitchen — one in which you can see the chefs and cooks preparing your food — can appreciate transparency. In fact, this kind of transparency in the restaurant industry has become rather commonplace. But why? Doesn't it cost money to open up the kitchen? Doesn't it risk having patrons see an employee sneeze on the food (or worse)? Why are so many restaurants then adopting this transparency?

It turns out that transparency leads to faster service and higher customer satisfaction. According to research[10] at the Harvard Business

10 Buell, Ryan W., Tami Kim, and Chia-Jung Tsay. "Creating Reciprocal Value Through Operational Transparency." *Harvard Business School Technology & Operations Mgt. Unit Working Paper No. 14-115.* (20 May 2015): n. pag. Web.

School, when diners and cooks can see each other, customer satisfaction goes up by 17 percent, and the food is served 13 percent faster. An open kitchen is an example of *operational* transparency because it reveals operating processes to customers. Previous research has shown that operational transparency increases customer perception of the work needed to produce a product, and also enhances their sense of appreciation and willingness to buy.

More astonishing is the effect of *cost* transparency. In similar research[11] by Harvard Business School, researchers found that online retailer Everlane generated 44 percent more sales by revealing the cost composition of a product (a wallet). The mere act of disclosing the costs, along with the price — even when doing resulted in a healthy profit margin — improved sales. According to the researchers, "revealing costs on competitively-priced products, managers can improve consumer attraction to the brand, and in turn, sales."

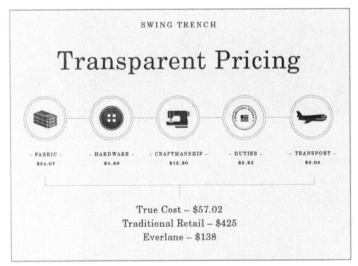

Figure 1-4: Everlane reveals cost composition of every product, thus improving customer loyalty and sales[12]

---

[11] Mohan, Bhavya and Buell, Ryan W. and John, Leslie K. "Lifting the Veil: The Benefits of Cost Transparency." *(29 May 2015). Harvard Business School NOM Unit Working Paper No. 15-017.* Available at SSRN: http://ssrn.com/abstract=2498174.

[12] Source: Everlane.com.

Now examine the comparison made between an IT-provisioned laptop and one purchased off the shelf. Do you suffer these unfair comparisons? If so, are you being transparent about your costs and operations? Do you show that your laptop costs include not only the hardware, but also the software, support, network, storage, and security? Do you spell out the quality and value of those ingredients to your business partners? (If not, perhaps it's time to open up your own kitchen!)

Just what is IT transparency? It's not merely exposing your costs or performance to your business partners, although that is an important aspect. Instead, IT transparency is the discipline of putting facts into meaningful contexts for decision makers. Transparency of IT for an internal service provider is different than what it is for a business partner, because they each have different decision-making needs.

Consider Everlane again. The cost transparency they provide in the above example is good enough for their prospective buyers. It helps them understand why the price being charged is fair; it even helps them understand value better. But the facts are inadequate for, say, the product manager who would need to understand better the breakdowns of materials costs, labor, and duties in order to make more informed decisions about product design, manufacturing, sourcing, and transportation. In this way, transparency not only helps shape demand, it helps shape supply decisions.

But transparency can also do more. In their book *The Real Business of IT*, Richard Hunter and George Westerman show that transparency is an essential force for changing the role of IT from order taker to strategic partner. By being clear about costs and performance, CIOs can take charge of the value conversation. They can show their capabilities as IT leaders, help business leaders to improve their processes, and then take on new strategic roles.[13]

---

[13] Hunter, Richard, and George Westerman. *The Real Business of IT: How CIOs Create and Communicate Business Value*. Boston, MA: Harvard Business, 2009. 12. Print.

Transparency is essential in today's enterprises, not just because it improves your customer satisfaction and brand loyalty. When employed by your IT organization and with your business partners, transparency allows you to exploit the forces of supply and demand, empower your people to make value-based decisions, and accelerate initiatives that are important to your business.

The Forces of IT Economics

If you've ever taken a microeconomics course, you learned about the forces of supply and demand. In a market economy, these forces respond to price. As the price of something goes up, producers will make more of it but consumers will buy less; as the price goes down, the producer makes less and the consumer buys more. At just the right price, therefore, the quantity that producers will make and consumers will buy is the same. At that point, you have equilibrium. It's a beautiful thing.

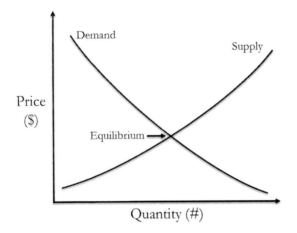

Figure 1-5: The supply and demand curve shows that price governs quantity based on perceived value

This supply and demand model (above), which originated in the late nineteenth century, illustrates a now well understood principle: Price and cost are essential to negotiating consumption between suppliers and consumers, as well as establishing the relative value of the good or service being offered.

Despite over a century of research that has supported and refined this economic principle, many business leaders fail to use price and cost to shape the demand for IT. Some CIOs and CFOs behave as if the concept will not work, that demand should be governed instead by a central authority like a steering committee. Some have said that shaping demand in this way is impractical or goes against other principles of their business. Yet, many CIOs agree that poorly governed consumption is among the leading causes of misallocated capital and IT resources. Clearly, demand must be shaped. Perhaps then it is time to use a more market-oriented approach.

It's also important to recognize that much of your demand is governed by individual choices, behaviors, and decisions. Application owners decide on the quality and quantity of needed infrastructure. Operations analysts decide where to focus problem management efforts. Architects set standards and adopt models that drive implementation decisions. Capacity managers choose when to purchase and install additional storage. These are all decisions and behaviors that can be shaped and managed using TBM.

Shaping demand with facts about cost and consumption is hardly a new concept. Consider how smart meters and detailed utility bills help optimize household electricity consumption. Studies have long shown that these and similar feedback tools are effective in reducing electricity consumption by 5 to 20 percent.[14] They also show that feedback is most effective when it:

- is tailored to the homeowner

- comes in an interactive and digital format

- provides consumption data by appliance

- includes advice for conserving electricity

---

[14] Vine, Desley, Laurie Buys, and Peter Morris. "The Effectiveness of Energy Feedback for Conservation and Peak Demand: A Literature Review." *OJEE Open Journal of Energy Efficiency 02.01* (2013): 7-15. Web.

- is put in the context of conservation

These lessons are useful for IT as well. How do you report IT consumption to your business partners? Are you advising your business partners on how to use IT more efficiently? Have you set and communicated savings goals? This analogy isn't perfect of course — electricity is a commodity with no choices about quality or delivery, attributes that are obviously essential to the IT value equation — but the point here is that transparency in the form of facts and figures leads to a desired change in consumer behavior that benefits everyone.

TBM helps your consumers make similar changes. When business leaders clearly see the total costs associated with the services they consume, and they understand their role in balancing cost, quality, and consumption, they will tell you when cost exceeds value. They will be empowered to make informed tradeoffs (more on these later) that not only meet their needs but leave IT without so many budget issues to resolve down the road.

The Power of Distributed Decision-Making

Even though your business partners know that technology powers their business, too many of them still ask a question they believe is critical to their success:

Are we spending too much, too little, or the right amount on IT?

Unfortunately, it's the *wrong* question. This question evaluates IT through the lens of a cost center, one that requires a specific predefined level of funding to serve the needs of the business. It evaluates IT only as a whole, using a metric that is far too simplistic. It risks harming the business by forcing ill-informed decisions, such as running too lean or cutting innovation spending that is clearly justified by its own merits. Most of all, it perpetuates the perception of IT as a black box, distinct from the rest of the business.

Asking a CIO this question is no different than asking a manufacturer how much, as a percentage of revenues, that company should spend on robotics. While relevant industry benchmarks may be available, the decision is best made by industrial engineers, product design teams, cost accountants, and others who are closer to the problem. They will spend what they need so long as it's cost-justified based on their product lines. They simply need to know the costs to acquire, implement, operate, and maintain their robots compared to the business benefits (e.g., labor cost avoided, quality improved).

It's not that high-level ratios, such as IT cost per revenue, are not useful. They encourage you to ask *why*. Why are your IT costs higher (or lower) than your industry peers, for example? With TBM, this question is a lot easier to answer. Instead of simply answering how much should you be spending on IT, TBM arms people throughout your organization with facts that are closer to the business, where they are *actionable*.

Consider this example. In 2007, Cisco began its IT-as-a-Service journey. Part of Jacoby's strategy at Cisco for this transformation was to shift more spending from two-thirds run-the-business (RtB) to two-thirds change-the-business (CtB). This was considered essential to Cisco's business strategy and growth.

In 2009, during the first year of Cisco's TBM rollout, Jacoby's leadership team defined a playbook that included a "P&L" for her IT services. While her organization did not charge back for its costs, this reporting got her entire organization talking about cost-for-performance tradeoffs. Most of the initial optimization decisions were made top down by a handful of executives.

The next year, Cisco accelerated the shift to change-the-business. By pushing P&L reporting and decision-making out to more than a hundred IT service owners, along with accountability for service cost and value, Jacoby was able to drive more than 20 percent of her cost optimization goal in a single year. This distributed approach dramatically accelerated the value and also the savings generated.

In another example, TBM provided First American's application owners the insights they needed to optimize their costs. As described earlier, Godec originally took a top-down, portfolio-oriented decision-making approach, partnering with his CEO, CFO, and line-of-business leaders on spend decisions and priorities. He also authorized a project to hunt for savings. While this focus led to many optimizations, it was just the start.

Later in the first year, Godec's team began delivering a bill of IT to his line-of-business leaders, application owners, infrastructure owners, and others. This act jumpstarted fact-based conversations with those leaders about how to optimize spending and how to find room in the budget for higher priorities.

Then, in 2014, Godec and his CFO implemented chargeback. By creating a high level of accountability, paired with an insightful bill of IT, Godec's application owners began to drive conversations around cost-for-performance tradeoffs with their business-side counterparts. This change led to many more decisions, including shutting down unnecessary applications and re-tiering of storage that reduced the need to continually buy more.

In both examples, these CIOs used TBM to create a structure that gave their people the insights — and the incentives — needed to improve value. Ivory tower approaches to making cost, consumption, and quality tradeoffs were much less necessary. Let's face it. Wouldn't we all rather have a culture of empowerment and accountability vs. a command-and-control hierarchy?

Accelerating Key Initiatives

TBM is rarely implemented for its own sake. It's rarely an overarching IT strategy;[15] it's usually part of a broader transformation of IT or the business, or both. By providing the right facts to decision makers, TBM helps accelerate imperatives or initiatives that often get stuck without the right information.

---

[15] This may not always be true. At least one CIO — for a large security software company — defined his IT transformation as a "TBM transformation."

Consider the shift to a service-delivery IT operating model, as Cisco did. If you've adopted this model, you've probably wrestled with managing finances and resources. Service costs are rarely exposed via traditional corporate financial reporting. As you will see in the coming chapters, TBM gets around this problem by translating a financial view of resources into terms and metrics that service owners and their business partners need in order to make better decisions about quality vs. cost (i.e., cost for performance).

Adopting cloud computing is another example. Cloud frustrates existing IT financial models. Much like virtualization did over a decade ago, cloud computing creates sprawl due to the ease of ordering and provisioning compute resources, such as servers and storage. Public provider bills also remain stubbornly difficult to analyze with any degree of detail. For both public and private cloud services, you need your business partners to be good stewards of the costs they drive. Meanwhile, your service owners need to manage those costs just like any other cost of doing business. TBM helps you accomplish these things.

Application rationalization initiatives are also bolstered by TBM. Efforts to rationalize application portfolios are often stymied by the unclear total costs of ownership (TCO) of each application. According to Gartner[16], "IT should be able to map its actual spending to application towers and to appropriate business areas, so that business stakeholders can understand the costs IT has incurred on their behalf. This information is vital for engaging these business stakeholders, creating a sense of budget ownership, and motivating business decisions that optimize application spending." TBM provides this precise mapping.

TBM has helped CIOs and CFOs accelerate other important initiatives as well, including:

- becoming a transparent broker of services to the business, encompassing internal, public cloud, and other third-party services,

---

[16] Van Der Zijden, Stefan, Matthew Hotle, and John P. Roberts. "Eight Steps to Revitalize Your IT Cost Optimization Initiative With Application Rationalization." *Gartner.* Gartner, Inc., 20 July 2015.

by providing clarity for third-party costs, internal consumption, and TCO

- tackling technical debt by providing a more complete view of TCO, including the costs to maintain and support applications and technologies that were put into production with less than optimal code

- negotiating better outsourcing contracts by providing a clearer perspective of internal costs and consumption so as to ensure that vendor proposals are complete

- accelerating synergies after mergers and acquisitions (e.g., Bank of America and Merrill Lynch) and drafting effective transition services agreements after divestitures (e.g., as eBay and HP did with their TBM implementations)[17]

Really, TBM has near universal applicability. Just ask yourself how would you use facts about cost, business consumption, resource utilization, and other aspects of what you deliver to accelerate the achievement of important goals?

Key Takeaways

- Technology Business Management (TBM) is a value-management framework for CIOs and their teams that centers on the transparency of costs, consumption, and performance. The TBM framework spans supply and demand to enable the fact-based tradeoff decisions needed to optimize spending and accelerate change.

- Transparency, or the act of disclosing facts to decision makers to empower better decision-making, is essential for value creation. In the restaurant and retail businesses, transparency has been shown to improve brand loyalty and the perception of value, goals that are

---

[17] These achievements were accomplished by clearly linking business applications and services to the underlying infrastructures, data centers, and resources they supported, allowing for more informed decisions.

similar to those of CIOs with their business partners. In IT, transparency has been proven effective for communicating value and shaping business demand.

- When technology services are free or the prices of those services are hidden and demand is not commensurate with value, use TBM to exploit the forces of economics and put a clear price on your services. Price shapes the forces of supply and demand, balancing value and consumption.

- By providing facts to accountable decision makers, TBM empowers distributed decision-making. Use TBM to spread the responsibility for making tradeoff decisions and delivering cost more effectively, thus accelerating business value. Give your people the facts they need to make decisions and create a culture of empowerment.

- TBM is a means to an end. Use it to accelerate your imperatives, such as organizational transformation or important initiatives like adopting the cloud, executing during and after M&A, rationalizing applications, or optimizing costs after a budget cut.

Chapter 2:
The Tools of TBM

It's no secret that many CIOs see IT very differently than their business counterparts do. In fact, as CIO Magazine's *2015 State of the CIO* research reveals, 54 percent of line-of-business executives view IT as an obstacle to their mission, while only 33 percent of CIOs feel the same way.[18] Technology business management (TBM) looks to change this calculation. Through a data-driven framework for measuring, managing, and communicating the cost, efficiency, and consumption of IT, TBM fosters fact-based value conversations about the supply and demand of the services that IT renders and the service applications it supports. In short, TBM gives you the tools to communicate the cost, quality, and value of IT investments to your business partners.

It does so by borrowing the same business management, finance, and accounting disciplines that technology businesses, including cloud providers, have been using for years. Like those earlier efforts at understanding the connection between tasks and resources to the products being produced, TBM allows both IT and business leaders to map and trace technology spending throughout an organization to see who is supplying technology and who is consuming it. This transparency gives everyone from IT tower owners to business unit leaders to the CIO, the CFO, and the CEO the ability to pull back the curtain and understand how and where IT spending is tied to specific business outcomes.

By providing a taxonomy that translates IT-speak into terms the business can understand (and vice versa), TBM breaks down the long-standing communication barriers that too often hamper alignment between IT spending and business needs. This taxonomy enables CIOs and their business partners to have far more productive *value conversations* about the supply and demand nature of IT services.

---

[18] State of the CIO Survey. *CIO magazine*. January 2015.

Value conversations are at the heart of TBM. A value conversation is an interaction that focuses on the tradeoffs between cost, consumption, capacity, performance, and risk in the pursuit of better business outcomes. It can be internal, between the technology leaders on your team, or it can be between your organization and your business partners. Here are some of the questions that can lead to value conversations:

- Should we increase our investment in disaster recovery to reduce the risk of business interruption?

- Should we cut spending on our back-office applications in order to fund improvements in our customer-facing services?

- Where can we improve efficiency without materially impacting service quality?

- Should we implement a policy to reduce email storage requirements?

- Can we dedicate more people to our innovation program by pulling resources from other teams? Which teams?

- Are we capable of absorbing the new application or service that's being proposed?

All these questions lead to cost-benefit considerations (tradeoffs). With TBM, these tradeoffs are informed by precise facts about the total cost, consumption, capacity utilization, hours of labor, and other metrics. Guesswork, conjecture, and intuition are thus reduced.

When these conversations do occur between you and your business partners, they revolve around the *value* of spending to the business. Put another way, are these partners getting the technology and services they need for the money they are spending? Business people know how to make that decision. They do it every time they buy something.

To make value conversations possible, however, both of you have to use the same terms to describe what you're providing and how much it costs. This is where so many technologists get it wrong. They talk about the purchase costs of assets when their business partners need to know the full lifecycle operating and capital spending of the service you're delivering. And they also need to understand what's included. Are you buying them a PC from Best Buy? Or are you procuring, installing, configuring, networking, supporting, troubleshooting, securing, and training them on how to use a PC and then wiping, decommissioning, and recycling it when it's kaput?

The TBM taxonomy enables you, your people, and your business partners to communicate better. When you have a value conversation, you are using the TBM taxonomy to break down the language barriers between IT and the business. By shifting the focus away from budgets and technology to the business outcomes those elements enable, you have made the first of many transformative moves that will help you realign your IT organization to run more efficiently and finally deliver on the true promise technology holds to drive business growth and productivity.

The Essential Elements of TBM

Like any formalized approach, TBM offers a set of tools that can be adopted by any enterprise. But unlike the tools of many other approaches, these have been forged in practice, not just theory. The TBM Council, its founder and technical advisor, Apptio, and partners like KPMG, EY, Deloitte, ISG, and McKinsey, have collaborated over the last several years through real-world implementations of TBM, industry workgroups, research projects, and product collaborations to precisely define and refine the tools for managing the business of IT.

The primary tools of TBM are:

- **The TBM framework**: The core elements — the organizational traits, management disciplines, and value conversations that make up a mature TBM program

- **The TBM taxonomy**: A common language that normalizes tech-speak and business-speak to connect IT and the business

- **The TBM model**: A data-driven method for mapping and allocating costs and resource consumption from their sources to their uses, powering the reports, analytics, and metrics that are needed for successful value conversations

- **TBM metrics**: The key performance indicators (KPIs) that allow CIOs to measure, improve, and communicate business value

- **TBM system**: The enterprise management software, data, and model needed to automate analytics and processes to manage your technology business

Each element is introduced and discussed below.

The TBM Framework

Many industry standards for IT have a framework that defines and stitches together all of the parts. Technology Business Management is no different. Ultimately, what sets the TBM framework apart from other industry approaches is that it focuses on specific business management practices for technology organizations. It is not designed to be a complete IT governance framework; rather, it goes deeper into the business management aspects of technology management than other frameworks go.

The TBM framework is additive in that it can be applied on top of other best practices, such as ITIL or COBIT. It exploits the disciplines of investment portfolio management, cost transparency, and business demand management. It is built on a foundation of quantifiable financial and operational data and the business knowledge base of IT people and their understanding of the business's processes.

The TBM framework provides a decision-making model for maximizing the business value of a technology portfolio — not its operational value. In other words, just because IT runs better, or costs less, or is more reliable does not automatically translate into value for the business. Instead, improved business value is the result of tradeoffs between those traits and other business needs, such as innovation and agility.

In the remainder of this chapter, we provide a brief tour of the TBM framework and introduce you to each component. In subsequent chapters, we discuss each component of the framework in greater detail. You will learn about the options you should consider when applying TBM, along with the pros and cons of each one of them.

For now, let's get started by understanding the TBM framework, as it is the foundation for everything to come. The TBM framework is comprised of the following ten elements:

- Two organizational elements — *Position for Value* and *Continuously Improve*

- Four core disciplines — *Create Transparency*, *Deliver Value for Money*, *Shape Business Demand*, and *Plan and Govern*

- Four value conversations — *Cost for Performance*, *Business-Aligned Portfolio*, *Investment in Innovation*, and *Enterprise Agility*

The overarching goal of the framework is to help IT optimize run-the-business (RtB) and change-the-business (CtB) spending in order to achieve greater business value, based on the strategy and goals of that enterprise.

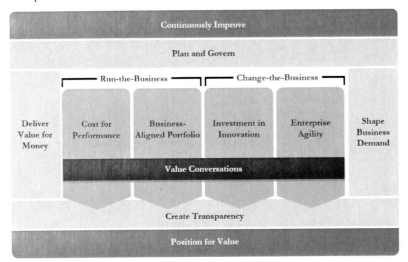

Figure 2-1: The TBM Framework defines the organizational elements, disciplines, and value conversations of an effective TBM program

The organizational elements of the framework — *Position for Value* and *Continuously Improve* — define the essential roles for TBM and associated value creation. We will talk more about the roles of TBM and how they function in the real world in Chapter 3. For now, it is important to note that implementing TBM does not require a massive round of new hires nor a whole new set of skills. Most of the people you will tap for your TBM initiative already exist in your organization.

The basis of this foundation is the discipline needed for generating cost transparency (Chapter 4). Cost transparency is the key to delivering value for money (Chapter 5) and shaping demand (Chapter 6). It augments and accelerates internal IT decision-making, highlighting not only areas of waste but also the cost of that waste, so you can drive both action and accountability. It provides the facts needed to generate a bill of IT, clearly designed to change behavior by showing the business the cost of its consumption (and also offer a good starting point for driving accountability of consumption).

Cost transparency also enables better financial planning and governance (Chapter 7). With transparency, IT leaders can better anticipate the impact of changing business needs on future IT resource requirements. Further, by putting those plans into business terms, CIOs can demonstrate the business value of the IT budget.

The value conversations (Chapters 8 and 9) of *Cost for Performance*, *Business-Aligned Portfolio*, *Investment in Innovation*, and *Enterprise Agility* sit at the center of the TBM framework. These conversations result in tradeoffs for optimizing the running of the business and shifting more investment to changing the business. As such, they are collaborative decisions based on facts.

The TBM Taxonomy

Taxonomies are a schema of classification, the purpose of which is to establish a common language and structure, so everyone is talking about the same thing in the same way. Many taxonomies, such as those in biology (think Tree of Life), are hierarchical, illustrating the relationship between the different ranks, branches, or layers of a schema. Similarly, the TBM taxonomy (see Figure 2-2) classifies and organizes IT costs, units, and other metrics from disparate sources, assets, and services in a hierarchical manner and provides a common set of terms to describe them.

The TBM taxonomy is not just semantics. It gives everyone the ability to compare technologies, towers, and services to peers and third-party options (e.g., the public cloud). Just as businesses rely on generally accepted accounting principles (or GAAP[19]) to drive standard practices for financial reporting — and thus comparability between financial statements — IT leaders need a generally accepted way of reporting costs and other metrics. The TBM taxonomy provides this tool.

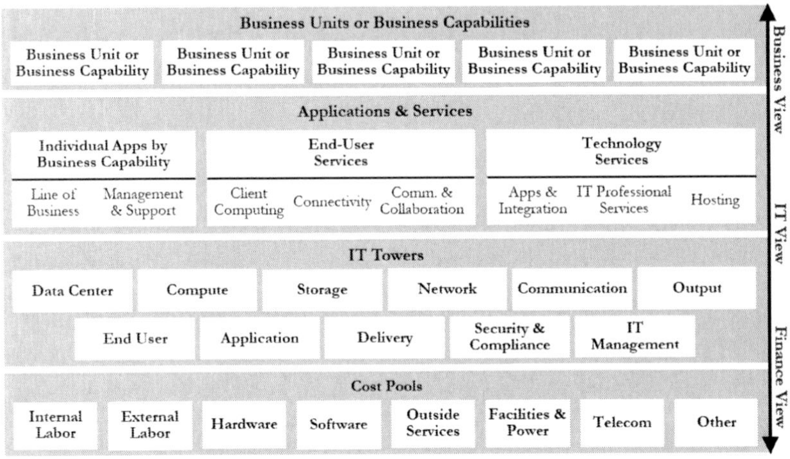

Figure 2-2: The TBM taxonomy provides a standard set of categories for costs and other metrics

There are four main layers of the TBM taxonomy — cost pools (and sub-pools), IT towers (and sub-towers), applications and services, and business units or business capabilities — that support three views. These three views represent the major steps of translation of costs and other metrics. From the bottom up, we have:

- **Finance**: This view begins with your general ledger (GL), but may include other cost sources unique to your organization. The taxonomy provides for a standard set of breakouts (e.g., CapEx vs. OpEx, Fixed vs. Variable) and a standard set of cost pools as in hardware, software, internal labor, external labor,

---

[19] Generally Accepted Accounting Principles.

facilities/overhead, and outside services. Cost pools not only make cost allocations easier, they enhance reporting because they can be traced through the model to reveal the composition of your costs and allow for comparability of composition (e.g., How much internal labor is found in this service versus that one?).

- **IT:** This view includes a common set of infrastructure towers and sub-towers, such as servers, storage, voice and data networks, application development, and support. These towers are in use by nearly all companies and are the basic building blocks of specific applications, services, etc. Regardless of where they come from (e.g., internally or via the public cloud), this view enables IT leaders to assess just how cost-effective IT is in its delivery of technologies and services.

- **Business**: this view provides a standard, generic set of applications and services along with the business capabilities they support. At this layer of the model, we anticipate the creation of industry-specific elements that will allow for more meaningful reporting and comparisons for each vertical. This layer also includes the business unit consumers or breakouts (allocations) by consumers.

The TBM taxonomy is the result of applied research and actual trial and error. It is based on the work of TBM Council technical advisor Apptio, which worked with IT benchmarking providers such as ISG and Rubin Worldwide and has deployed the taxonomy at hundreds of companies. It was designed to facilitate apples-to-apples benchmarking and support the hundreds of reports, KPIs, and other outputs needed by real decision makers. The TBM taxonomy was reviewed by the principal members of the TBM Council and later endorsed by the council's Board of Directors. It will continue to evolve based on experience and feedback.[20]

---

[20] As of this writing, Version 2 of the TBM taxonomy is currently in draft as a working standard approved by the TBM Council board of directors. Updates will be shared with TBM Council members and the broader community as they are available.

The TBM taxonomy is a recommended template, and also one that allows for customization and extensions. Many firms use it as the basis of their own somewhat unique taxonomy. For example, the State of Washington Office of the CIO created its own TBM taxonomy for all its state agencies to use.[21] The state's taxonomy includes many unique elements, such as "state hosted cloud," "agency storage," "radios," and "building automation systems." These reflect towers that are provided by state agency IT organizations but not normally found in corporate IT shops.

Of course, there is a drawback with creating a non-standard taxonomy. One financial services company deployed a taxonomy and cost model that reflected the various Excel-based approaches in use for years to support various reporting requirements. The model functioned, but it did not provide all of the reports, metrics, and comparability that were needed to take their TBM program to the next level. As their SVP of Infrastructure explained, "The model we built is somewhat of a Frankenstein. We are seeing gaps in our model where some reports don't tie into others, so my people think the numbers don't tie out when they really do. And we're seeing new opportunities for reporting that this approach doesn't support. What we really need is a best practices model."

This company then deployed a model based on the TBM taxonomy. The model not only supported most of the their unique reporting requirements, but it also delivered a foundation for addressing new requirements that were beginning to surface as more TBM principles were exploited. The model accelerated the company's TBM journey by giving them comparability for benchmarking and it proved that the TBM taxonomy can be applied to what were previously considered unique and complex circumstances.

The TBM taxonomy is a game changer for financial and business-minded technology leaders, as it is the first generally accepted approach

---

[21] You can find the State of Washington's FY16 taxonomy online at https://ocio.wa.gov/policies/standard-11330-tbm-taxonomy.

for translating finance, IT, and business perspectives. It also enables TBM adopters to participate in a community of like-minded peers to gain knowledge, share experiences, and gather benchmarking data. When the TBM taxonomy is implemented in a technology solution for TBM, the benefits are numerous. Four of these benefits, in particular, can be transformative:

- **Standardized Cost and Resource Modeling** — The Taxonomy supports standard models with predefined metrics and KPIs, so that business and its IT leaders can rapidly define their own IT business model for managing cost, consumption, utilization, and the quality of its technologies, products, and services.

- **Accelerated Benchmarking** — The Taxonomy was built with benchmarking in mind, and was designed to support meaningful comparisons so as to benchmark data from leading third parties.

- **Extensibility** — The TBM taxonomy is extensible, allowing organizations to add their own specific categories or subcategories without losing the benefits of the standard categories.

- **Ecosystem Leverage** — The TBM taxonomy makes it easier for TBM Council members, technical advisors and partners, and the broader practitioner community to collaborate and learn from others. It is a common language used in the TBM ecosystem.

Thus, the TBM taxonomy, with continued feedback from the TBM Council, is an invaluable tool for IT leaders, and it will continue to evolve and improve over time.

The TBM Model

The TBM model provides the elements needed for mapping and allocating costs and other resources from one layer of the TBM taxonomy to another. The TBM model includes the taxonomy objects and layers plus the data requirements, allocation rules, and metrics needed to create transparency and enable the reporting that is needed for the value conversations of TBM.

The model creates the financial, technical, and business views that are meaningful to your various decision makers and stakeholders. The TBM model depends on certain technical capabilities, such as the ability to consume data from third-party sources and dynamically allocate costs using that data. As such, the TBM model lives in software. The requirements for such a modeling system, and more broadly the enterprise TBM system as a whole, are discussed below.

To "populate" the model, costs and other data are extracted from sources like your GL (the most common source of cost data), asset inventories, payroll systems, trouble tickets, project management systems, server and storage management tools, and more. That data is then used to allocate costs from the GL up through the model, as illustrated in Figure 2-3.

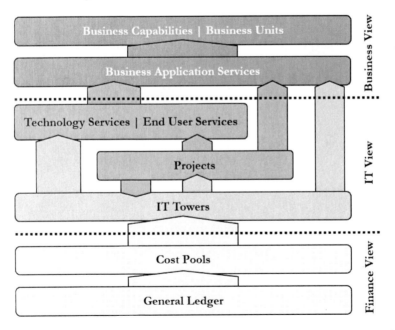

Figure 2-3: The TBM model (conceptualized here) allocates costs from the GL through the financial, IT, and business layers

The cost data is allocated based on consumption data where possible. For example, if an application consumes 30 percent of the storage, it would receive 30 percent of the costs. Sometimes data is not available for allocating costs, so estimates are used until the data is sourced.

Although your model should be standards based (using the standard TBM taxonomy), it should be flexible enough to allow for a mix of cost allocation strategies that can best match your organization's maturity, unique business needs, and available data. Sticking close to the standard TBM taxonomy, which was aligned to several benchmarking data sources (e.g., ISG, Rubin Worldwide), means it will be easier to make comparisons with other TBM adopters. (Benchmarking is discussed in more detail in Chapter 5.)

TBM Metrics and KPIs

W. Edward Deming, the father of total quality management (TQM) and numerous other forward-looking business management practices, is often quoted as saying "You can't manage what you can't measure." Unfortunately, the quote is wrong: what he really said is, "It is wrong to suppose that if you can't measure it, you can't manage it — a costly myth."[22] (He does concede that measurement does help, however.)

So why bring this aspect up here? Once you begin to understand TBM, you will realize the concept is actually a bit paradoxical. On one hand, it's all about improving IT's value and contribution to a business. However, value is largely subjective. Like all things, value is defined by the buyer (in this case, your business partners), and the very definition of value is different from person to person.

On the other hand, TBM is based on the idea that in order to improve value (even if it is just the perception of the value you already provide), you must present the business as facts and figures for how well IT is performing relative to cost and business outcomes. Key performance indicators, or KPIs, give you something to show your business partners to foster the right discussion. They also show them that you're using data to run your business, just like they do to run theirs.

But KPIs are not just for show. They allow you to set meaningful and achievable targets for your team. If you set a target for meeting or beating

---

[22] Deming, W. Edwards. *The New Economics: For Industry, Government, Education.* Cambridge, MA: MIT, 2000. 35. Print.

unit cost targets for key IT services, you will leave little room for second guessing. It focuses your leaders on figuring out how, rather than what. KPIs should be used first of all to set targets and goals, and then secondly to demonstrate progress or success.

Specific KPIs are discussed in more detail in Chapter 8, but the outcomes highlighted by these metrics revolve around the following value conversations described earlier:

- **Cost-for-Performance** KPIs help IT continuously improve the cost efficiency of its services while maintaining quality.

- **Business-Aligned Portfolio** KPIs enable IT to focus its time and resources on the services, applications, technologies, and vendors that drive the most value for the business.

- **Investment in Innovation** KPIs help IT and its business partners to better govern and collaborate on the right level of project spending.

- **Enterprise Agility** KPIs facilitate the creation of a more agile cost structure for IT and accelerate effective decision-making.

Of course these KPIs are not an exhaustive list for IT leaders. There are operational and service health KPIs that should be balanced with these. Technology leaders may also have very unique KPIs based on their own specific business outcomes. For example, a hospital system may have a goal to reduce patient care professional time spent completing online forms; TBM does not address these specific situations, but it can help any IT organization balance its investment in unique business outcomes like this one.

The Enterprise TBM System

A complete discussion of an enterprise management system for CIOs is beyond the scope of this book. However, no discussion of the essential elements of TBM would be complete without mentioning the software system that is needed. As described at the beginning of this book, it is an unfortunate reality that so many CIOs and technology leaders are operating without their enterprise management system. Too many have tools for managing the parts, but none for managing their businesses holistically.

There are many tools to use to build your TBM system. These can include everything from spreadsheets and business intelligence software to custom-developed software and purpose-built packages. Each approach has its own pros and cons. But before determining how you want to build it, you need to understand your requirements. Below are several to consider.

The first requirement is the system's ability to **create, support, and process your TBM model** (or models). The allocation of numerical data using other tables, lists, or rule sets as weighting criteria sits at the core of the TBM model. Since your model and the amount of data can be both very large and very complex, your TBM system must scale to meet the task.

Next, your system must be able to **extract, transform, and load data from other tools**. It should do this task automatically, so that the system is easily maintained. The system must work well with imperfect data because that is what you're likely to have, especially in the beginning. It should also allow you to easily upgrade your datasets, so that as your source data matures or your needs evolve, you can integrate new data without a significant amount of rework.

Your system must **provide the reports, metrics, dashboards, and analyses** your people actually need. Since you cannot predict all of their reporting needs, the ability of your report consumers to access and manipulate data and create their own reports is also essential.

Your system must **enable your decision makers to interact with the data and reports**. Many users such as financial planners, technology owners, architects, and application owners will have complex, multi-dimensional questions. For example, an app owner might want to know why her infrastructure costs are so high: Are the unit costs of infrastructure components like storage and servers high compared to others? Or, are those components utilized inefficiently by her application? Commonly, a decision maker needs to explore the data in order to answer a complex question.

Finally, your **system must be secure**. Your models often will integrate a lot of sensitive data, such as asset lists, payroll data,[23] transaction volumes and more. When sensitive fields are not needed, they should be excluded from the system. Since sensitive data is often required in our model, you need good security, including user authentication, role-based access controls, and the ability to redact sensitive information within reports.

This book will remain as neutral as possible about the vendors, tools, and services that comprise TBM solutions. However, please do understand that the disciplines, taxonomy, models, and other elements of TBM were not born on paper; they were forged in hundreds of enterprise IT shops around the world. Most have relied on packaged software, consulting services, and data provided by dedicated vendors and partners. The experience of these engagements and deployments is indeed reflected in the chapters that follow.

Key Takeaways

- TBM borrows the same business management, finance, and accounting disciplines that technology businesses, including cloud providers, have been using for years.

- The TBM framework defines the essential elements of a TBM program, including organizational considerations, essential disciplines, and the value conversations TBM inspires. The TBM framework complements governance frameworks and models like ITIL and COBIT, rather than replacing any of them. This book is organized according to the TBM framework, with later chapters exploring each element in much greater depth.

---

[23] Average pay rates are normally used instead of actuals so as to protect specific employee salaries. However, even names, rates, and other figures are sensitive and must be protected.

- Use the TBM taxonomy to create a common language for finance, technology, and your line-of-business partners. Leverage this common language to foster the value conversations of TBM, which then give you the shared facts to make tradeoffs of cost, consumption, capacity, risk, and performance.

- Use the TBM model and recommended data sets to allocate costs, resources, and other metrics to the towers, applications, services, projects, and other objects that are consumed by the business and other decision makers. The model gives you transparency based on the delivered TBM taxonomy.

- Use TBM Metrics and KPIs to help convey the value your technology organization delivers. More importantly, leverage these metrics to establish clear, measurable, and achievable goals for your team.

- Implement an enterprise management system for your technology business. It should meet key requirements for functionality, scalability, security, data integration, reporting, and analytics. No TBM program can be complete without including and using the proper tools.

ViewPoint: **Assessment Reveals Key Habits for TBM Success**

The 2016 KPMG Global TBM Proficiency Assessment Report is the second in our series on TBM. The report provides an overview of the maturity and the drivers for TBM practitioner success based on today's challenges for an IT organization and its CXO roles — the people, processes, enablement data, and technology that support IT cost, performance, and value.

Our research is based on more than 200 respondents from over 170 companies with a global presence, representing major industries that include banking, insurance, energy, consumer product goods (CPG), healthcare, manufacturing, transportation, and technology, media & telecommunications (TMT).

The research has revealed key factors for TBM proficiency and why they matter. Using our growing global TBM database, we provide practical advice about the best ways to prioritize and sequence the activities that move a company's TBM proficiency from good to great.

Working with a diverse set of companies worldwide, we have learned that financial transparency over the IT services delivered by the organization — *namely, the ability to clearly capture the cost/price, quality, and performance of IT services* — is at the root of true IT value generation for the business.

At a global level we have found that more than 55 percent of respondents have used TBM to drive greater visibility into IT spend while reducing operational costs and increasing spend control.

Based on numerous TBM engagements across a diverse set of industries and two years of survey data, we have found a correlation between a set of practices or habits and a high level of TBM proficiency, including the ability of an IT organization to articulate and deliver business value to its stakeholders through TBM.

Different habits are required depending on the TBM maturity level of the IT organization. Companies just starting their TBM journey should consider the following:

- start defining and publishing a list of technology infrastructure services

- focus on data to support transparency. The data does not need to be perfect, but processes need to be in place for improving data quality

- move away from spreadsheets and use a bespoke tool to sustainably manage IT finance and reporting

- acquire the skills to articulate IT value in a language that is understood by the business

- conduct regular reviews across IT portfolios — technology, applications, and vendors

- put the CIO in charge of TBM

For organizations further along their TBM journey and seen as TBM leaders, the following activities can help advance their TBM maturity:

- collect and maintain *all* technology costs, service consumption information, and resource utilization information

- hone the ability to articulate the value of IT in terms that appeal to business partners

- maintain a tight connection between technology and business goals, especially as these goals evolve due to market forces

- make it very clear to the company's business partners the complete set of services they can leverage

TBM increases transparency around the value of IT through better and more accurate cost and performance management. This builds trust with consumers in the business and enables the CIO to identify appropriate optimization opportunities that will drive sustainable value from the IT investment and support the organization's overall business goals.

Properly designed and implemented, TBM can help transform the IT function from being only a technology provider to becoming a true value creator and strategic enabler for the organization. TBM, quite simply, is the set of disciplines that supports this transformation.

Steve Bates
Principal, CIO Advisory
KPMG

Chapter 3:
Positioning for Value

TBM is value management for technology leaders. The foundation of TBM is clearly defining where and how you deliver value (i.e., your value proposition) to your enterprise. Your value proposition may seem obvious, but the business attributes of many technology organizations (see Appendix A) aren't aligned to their specific value proposition. For example, many service provider IT organizations are funded based on a percentage of revenues or cost per employee to deliver their services instead of a well-informed cost. This mismatch jeopardizes the organization's ability to serve its designed purpose by misallocating key resources.

On top of this misalignment, many leaders mistakenly assume their technology organization's value proposition should mirror the corporate strategy. They might assume, for example, that IT should be cheap if the corporate strategy is based on cost leadership, or conversely an enormous technology investment is warranted by a business strategy of product leadership. This line of thinking is overly simplistic, imperils the corporate strategy, and stems from a failure to understand or communicate how technology can help the business succeed. It's as bad as looking for that magical perfect amount for the company to spend on IT.

While IT's value proposition and corporate strategy are linked, they are not interchangeable. Instead, IT's value proposition must clearly articulate how IT enables the business to execute *its* strategy. This depends on how and where you fit into the value chain for your enterprise. To illustrate, let's explore the value chain model for a technology-enabled business (Figure 3-1).

In this chain, business value starts by the capabilities the business uses to create revenue or serve customers. IT enables that value through business services and applications, which are built on technology and end-user services. In turn, those services are assembled from the resources we call IT towers.

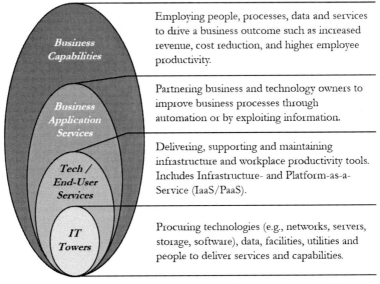

Figure 3-1: The value chain helps you understand where your organization fits

Starting business conversations from the point of view of your IT resources sets you up for failure, since they're not in a language or level of detail that business leaders care about. Starting instead from business capabilities and consumption provides you a language to work with business leaders to improve the way you provide capabilities and value, how they can help you optimize costs (and vice versa), and ultimately how you can work together to improve business outcomes.

You may or may not yet be service oriented. If you aren't, you should be headed in that direction.[24] In the meantime, business applications are a close proxy for services for the purposes of TBM and can serve as an effective point of focus for the top of your value chain. Creating transparency in your application costs and consumption provides similar

---

[24] Simply put, service orientation means that you define what you deliver in terms that are understood and agreed upon by your business partners and you take on end-to-end ownership of those services. Public cloud services have today altered the expectations of your business partners, so that anything less than a service-oriented technology department is no longer acceptable.

decision-making value to what you get from transparency of services. As you read this book, interpret the word "services" to mean those applications that you deliver to your business partners, if that is all you have.

Now ask yourself, what is your part in that value chain? Do you acquire resources, manage towers of infrastructure and applications, and deliver services? Do you build custom applications? Your organization may not execute all four layers of the value chain; your business partners probably deliver just parts of it, such as line-of-business applications or business capabilities. But you do own and perform certain parts of it. In practical terms, this aspect defines your value proposition.

To illustrate this point better, let's look at several technology leaders who are actually practicing TBM:

- Don Duet, head of the Technology Division at Goldman Sachs, delivers and manages technology, which enables commercial opportunities and facilitates consistency and control within the firm. The Technology Division bills the firm's lines of business each month for products they consume. These products include the full end-to-end cost of business applications as well as workplace products, market data, mobile communication, and more.

- Phuong Tram is the CIO of DuPont. As his organization increasingly relies on the public cloud for its technology services, Tram has focused more on transactional process support for his businesses, functions, and regions. His emphasis has shifted to *business application services*. His business partners rely on them to develop and produce the products and take them to market.

- Debra Bailey, CIO at Nationwide Building Society, is responsible for IT development, support, operations, and risk control along with Group Security; but she also owns ATM services and payments. Her span of control includes *technology services, business application services,* and many back-office *business capabilities*, some of which generate revenue for the firm.

Regardless of where you fit in terms of the value chain, you must understand the unique value that you are providing. It is not enough to cost-effectively deliver technology. Many third-party service providers offer equally cost-effective solutions. Fortunately, you being an integral part of your business provides an advantage when delivering a value proposition that external vendors cannot match. Do you possess advantages for safeguarding customer data, for example? Are you in a position to deliver the end-to-end ecosystem of services that your business needs to connect customers, stakeholders, vendors, suppliers, and partners? Are you able to build and support differentiated business applications because you have a more intimate knowledge of your business and its customers, products, and services?

If you possess these and other advantages, use them to define your unique value proposition. If you are unsure of which advantages you possess, ask your business partners the following questions:

- Why do you source services from my organization and not a third party (and vice versa)?

- Do you build or source your own technology-enabled services and applications? If so, why not source them from me? If not, why do you rely on me?

- What does IT provide that you cannot get elsewhere? Is there anything unique about the services we deliver?

- How do we help you execute against your business strategy?

- Do you consider IT a business partner?

If your business partners struggle to answer these questions, or if they feel they are forced to rely on your organization instead of seeking outside alternatives, spend time to develop or refine your unique value proposition.

Understanding Your Technology Business Model

The value chain is important because it helps you identify and understand your specific technology business model. This model determines the choices you make for the way you actually run your technology business, such as how you're funded, what type of transparency you should provide, what roles you rely on for business alignment, and what your service portfolio looks like.

There are four archetypical technology business models: expense center, service provider, value partner, and business driver. We'll explore each of these below. These archetypes vary based on focus of the technology organization and its placement in the value chain. Indeed, these two elements are highly correlated. An internally focused technology organization emphasizes asset and cost management; an externally focused one emphasizes business-focused services and capabilities that more directly create business value. This correlation is illustrated in Figure 3-2 below.

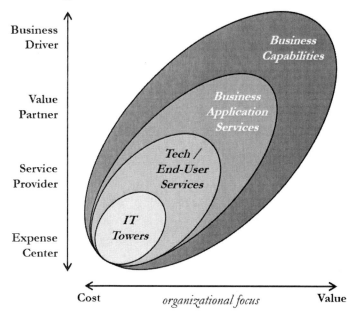

Figure 3-2: Use transparency to move IT up the value chain from towers to services and capabilities, raising strategic business impact

Due to the linkage between organizational focus and the value chain, you can aspire to lifting your organization to a higher plane. As you'll read below, the business driver archetype, where CIOs own a revenue generating business unit, is attainable. TBM's ability to help you shift your focus higher in your value chain can also help you make that transformation.

To understand this better, let's take a closer look at each of these technology business model archetypes.

Expense Center

Expense center organizations are characterized by a lack of service orientation. Because of this, they struggle to connect business demand to their internal resources. They are usually funded as a percentage of revenues, based on headcount or through a baseline budget adjustment, methods which inadequately reflect or satisfy business needs. The expense center model is not appropriate for any corporate strategy today. It is the vestige of an era when technology wasn't essential to business growth and transformation.

As its name implies, an expense center IT organization is focused on cost containment. This aspect mistakenly leads many business leaders to assume it is the right model for a company with a price leadership corporate strategy. After all, low price is tantamount to market leadership for these companies. Yet, investing more in technology often helps reduce the cost of products and services due to productivity gains.

Take Walmart. For this retail giant, cost leadership often results from *outspending* its competitors on business technology, not cutting it to the bone. Its technology business model is best described as a value partner even though its customer-facing value proposition is largely about low prices. For example, in 1987, Walmart built its own satellite network. At the time, it was the largest private satellite communication system in the world. It gave the retailer a distinct advantage in managing its inventory and supply chain.

The company continues to make dramatic investments in IT to support its "every day low cost" strategy. But it's now more than that. This Bentonville, Arkansas-based retailer acquired the Silicon Valley firm Kosmix (shopping search and advertising engine) in 2011 to form @WalmartLabs, Walmart's digital research and development program. It formed Walmart eCommerce in the Valley as well, and it runs

Walmart.com. More recently, in October 2015 Walmart CEO Doug McMillon announced that the company would increase its capital expenditures on eCommerce and digital initiatives from $700 million in FY15 to a projected $1.1 billion in FY17.

It is this retailer's strategy of price leadership, and its linking of IT services to unique business value, that justifies Walmart's investments and drives its technology business model. Walmart is clearly demonstrating that an expense center model is inappropriate even for a cost leadership corporate strategy.

The following discussion summarizes how the expense center archetype fails to implement even the basics of each TBM discipline:

- **Create Transparency:** IT leaders see their costs through the standard financial reporting model of the enterprise by relying on a structure of general ledger (GL) accounts and cost centers. They have few meaningful metrics to discuss cost and performance tradeoffs with their business partners.

- **Deliver Value for Money:** Measuring cost efficiency depends on traditional systems management practices, such as capacity planning, with little insight into financial tradeoffs. Thus, benchmarking, if performed at all, is a project undertaken once every one or two years. Spending cuts are driven top down and usually without understanding the impact on service levels or risk.

- **Shape Business Demand:** Business partners are not allocated costs at all *or* are allocated costs based on a predetermined rate, such as their percentage of the firm's total revenues or its number of employees. Cost allocations provide little incentive for a business unit to change its consumption of technology.

- **Plan and Govern:** The technology budget is often based on a percentage of revenues, cost per employee, or another arbitrary formula. Budgets are managed at the cost center level, and cuts are often made top down without any understanding of how services will be impacted afterwards.

Service Provider

Service provider organizations have defined a portfolio of services and formalized roles for service owners and business relationship managers (BRMs). Service providers focus on the maturity of service management processes (e.g., IT Infrastructure Library [ITIL] or Microsoft Operations Framework) to define and deliver services efficiently at the promised level of quality.

Service providers often operate at arm's length from their business partners, much like a vendor-customer relationship. They rely on the BRM to understand their business partners, anticipate their needs, and position solutions to meet those needs. The BRM also discusses IT performance and consumption with your business partners. Service providers employ service owners to define and deliver services, create service packages (i.e., different service levels), establish service level agreements, and more. The service owners will collaborate with BRMs to negotiate service level agreements with your business partners, set expectations, review performance on a regular basis, and make service level adjustments.

The service provider model is well suited for most shared services organizations. Since these organizations must serve the needs of multiple business constituencies, the service provider model delivers standardized services at clearly specified levels of quality and costs. Indeed, businesses that choose a shared services approach generally do so to improve their operations, something this model also supports quite well.

In the service provider model, projects and other change-the-business investments are often restricted to technology services, such as new applications, even though these may be driven by transformational or other high-value business initiatives. However, the role of the business technology organization is often limited to the technical aspects of those projects or investments.

The following discussion summarizes how the service provider archetype typically implements each TBM discipline:

- **Create Transparency:** Tech leaders know the total costs of delivering services, including services/costs on a per-unit basis. Asset owners understand how their assets are consumed by providing services. Service owners understand how their services are consumed by their business partners and at what cost.

- **Deliver Value for Money:** Tech leaders monitor the unit costs of their services and towers (including assets). They benchmark their costs and cost ratios regularly to identify variances internally, over time, and against industry peers. They also regularly set targets for improving cost for performance and to measure attainment.

- **Shape Business Demand:** Business partners are allocated costs based on the actual or planned consumption of services, which are often based on pre-established rates (prices). They receive a bill of IT that provides the details of consumption. Business partners are thus incentivized to balance consumption with service value.

- **Plan and Govern:** The budget is often set based on the amount of services to be delivered and consumed by the business, after considering the headwinds (e.g., salary increases) and tailwinds (e.g., depreciation roll-offs). Project funds are then established separately based on business requirements and IT4IT improvements.

Value Partner

Like service providers, value partner technology organizations are distinct from their business partner organizations. They are headed by a technologist,[25] not a line-of-business leader, and usually support multiple business units or product lines. However, value partners are more ingrained in the business than most service provider organizations are.

The value partner depends on trust and also knowledge of the business because they are responsible for delivering bespoke business applications or integrated solutions. They must know not only how to

---

[25] Value partner leaders often have business leadership backgrounds.

serve their business partners, but also know how to collaborate closely with them on innovating business capabilities, distinguishing the business from the competition, lowering business costs, and so on. Value partners own the business technology and make decisions on how that technology will be used by the business, but they do not own the line of business itself (which is what distinguishes value partners from business drivers, as described below).

Value partner relationship status is earned by:

- Creating a governance program that enables you, your business partners, and your corporate leadership to review, discuss, and manage the IT investment portfolio against business goals and needed capabilities;

- Clearly differentiating the business value of your IT services through a regular review process that involves process representatives (service owners, BRMs, etc.) and other stakeholders from the business and IT;

- Delivering professional services, such as application development, information security reviews, business application design and planning, business process analysis, enterprise architecture, and so on. These services demonstrate that your organization understands the business it is supporting, not just the technology it is enabling; and finally

- Meeting other core financial requirements, such as minimum performance levels, the establishment of KPIs, competitive unit costs, and expedient problem resolution.

Today, there is no better example of value partnership than those technology leaders who are leading the digital agenda for their firms. It means they've gained the trust of their business partners (including the CEO) and understand the business very well. Still, it's more than that. In *Leading Digital*, authors George Westerman, Didier Bonnet and Andrew McAfee argue that three elements are needed by technology leaders in digital enterprises: (1) forging a strong IT-business relationship, (2) building the necessary digital skills, and (3) delivering an effective technology platform for digital processes.[26] Successfully leading the digital agenda means you excel at being a value partner.

The following discussion summarizes how the value partner archetype typically implements each TBM discipline:

- **Creating Transparency:** Value partners know the total cost of delivering business application services, including those on a per-unit basis. They often know the total cost of delivering business capabilities (as discussed in Chapter 11) so they and their business partners can decide on tradeoffs. Service owners also understand how their services enable business outcomes and at what cost, such as the cost per business transaction.

- **Delivering Value for Money:** Tech leaders monitor the unit costs of business application services. They balance tech spending across their portfolio and make tradeoffs to improve value. They also measure and manage investment levels in their services as a portfolio over time.

- **Shaping Business Demand:** Technology costs are evaluated as business costs. Investments in technology are based on the business impact on product-line P&Ls.

- **Planning and Governing for Value:** The budget is based on business plans that have a clear connection between innovation and service demands and IT resource needs. Investment targets are evaluated to ensure good alignment between portfolio needs and funding levels.

---

[26] Westerman, George, Didier Bonnet, and Andrew McAfee. Chapter 8. "Building Technology Leadership Capabilities." *Leading Digital: Turning Technology Into Business Transformation*. Boston: Harvard Business Review, 2014. Kindle ed.

Business Driver

Business driver organizations *are the business*. This model is only possible when the products or services delivered to external customers are technology-centric. If your company provides Software- (SaaS), Platform- (PaaS), or Infrastructure-as-a-Service (IaaS) *to generate revenue*, then this is your business model. If you are not in the as-a-service business per se, but you still provide technology-based services to your company's customers, then you fall into the business driver category as well.

For example, the online store of a brick-and-mortar retailer represents a business driver. Even an investment bank where services rely heavily on technology may fit this model. Or perhaps the business unit of an aircraft manufacturer that provides online flight scheduling services is a business driver. In each case, the services of these technology organizations demand such an intimate relationship between business process owners and IT service owners that the two roles are largely indistinguishable.

Many business driver technology organizations start out that way; but a service provider or value partner often becomes ("earns the right to become") a business driver. For example, shared technology organizations are sometimes spun out as a separate business unit with its own P&L. In those cases, technology services become the actual business.

In this way, CIOs become leaders of business driver organizations. Indeed, with the emergence of the cloud, CIOs are often given responsibility for their company's external "Technology-as-a-Service" business lines. This scenario happens when the CIO has proven his or her ability to run IT like a business. This is something noted by Hunter and Westerman as well: "When CIOs focus on business performance and then deliver it, sooner or later they are perceived not merely as leaders of a technical organization but as business executives capable of contributing beyond their immediate organizational specialty."[27]

The following discussion summarizes how the business driver archetype typically implements each TBM discipline:

- **Creating Transparency:** Business (tech) leaders know the total cost of delivering business capabilities, including the per-unit basis. They understand their business cost dynamics and how all costs are shaped by changing business conditions and demands.

- **Delivering Value for Money:** Business leaders monitor both their technology and non-technology costs. They manage the unit costs of their business capabilities, such as cost per trade or the monthly cost to serve a subscriber. They aggressively seek cost efficiencies by trading labor costs for technology costs (via process automation) or by improving reliability.

- **Shape Business Demand:** The cost of technology is baked into the firm's product prices. Demand is shaped through the market of which the firm is a part.

- **Planning and Governing for Value:** Technology budgets are integral to product-line fiscal plans. Business planning is also tech planning.

The following pages summarize these and other attributes for all four of these archetypes.

Moving Up the Chain

No CIO should aspire to running an expense center. Time and again, expense centers are forced to evolve or are replaced. What started with an outsourcing of expense centers has merely accelerated with the public cloud. This competitive intensity means IT's investments in technology

---

[27] Hunter, Richard, and George Westerman. *The Real Business of IT: How CIOs Create and Communicate Business Value.* Boston, MA: Harvard Business, 2009. 12. Print.

must directly benefit business strategy. Expense center providers rarely do this task well.

For expense center CIOs who are trying to migrate up the value chain, the service provider business model is the logical starting point. By adopting a services strategy, developing a service portfolio, defining a unique value proposition, and creating roles for service owners and BRMs, your organization will become less dispensable. It will attain an identity beyond just that of "IT."

This is only a step in the right direction, however. Service provider IT organizations are increasingly at risk of being replaced in whole or in part by external service providers, including the cloud. There is an exception, however. Some technology organizations are built just for the purpose of delivering cost-effective technology services at scale. Common in large organizations, especially in global banks, CTO-led technology organizations often provide hosting services and shared applications to their lines of business. These organizations often operate like internal cloud providers, even billing the lines of business based on consumption.

The unique value of these internal providers stems from being more cost-effective than external providers while delivering high-performance and specialized (e.g., via security, privacy) technology services. They are in a better position to offer unique value through their extensive internal knowledge of the organization — knowledge an outside provider simply cannot match. This advantage gives these service provider organizations the ability to suggest best practices for streamlining existing business processes as well as identifying areas where technology can add value (either through integration with partners or via new technology-enabled services) to the customers, partners, and affiliates of that business.

The value partner is the most indispensable model for any purely "IT" organization. At this level, you've achieved the business partner intimacy and business acumen that allows you to create unique value at will. You're leading the firm's digital agenda. Value partner CIOs have earned a seat at the table alongside their business partners because not only do they understand IT, they understand how it applies to the business. These CIOs have also demonstrated that they can run other shared services beyond just technology, such as procurement, human resource management, and even legal services.

With the credibility provided by an intense focus on value through business capabilities, and a proven ability to manage their own "P&L," IT leaders earn the right to lead more. Many assume the business driver archetype, often while holding onto their value partner and service provider roles.

Many businesses rely on technology organizations that operate in more than one business model archetype. Does this fact mean you can adopt a hybrid model, too? Yes, you can. Those that operate in multiple model archetypes often span service provider and value partner roles. They've earned the trust to be a value partner, thus taking on additional responsibilities without giving up what made them trustworthy in the first place, namely their services. Providing services (or products) to earn revenue is a logical next step.

The concepts in this book and for TBM in general apply to organizations that exhibit the characteristics of all four model archetypes. For expense center organizations, the principles of TBM will help them become better service providers. For the others, it will help them focus higher in the value chain and then optimize the business value of what they deliver.

Accountability for Service Value

Regardless of your technology business model, services are crucial to the value you deliver. They power the capabilities your business needs. Projects, while important, merely implement *new* services or *change* the ones you have. Still your business runs on your services, not your projects. Because of this fact, you must define your portfolio of services carefully and continuously improve the value of that portfolio. In reality, it is a constant balancing act. TBM helps improve value by giving you and your people important tools and metrics to make tradeoff decisions regarding cost for performance, business alignment, innovation, and agility.

Service value can be evaluated for two dimensions. The first dimension is the intrinsic **business value** of a service.[28] It describes how the service uniquely enables your business to achieve its corporate strategy and performance goals. For simplicity's sake, business value is defined using the following three categories:

- **Essential:** A service in this category is essential to business capabilities that *do not provide a competitive advantage*. Instead, the capabilities supported by this service are important or necessary for running the aspects of your business. An example is your corporate financial reporting system;[29] it is essential, but it won't help you outperform your competitors. The services that support your financial reporting are therefore *essential* and fit into this category.

- **Advantageous:** A service here supports business capabilities that provide a competitive advantage, but the service itself is not unique or difficult for others to provide. An example might be your customer relationship management (CRM) application service; customer service may represent a competitive edge for your company, but you buy public Software as a Service to support it. Unless you modify your software to the point where it will be considered unique, it's merely *advantageous* in our model.

- **Differentiator:** Services here significantly contribute to your competitive advantage and are unique and difficult for competitors or external service providers to replicate. An example might be your supply chain services; if done right, these distinguish your

---

[28] If you're familiar with ITIL, you might know this business value attribute as *service utility*. However, we consider utility in the context of corporate strategy and performance and, in particular, how well it creates a competitive edge.

[29] This does not include your ERP system as a whole, which often includes applications for which the services are "Advantageous" or "Differentiators."

business from your competition. You might even consider supporting IT services trade secrets. They are *differentiators* in our model.

You probably provide services in each category. It is unrealistic to think, however, that you can deliver only differentiators; many of your competitive advantages may not be products of your technology-enabled services. They may have more to do with the design and quality of products (e.g., Apple), the strength of your brand (e.g., The Coca-Cola Company), the efficacy of the supply chain (e.g., Walmart) or the skills and knowledge of your employees (e.g., McKinsey). Your services may be essential to exploiting these advantages, but they may not be unique in and of themselves. This differentiation is to be expected.

Furthermore, your business partners need services that do not support the competitive advantage of your business. For example, a collaboration service may not directly support a competitive advantage, but your business partners will insist on having it. The point here is that you must invest in each of your services based on their contributions to your overall corporate strategy and performance.

The second dimension of service value is **cost for performance and alignment**. This attribute is managed through value conversations on the left half of the TBM framework (see Chapter 2, Figure 2-1). They're reflected by metrics like unit costs meeting or beating targets, service level attainment, and service TCO compared to business expectations. To assess this dimension, ask the following questions about each service:

- Is the service cost-effective when compared to business expectations or equivalent alternatives?

- Is the service meeting service level agreements, satisfying users, or otherwise meeting performance expectations?

- Is your total expenditure on the service — operating and capital — aligned to your business needs and expectations? Or are you spending too much or too little on running and enhancing it?

These two dimensions of service value — business value and cost/performance/alignment — work together in the world of TBM. To illustrate, let's use the Service Portfolio Matrix shown in Figure 3-3 below. This is a mental model that will show you how the tools and metrics of TBM help you and your service owners, the business relationship managers and other decision makers to improve value.

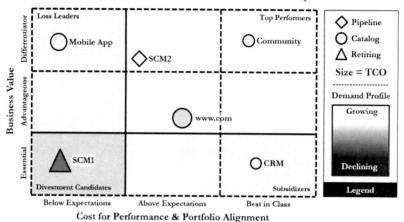

Figure 3-3: The Service Portfolio Matrix plots cost, alignment, and performance against business value for your services and their capabilities

In addition to the dimensions of the X and Y axes, the matrix shows where a service sits in the portfolio (pipeline, catalog, and retiring), the TCO of the service (both operating costs and investment spending), and the demand profile (growing vs. declining). These are all factors related to managing the value of services. Now let's examine how.

Improving Value: The Supply-Side Perspective

There is no more important role when managing the value of services than that of your service owners. They may go by other names,[30] but these are the people who own the supply-side decisions for what you deliver. Your service owners are like the product managers of a software company. They are accountable for the success of their services,

---

[30] A service owner is sometimes called a product manager or service manager. The ITIL v3 Service Strategy book refers to this role as product manager, while other ITIL v3 books refer to it as service owner.

beholden to key performance indicators set by the IT service portfolio manager and the executive management team. Good service owners deliver successful services by:

- understanding their customers, business, and markets

- monitoring and assessing service alternatives

- rationalizing the technologies used to deliver their services

- building different service level packages or tiers of service to give their customers choice

- managing costs, budgets, and financial performance

- managing and setting rates (unit rates, prices)

Service owners[31] are responsible for the entire lifecycle of the service. Without a lifecycle perspective, service owners will struggle to apply a portfolio mindset, especially when it comes to making or recommending investments in new services, introducing new service packages, and retiring other services.

Service owners are not service *delivery* managers. They are not responsible for the day-to-day operation and support of the service. Instead, service delivery managers work with service managers, application owners, tower owners, and others to ensure that their services are being performed according to expectations and commitments.

---

[31] A good description of the service owner role is provided by Rebecca Jacoby of Cisco and can be found online at:
http://www.cisco.com/c/dam/en_us/training-events/le21/le34/assets/events/i/CIOSummit-Handout.pdf

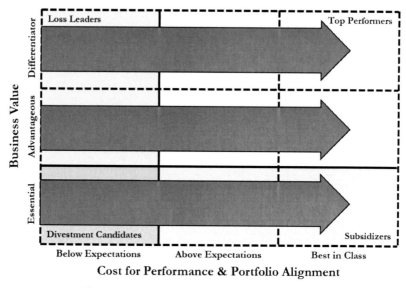

Figure 3-4: Service owners improve the cost-effectiveness and
business alignment of service spending

Service owners are responsible for improving the financial performance of their services. They work to right-size their spending levels, using the cost-for-performance tradeoffs made possible by TBM, e.g., better performance at a higher cost, tighter capacity for a lower cost.

Your service portfolio managers work with service owners and business relationship managers to manage the service portfolio. They set the services strategy to deliver on your value proposition and support the company's strategy. They create the management model for service value and the service portfolio value. They also decide on tradeoffs between service investments (or settle disputes between service owners in the quest for resources, as the case may demand). In doing so, they help service owners improve alignment of service spending to business value.

Improving Value: The Demand-Side Perspective

Once services are defined and owned, there is nothing more important for linking the supply of those services with business demand than the role of the business relationship manager (BRM). While service owners and service portfolio managers are accountable for the success of what is delivered, BRMs ensure that business partners are successful and satisfied with that effort. They fulfill this role by:

- liaising with business partners to understand their needs and their business plans

- working with service owners, enterprise architects, business process owners, and others to define and propose solutions for new business problems

- communicating the business value, business consumption, and cost of the services in the portfolio (or, more specifically, the catalog)

- assessing and negotiating the business demand for your services

- identifying and addressing service-related issues by working with service owners, service managers, enterprise architects, and others

BRMs are like the account managers of a services vendor (and are sometimes called account managers or client relationship managers). They listen to their business partners, understand their plans and pains, and propose solutions. They also wield the service catalog[32] and identify the need for new services in the pipeline. In this regard, the BRMs influence the technology supply.

They are also authorities on demand patterns and trends. They serve a critical demand management function by prioritizing what your business partners think is most important, communicating the cost of service choices, and helping defer or eliminate low-value requests from the business. They are mindful of supply-side constraints but manage to meet the goal of ensuring the business partner's success.

Business process owners also play a key role in demand management. They are business partners, but they differ from line-of-business owners. They often reside in a shared services organization and are responsible for the design, implementation, and continuous improvement of

---

[32] The service catalog is usually owned and managed by a service catalog manager and/or service portfolio manager.

common processes across the enterprise. They are accountable for achieving the promised benefits of their processes.

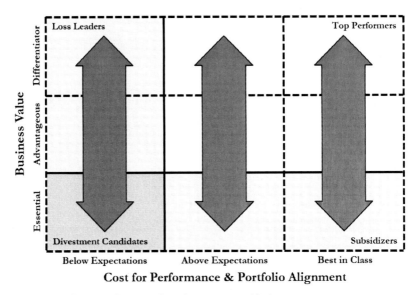

Figure 3-5: Business relationship managers and business process owners manage the business value of services

Because their roles are so interdependent, business process owners should be paired with the service owners who support their processes. In many cases, this is a one-to-one pairing. Pairing service owners with process owners provides the necessary supply-to-demand linkage between your services and the business.

Taken together then, BRMs and business process owners are responsible for defining business value and managing demand. It may be counterintuitive to make these roles responsible for defining value, but value is indeed a function of business need. These roles bridge the gap between the business's processes and its IT services. Therefore, they are essential to delivering value.

Overcoming Resistance

For your service owners, business relationship managers, and other decision makers to be successful in managing value, they need the power to make changes. But that's not easy. Changing cost for performance and business alignment of service spending is often frustrated by a lack of agility, especially in the form of fixed costs. Improving the intrinsic business value of services is often frustrated by a lack of innovation funding or capital.

The TBM framework addresses this issue. The right-side value conversations are all about agility and investment in innovation. Decisions made through TBM help you make intelligent tradeoffs to improve agility, such as adopting public cloud services to "variablize" your costs. They also help you properly invest in an innovation program and evaluate your portfolio spending.

That's how left-side and right-side value conversations work together. The left side is about managing the value of services; the right side arms IT with the agility and investment needed to make necessary changes.

Key Takeaways

- The foundation of TBM is positioning your organization properly to deliver value. This position depends on what you deliver and why the business needs to get it from you.

- Evaluate the alignment of your technology business model and your position. What services do you provide? Are you funded properly? Do you provide the right level of transparency? How do you deliver value for money? How do you shape demand? Do those practices align to your unique value proposition?

- It is no longer acceptable to operate as an expense center. Be careful to avoid this often accidental technology business model by instead adopting the right disciplines of TBM.

- Manage the business value of your services by optimizing their intrinsic value along with cost for performance and business alignment. You can do so by establishing roles for service ownership, business relationship management, and where needed, business process owners. Then, use TBM to arm your people with the insights they need to make good business decisions.

ViewPoint: **TBM Enables Commercial-Style IT Organizations**

IT organizations continue to face increasing pressure as demand for IT services explodes while cost and budget pressures increase. In addition, the growing adoption of public cloud and shift to digital are challenging corporate IT cost structures and financial models by pushing them towards true consumption-based (vs. allocations) and cost of goods sold, or COGS (vs. General & Administrative) measurement. To respond to these pressures and to prevent being circumvented by business units/end users, leading IT organizations are going beyond process optimization and are increasingly rethinking how they operate with a more "commercial-style delivery model" — or running internal IT as an IT service provider.

While exposing commercial-style delivery models to businesses and end users is a trend, its real impact is not yet fully understood. McKinsey collaborated with the Technology Business Management Council to develop an assessment instrument, the **TBM Index™**, to measure organization maturity across several core practices and capabilities and understand their link to measurable business impact.

The TBM Index assesses the maturity of IT organizational practices along four dimensions:

- **Service orientation** — degree of service orientation in the interface IT exposes to business, and how demand and costs are measured and billed at a service level

- **Operating model and organization** — how IT is organized to deliver on service expectations and operate in a "commercial style"

- **Data and Tools** — data management and automation in place to manage IT cost flows

- **Management capabilities** — specific practices and capabilities to enable a commercial-style IT organization (e.g., design-to-value)

Additionally, the assessment links these underlying practices and their maturity to the business impact as measured along three dimensions:

- **Service quality and satisfaction:** improvements across the interface and collaboration between business and internal IT stakeholders

- **Financial:** reduction of per-unit and absolute costs, change in variable vs. fixed cost structure, and run-the-business vs. change-the-business spending mix

- **Speed of delivery:** increase of speed of delivery, optimization of time to market, and demand process

We conducted in-depth interviews and surveyed more than 50 global organizations to build a knowledge base. The exercise spanned nine different industries (e.g., banking, insurance, healthcare, high-tech, media, manufacturing, oil & gas, retail and transportation) including organizations with less than $500 million in IT budget to those with more than $1 billion.

Our assessment indicates that organizations in general have only achieved basic maturity across all dimensions. Indeed, more than two-thirds demonstrated a baseline level of maturity. However, a business improvement of up to 20 percent in key areas (cost, quality, speed) is highly correlated with the level of maturity.

This research also revealed that organizations fall into one of five archetypes representing different levels of TBM maturity:

1. **Transparency Driven:** Creates IT cost, performance, complexity, and consumption transparency

2. **Cost Optimizer:** Achieves cost optimization from transparency while meeting business needs

3. **Business Portfolio Alignment:** Better aligns IT portfolio to business objectives

4. **Business Capabilities Enabler:** Enables new business capabilities while continuing to provide existing services optimally

5. **Enterprise Transformation:** Drives business transformation

When analyzing business impact, we found that in terms of TBM maturity, the top-quartile companies have achieved twice the impact of average companies in three areas:

- **Quality of service** improved 15 to 25 percent for top quartile versus 5 to 15 percent on average

- **IT cost** reduced up to 20 percent for top quartile versus up to 10 percent on average

- **Speed of delivery** increased 15 to 25 percent for top quartile versus 5 to 15 percent on average

Moreover, three primary dimensions set the top-quartile companies apart from their peers:

- Services defined across applications, infrastructure, and end-use, organized in a catalog with standard platforms and packages

- Costs broken into unit costs, amount consumed, and service levels utilized

- Tools and data in place to let transparency motivate actionable IT cost structure

While organizations have adopted TBM practices over the past few years, many still lack overall strategy for moving towards more mature practices (archetypes 3, 4, and 5 in our model). Some of the areas that would need immediate attention in order to fully realize the benefits of TBM practices include:

- Setting a clearer aspiration or vision for what great looks like, followed by articulating the value at stake by defining IT cost savings or IT effectiveness targets, and then measuring and communicating against these targets

- Ramping up services-oriented transformation (e.g., evolving showbacks into chargebacks reflecting true cost drivers, offering more standardized services)

- Moving towards a commercial-style management of IT services and clear separation between demand and supply

- Investing in tools to improve data and service quality (e.g., rigorous collection and tracking of inventory, measuring usage down to consumption drivers, improved financial and operational reporting)

- Focusing on innovation and continuous improvement to enable service efficiency/effectiveness (e.g., performance management framework, use of IT economics in decision-making)

From these findings, we conclude that organizations that have not yet started the TBM journey can adopt these practices and drive bottom-line financial impact and operational improvement of approximately 10 percent. Organizations that are already implementing TBM can push towards top-quartile maturity, which can double the business impact they've had to date. Furthermore, organizations aspiring to even greater impact have ample room to truly transform the IT role and overall business engagement.

If you would like to self-assess, the TBM Index is available at http://tbmcouncil.org/learn-tbm/tbm-index.html

Leandro Santos
Partner
McKinsey & Company

Himanshu Agarwal
Associate Partner
McKinsey & Company

Giovanni Maglia
Engagement Manager
McKinsey & Company

Ritesh Agarwal
Engagement Manager
McKinsey & Company

Chapter 4:
Creating Transparency

Beginning in the 1970s, the manufacturing sector made fundamental changes to how they costed their products. Many employed a new accounting model, called activity-based costing (ABC), that empowered changes in both management and design and transformed how manufacturers deliver products. The techniques inspired by ABC have survived to this day.

What led to these accounting changes? During this time, manufacturers began automating more and more work using robotics and computing. They also equipped their production personnel with advanced tooling. These changes boosted productivity dramatically. But by making production ever more capital intensive, automation shifted costs from labor, a direct expense, to overhead, an indirect expense. It also added new cost categories to overhead, such as engineering, support, and maintenance of equipment. Suddenly the indirect costs of capital and overhead were dominating the manufacturing cost structure.

Traditional cost-accounting methods could no longer provide accurate product costs. They relied too heavily on direct costing, usually based on labor. Accountants would allocate overhead (e.g., facilities, utilities, equipment, management labor, and supplies) to products based on labor and other direct costs: the more labor-intensive the product, the more overhead they would allocate to it. This approach distorted the true cost of products when automation (an indirect cost) began to reduce labor (the primary direct cost) while itself consuming a greater share of the total cost of production.

For many manufacturers, the solution was ABC. Instead of allocating overhead directly to products, ABC assigns overhead first to manufacturing activities, such as inserting a rivet, soldering a wire, applying a quart of paint, performing a test, or fixing a defect.

The cost of each activity includes the direct cost of its labor and materials as well as the indirect costs of things like equipment depreciation, facility leases, and utilities. So, instead of simply calculating direct costs, the cost of a product became the combination of its activity-based costs.

This change proved powerful. Not only did it create more accurate product costs, it also provided the levers — the activities — that plant managers, engineers, designers, and accountants could pull to change the cost of a product. So instead of making designs that were practical only from an engineering point of view, engineers could work more holistically, assimilating assembly costs within their designs. This change drove down overall costs and improved quality.

ABC helped transform manufacturing by empowering decision makers at all levels of the organization. It enabled new approaches and helped many firms adopt Total Quality Management (TQM) by exposing the true cost of defects. The impact of this change was dramatic. Because TQM was first adopted by Japanese manufacturers, it shifted the balance of power of automakers from the U.S. and Germany to Japan. Companies like Toyota redesigned production by using these new insights, creating their own production system frameworks (e.g., the Toyota Production System) and becoming both global cost and quality leaders by the end of the 1980s.

If a simple accounting change can have this level of impact on an entire industry, imagine what IT could do by applying the same principles to its operations.

Transparency via Your TBM Model

Why is transparency elusive for so many CIOs? It's not due to a lack of financial reporting. Instead, the method of reporting IT costs fails to show the cost of the things that matter to decision makers. For example, your business partners want to know what services they've consumed and how much those services cost them. Your application owners need to know the TCO of their applications, including the infrastructure they consume. Your service owners need to know the cost and consumption of their services. In most companies — and probably yours as well —

your IT costs are reported from only a single perspective: that of your corporate financial reports.

In most companies, costs are captured and reported using general ledger (GL) accounts and cost centers. GL accounts represent types of expenditures, such as hardware, software, salaries, consultants, contractors, utilities, or taxes, and expenses that are realized such as depreciation and amortization. Cost centers usually reflect organizational units, such as teams within a department. This structure is two-dimensional, as illustrated by Figure 4-1.

But what is needed is a multi-dimensional perspective of costs, married to other metrics such as units (e.g., users, servers, applications, hours of labor). The dimensions (think of these as slices or perspectives) you need include your services, applications (TCO, not just purchase costs), business units, business capabilities (if you know them), locations (e.g., data centers), vendors, and so on. These dimensions give the right people the right information to make good decisions, not possible with a GL-only view of costs.

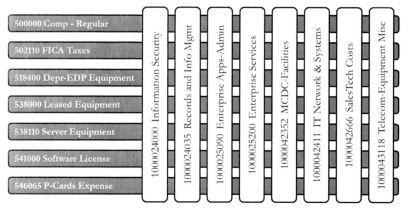

Figure 4-1: Most companies employ GL accounts and cost centers to report their costs and expenditures — a finance view that meets GAAP or IFRS reporting requirements

To create transparency, you will rely on a TBM model of costs, resources, towers, services, and consumption. This model unifies the finance, technology, and business perspectives (and data) using the TBM taxonomy introduced in Chapter 2. It does so by combining five types of data — financial, technology, service (or application), project, and business — to provide the analytics and metrics for TBM value conversations.

The value conversations of TBM depend on clarity regarding the consumption of your resources — money, people, infrastructure, software, and so on — and of your services and projects. Since money is a proxy for most other resources, most TBM models in practice are focused on financial costs, so this is where you will start. It is also where we will begin describing how to build a TBM model.

Building the TBM Model, Layer by Layer

Introduced in the last chapter, the value chain model (repeated below) for a technology-enabled business provides a good reference for modeling IT's costs and linking them to the business's consumption. Like that model, which is built in layers — resources, technology services, business services, and business capabilities — the TBM model is also built in layers, starting with your financial data. Costs and other resources are then allocated up through the model, layer by layer. In this way you can analyze your costs and consumption at each layer.

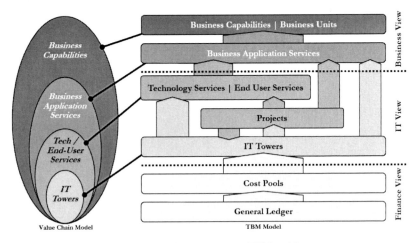

Figure 4-2: Your value chain maps to your TBM model to empower decision making at every step in value creation

You start by assigning costs to cost pools, which are high-level groupings of similar costs. In your TBM model, these will include hardware, software, labor (internal and external), outside services, facilities and power, telecom and "other" (a catch-all for miscellaneous costs). While not a layer of the business process value chain model, cost pools make cost allocations easier. Instead of allocating costs for each and every general ledger account and cost center combination, you can allocate costs upwards through the model based on fewer, more generalized rules.

Cost pools also enhance your reporting because they can be traced through the model to reveal the composition of your towers, services, capabilities, and more. They are like chemical elements, as no matter what compound you have, you can always express its composition in elemental terms. Water is H_2O. Caffeine is $C_8H_{10}N_4O_2$.

Similarly, an application might cost $48 per user per month in labor, $72 for software, $36 for hardware, $15 for facilities, $12 for outside services, $3 for telecom, and $1 other costs. You can then compare this composition to that of another application, business unit, or geography, as illustrated in Figure 4-3 below.

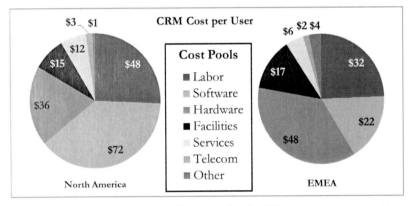

Figure 4-3: Cost pools can be traced to technologies and services helping to compare cost composition

In the example above, you might then ask why your software costs, as a percentage of total, are so much higher in North America than in EMEA. Is it due to a data problem in your model? Or perhaps North America drives more enhancements and customizations than their European counterparts? This type of comparison, which is described further in Chapter 5, can quickly highlight optimization opportunities.

From your cost pools, you assign or allocate costs to IT towers. These include applications (including app dev, support & ops, quality assurance), data centers, distributed computing, mainframe, storage, network, databases, communication, and end-user technologies. They also include elements like IT management, security and compliance, service desk, project management (PMO), and other categories of overhead. Many of your tower costs can be assigned directly from the cost pools based on your GL account and cost center structure, but some may have to be allocated based on other factors (e.g., percentage of a team dedicated to one tower versus another).

Your IT towers form the building blocks, the compounds if you will, that you use to both build *and* support services. Your TBM model will allocate some of your IT towers to projects based on how they consume application resources (e.g., app dev, quality assurance), distributed computers (e.g., servers, databases) and more. These represent the costs to build new services. But the lion's share of costs are usually allocated to existing IT services. These amounts are the costs to run those services.

Allocating tower costs to your services is best when they are data-driven because doing so drives greater fidelity in your costing and reporting and further links your team's management decisions to your company's bottom line. In some cases, you won't have the data needed to drive the allocations; estimations will have to do. In others, you will have data, such as a CMDB or asset mapping, project time tracking, service desk tickets, or storage reports to use to allocate your costs and resources. This is where data quality is often a challenge; we'll discuss this topic later in the chapter.

Finally, your service costs are consumed by your business capabilities and business units. Business capabilities are mostly unique to your organization or industry; most enterprises define their own. There are third-party models, such as the Bank Industry Architecture Network's Service Landscape models or Microsoft's Industry Reference Architectures. However you define them, you can use the TBM model to map your IT costs into those capabilities.

More often, CIOs use the TBM model to show how their services are consumed by their business units. This modeling should be done, regardless of whether or not your businesses are charged for those services. (More on charging in Chapter 6.) This business consumption should be modeled, where possible, on consumption data such as user entitlements (e.g., who is authorized to use which applications and services), user logins, desktop counts, and other statistics that reveal consumption.

Choosing the Right Allocation Methods

Correctly allocating costs and other resources is the most difficult aspect of modeling. In a perfect world, you would have high-quality consumption data from which to allocate costs from one layer of the TBM cost model to the next. Unfortunately, you rarely have all this data.

Further, most data is far from perfect (see the data quality discussion later in this chapter). For this reason, your model must also support allocations not based on consumption data, which can include approximations for resource consumption (e.g., equipment power ratings), estimates, or even-spread allocations.

However you choose to define and allocate your costs data, those choices will affect the quality of your decision-making down the road. If high-quality consumption data is used, your reporting will give you more precise levers for controlling costs and quality. If you use even spreads and educated guesses, your reporting will reflect that focus.

For example, if you allocate data center power and cooling costs (from cost sources to IT towers) based on the actual consumption of power (using data from power distribution units or hardware monitoring tools), you could target the least efficient servers and even identify applications that are driving the greatest power consumption. Using less sophisticated methods such as even spreads robs you of such a precise lever.

Incorporating Service Performance

With a cost model in place, you can create reports, dashboards, and other outputs to give your business partners a true cost perspective of what they own and use. This transparency allows service owners to see the total cost of their services. Service portfolio managers can see the total investments they are making and everyone can see how IT is investing in business capabilities. Still, cost is only one part of the cost-for-performance equation. Performance is the other. You need performance data to see where tradeoffs can be made without adversely affecting quality.

Performance comprises attributes such as responsiveness, fault tolerance, ability to recover from a disaster, and the security of your technologies, services, and data. These attributes help ensure that your services meet business expectations for performance under both normal conditions and more extreme circumstances after a disaster, such as during a cyber-attack or while under peak load.

There are several ways to incorporate service performance into your reporting. First, you can show the attainment of SLA metrics and other service quality specs in your cost reporting. Second, you can report user satisfaction levels for your services — provided you have these numbers, of course. If so, also include those results in your reports. Third, you can report the amount you're investing in performance (i.e., for each service, how much spending goes to disaster recovery, security, load balancing, Tier 1 storage, etc.).

Finally, you may be able to report the cost of any outages or disruptions. This aspect is often difficult (or impossible) to measure, but some organizations create an assumed rate for outages of mission-critical services. By multiplying the minutes of service outage by the assumed cost per minute, a cost of downtime can be calculated and shown.

Annual Run Cost	System	Function-ality	Cost to Move to Green	Reliability & Scalability	Cost to Move to Green	Efficiency Opportunity	One time Cost to Efficiency
$75M	Trading	Green	N/A	Yellow	$3M	$10M/Yr	$15M
$40M	Clearing	Yellow	$5M	Green	N/A	$5M/Yr	$8M
$30M	Customer Service	Red	$10M	Yellow	$6M	N/A	N/A
$20M	Settle-ments	Green	N/A	Yellow	$4M	$2M/Yr	$1M
$165M	Total "Base" Budget Includes "run" and in the pipeline "change" activities	$15 M Functionality Opportunity "Give you what you want to quickly meet business needs"		$13 M Reliability and Scalability Opportunity "Improve performance, reduce outages, and reduce systemic risk of failure"		$24 M Efficiency Opportunity "Spend money today to eliminate old systems and processes to reduce costs in future years"	

Figure 4-4: Dashboards integrate cost and performance data for more balanced decision-making[33]

By providing a service performance perspective, not only do you deepen the data supporting your true total cost numbers, you empower your people to spot opportunities for change. Do you need to invest more in load balancing? Has spare capacity been cut to the bone? Did your recent reduction in support spending then cause missed KPIs? This kind of transparency is critically important when making cost-for-performance decisions.

The bottom line for cost models is that they give you the ability to understand what drives the consumption of IT's resources.

Different Models, Different Perspectives

Using the cost model as a template, you can build other models as needed. When do you need these other models? One situation is when you need to set rates (prices) for your services at the beginning of the year. This is often done to create a bill of IT that is more predictable to give to your business partners than using actual costs.[34]

---

[33] Source: Carl Stumpf, Managing Director (former), CME Group. Data is fictional, for illustration only.

[34] We will discuss the bill of IT and rates management further in Chapter 6.

In this case, you would model business consumption and costs using your published rates instead of actual costs (e.g., price multiplied by quantity, or PxQ). This scenario doesn't mean you stop modeling your true costs. With a rates-driven bill of IT you still need to understand the true costs. But by having both models, you can compare the amount recovered to the actual costs incurred. It then becomes your IT services P&L statement.

You may also want a model for what-if scenarios. Here, you introduce new data or allocation assumptions to compare one scenario to another. For example, you may want to compare historical service costs against those using new sources of consumption data (say, prior estimates vs. new actuals). In this case, you would build the new model *based on* the current model, using as much of the data from your original model as possible. You would change only the data that you need to change for the new scenario and then compare the two outcomes.

TBM models may also be used to measure and manage non-financial resources as well, including labor hours, server units, power and cooling (e.g., kilowatts, carbon), WAN bandwidth, and more. A good example was shared in the introduction of this book: eBay models its environmental impact along with costs on a per-transaction basis. In theory, any resource for which you have a limited capacity can be allocated to show how it is consumed, not only directly, but also indirectly, up through the layers of your value chain.

By modeling non-financial resources, you will begin to understand how they are consumed by your services, projects, and business capabilities: How much power is consumed by each application? How many servers are needed for each CRM user? How much project labor is consumed for a service? What percentage of our data center capacity (rack space) is consumed by your storage infrastructure?

Understanding the answers to these questions and many others will help you better manage fixed- or limited-capacity resources like floor space, skilled labor, or bandwidth. In turn, that understanding will help you avoid unnecessary investments in new capacity. For example, if you optimize for the power consumed by business transactions, you can support more transactions using the same power supply. These insights then allow you to accurately translate business plans (e.g., revenue growth, hiring employees) into capacity plans and budget requests.

While these other perspectives will come in very useful as you mature, it's important to begin by modeling costs, because that is what everything comes back to over time.

Creating Trust in Your TBM Model

Your TBM model is judged first on whether or not it fairly and accurately represents what it is supposed to represent. In other words, can it be trusted? Trust in your model is difficult to earn and depends on many factors. It's not simply a matter of accuracy.

This is especially true when you're changing your model or the way in which it is used. For example, are you changing how the performance of your managers is evaluated? Are you modifying how you allocate costs to your business units, the leaders of which are compensated according to their P&Ls? Your TBM model affects livelihoods, so this trust is essential.

For this reason, your TBM model must be transparent and easy to explain. Allocations must be logical and perceived as fair[35] by your business partners and other stakeholders (e.g., application owners). Where possible, it must provide levers for decision-making, and those levers must affect the primary outcomes being reported by your model.

Do not overlook the importance of trust. Trust is essential for not only driving the adoption of the model by IT and your business partners but also for building commitment to the program. Apply the following measures to build trust through transparency in action:

---

[35] Here, fair means that the allocation of cost appears reasonable based on who or what is driving the cost and by how much. Consumption-based allocations are generally perceived as the fairest when the consumption data is considered accurate.

- Beta test new model changes with a trusted business partner. When the beta is successful, ask the business partner to help articulate the benefits of the new model.

- Prove your model accounts for every dollar. For every dollar in, there should be a dollar out.

- Explain how the majority of your costs are allocated through a plain-language, one-page document. Illustrate allocations with a simple conceptual model. This illustration also comes in handy with auditors who need to review or test your allocations.

- Ensure your peers understand how costs are allocated, how to interpret the reports, and what changes they are allowed to make. Resolve any concerns or objections they may have.

- Provide drill-downs in your reporting. Empower your consumers to see what makes up their costs so they can verify them. Are their allocated costs based on the right number of servers, users, or transaction volumes?

- Work with your CFO on an effective grace period for changes that might affect incentive payouts. Ensure that you address any potential "winners and losers" caused by switching to a new model, thus giving your business leaders time to adjust to the new model.

An Enterprise IT Model Based on Data

Data is the lifeblood of TBM. Not only does TBM provide the data needed in the right perspectives for you and your people to make better decisions, it relies on data to create those perspectives. TBM is unique in its approach to linking financial data to operational data to business data.

This is a powerful thing. Not only does this linkage help you provide the right perspectives of cost and consumption, it helps you accelerate many different types of decisions based on that data. For example, TBM uses financial accountability (which relates to incentives such as bonuses) to improve the linkage between applications and infrastructure, a challenge that perplexes so many IT leaders today. By improving this linkage, other decisions such as evaluating the impact of an infrastructure problem on your applications, services, and users, can be made more quickly and confidently.

This linkage, which depends on financial accountability, works best when it is grounded in your financial system of record.

Your Own Sources of Truth

Of all the data types you will employ, there is only one essential source of truth, and that is your corporate financial data. You must ground your cost models in this data for several reasons:

- Unlike most other data, corporate financial data is maintained independently under a tested set of internal controls.

- Corporate accounting practices are fairly standardized by industry, meaning you can compare your IT financial metrics to those of other companies because similar IT cost accounting models are employed.

- Since corporate financial data measures *corporate* performance, using it as your data source maintains the link between your technology decisions and corporate outcomes (i.e., your firm's income statement).

- Financial data often includes more than just your general ledger (GL). Sub-ledgers, such as fixed assets and payroll, provide more granular information, which improves the allocations you can make.

Once your financial data is in hand, you can use the other data types mentioned here to begin to understand the true total cost of IT. For example, technology data is created by the tools IT uses to manage infrastructure, applications, people, and projects. Sources of useful IT data include asset inventories, help desk or service desk applications (for tickets and requests for changes), monitoring and metering tools, and other IT management systems.

Services data includes the service catalog (if you have one) or a list of IT technology and business services. You can also leverage tools for mapping technologies to services, such as a configuration management database (CMDB). With these mappings, the costs of those technologies can be accurately allocated to the people, processes, and other technologies that consume them based on usage.

Project data includes both time and expense information. These are normally maintained by project management tools or time tracking systems and are important for creating granular change-the-business perspectives.

Finally, business data may include business transaction volumes, business unit revenues, headcount, and other data — historical, current, and projected.

These data sets are useful for creating the powerful perspectives your team needs to make good decisions and empower the value conversations we'll discuss later. Yet few technology organizations have all of this data. Does that mean they're not ready to embrace TBM? The answer is no, for the simple reason that TBM is a journey, and data maturity and robustness are key parts of it. The very transparency that you are creating with these data sets also will help you assess and improve your data quality.

Improving Data Quality

Obtaining good data is the most common roadblock to building a good model. Missing or low-quality data can impede accurate allocations, degrade your reporting, and impair trust in your model. For this reason, data quality is an essential element of any TBM program.

TBM leaders often struggle with a variety of data quality challenges. They often have trouble getting good data in a timely manner. This is often true when they first create their model or change it. After they've sourced new data for the first time, that process is often easily repeated. In contrast, getting complete datasets[36] with referential integrity tends to

---

[36] Referential integrity is essential for using data to drive allocations.

be a more persistent problem. To address these challenges, TBM applies a four-step approach:

1. **Use tools to transform and clean data** of obvious errors and inconsistencies. Tools may be able to correct things like improper formatting without requiring data source fixes. This process often will address a large portion of your errors.

2. **Use the model and benchmarking to help identify errors**. Load the data into your model and use (or create) reports to reveal how much of your costs cannot be allocated due to referential integrity issues and gaps in your data. (The right system will provide for data quality reporting.) Also, compare your costs to industry benchmarks; major differences are often caused by gaps in your own data.

3. **Fill gaps by using generalized allocation rules**. For example, if your data allows you to accurately allocate 80 percent of a cost pool, spread the remaining 20 percent using weights inferred from the allocated amounts.

4. **Fix source data quality problems over time** by working with data source owners. This process should include not only one-time fixes but also setting standards and procedures to prevent data quality problems from recurring.

Taking these steps to address data quality challenges depends on your system and its processes. Still, it's important to start with the data you do have and then work toward gathering (or creating) better data. You will never have perfect data of course, but the very act of modeling and using data will lead to better data — and greater decision-making power — over time.

A good example is Kaiser Permanente[37]. In addition to being the largest integrated healthcare provider in the United States, Kaiser Permanente is also a very large consumer of IT, as it uses technology to improve its healthcare services for its members. The company employs TBM to link demand to supply and, more importantly, link business strategy to its IT investments. Data is essential to these linkages.

"[Before TBM] the business was resigned to accept the costs that they were being charged and view it more as a tax than something that they could influence," recalls Steve Adams, Executive Director of IT Finance at Kaiser Permanente. "Conversations between IT and the business were repetitive, however, and not very productive. They'd ask us what decisions could they make that would affect their IT costs. We simply couldn't tell them."

"What I found with Technology Business Management is a template we could apply to get a jumpstart at building up the cost of services IT was delivering," explained Adams. Adams's team used the TBM taxonomy as the framework for their cost model. They configured mappings of raw data from their financial and IT management systems to standardized TBM terminology and formats, then configured costing rules that used their IT data to distribute costs to the taxonomy. They could immediately see the results of their cost model using the system's reports.

"Just like every other TBM practitioner we talked to, we found that our data was really dirty, especially around storage and applications," Adams recalls. The system highlighted where data were missing and were duplicated and measured "unallocated costs" to show where improvements in source data quality would place generalized costs into more granular and descriptive categories.

Adi Israel, TBM Consultant at Kaiser Permanente, built a TBM model for Yahoo before coming to Kaiser Permanente. She recognized

---

[37] Vignette built from 2015 TBM Awards interviews and case study. Kaiser Permanente was a finalist of the 2015 TBM Council awards. See video: https://youtu.be/2-oZCP6oEDY

the need for an iterative approach to data quality that involved IT stakeholders. "We worked on the process [for] acquiring the data and making sure it was available, complete, high-quality, reliable, and automated," she explained. "Then we started socializing and validating our cost engine in all levels of the organizations."

Along with improving data quality, the TBM team simultaneously worked to gain organizational buy-in. "We needed to clearly explain to business units how the new cost model was different than previous ones," Israel says. "We worked through concerns with financial analysts who were accustomed to their own tools and cautious about a new platform. Also, IT needed to create role-based accountability for the more holistic total-cost views of application services and technical services."

This story is a familiar one within TBM circles, and the advice is always similar: "When we first started our journey, everyone [in the TBM Council] said, 'Your data is not going to be perfect. You're not going to be able to model everything the way you want, but start,'" recalls Adams. "And I can tell you that's proven to be so true. We just needed to start and things started to fall into place. Are we where we need to be? No, but we are way further down the path than if we had waited for perfection before starting."

Sourcing Data from Vendors

Much of the data needed for your own cost models is often owned or managed by vendors and outsourcers. Third parties maintain asset lists, produce utilization and consumption data, track project hours, and manage support tickets — all of which can be used for consumption-based modeling.

This circumstance can be problematic, because despite your best efforts to create transparency, IT vendors obscure true perspectives by delivering bills (i.e., financial data) separately from assets, utilization, and consumption reports, thereby hindering any meaningful analysis of cost for performance.

As a result, it is imperative you include (or add during your next round of negotiations) contract provisions for obtaining this kind of data from your vendors. This "TBM clause" helps you hold vendors accountable for providing cost data you need to manage the same way as other costs using TBM. This data should arrive on a timely basis, such that it becomes a routine, monthly deliverable. This is not an academic exercise. Only by creating transparency of your vendor's services and technologies can you negotiate cost-effective contracts and hold vendors accountable for *their* performances.

How Much Data Is Enough?

With all this talk about data, you may be asking how much do you need? Of course, the answer depends on which outcomes you want to drive. To build a foundational transparency of costs by cost pools and IT towers, you'll need your general ledger, fixed assets, and HR data at a minimum. These data sources exist in virtually every organization. Still, to create application TCO, the data you need will depend on your TBM roadmap.[38]

Many teams begin by costing a selected set of applications, perhaps starting with their corporate ERP applications. Indeed, these may represent a large percentage of corporate IT spend, consuming a large share of both infrastructure and labor (support and projects). The data to cost ERP applications is illustrated in Figure 4-5 below, with good/better/best options sorted from bottom to top.

---

[38] The TBM roadmap is discussed in greater detail in Chapter 10.

Best	• List of ERP apps • Infrastructure mappings • Support time • Internal project hours • Consultant hours	• Simple app list • Server and storage mappings • Support time tracking • Project data (hours)	• End user devices • Inventory of apps • Infrastructure mappings • Network mappings, incl WAN links • Support time	• Corporate, BU and cloud apps • Infra mappings, incl. public cloud • Support time tracking • Project hours
Better	• List ERP apps • Infrastructure mappings • Support personnel with time estimates	• Simple app list • Server and storage mappings • Support personnel with time estimates	• Inventory of end user devices • Inventory of all workplace apps • Server counts and storage estimates • Support estimates	• Inventory of corporate and BU applications • Server counts and storage estimates • Support estimates
Good	• List of ERP applications • Infrastructure estimates • Support estimates	• Simple app list • Server counts and storage estimates • Support estimates	• Desktops and laptops • Office & other workplace apps • Server counts and storage estimates • Support estimates	• Inventory of corporate applications • Server counts and storage estimates • Support estimates
	Corporate ERP	Top 20 Applications	Workplace Services	All Applications

Quality of Data (vertical axis label)

Scope of Data

Figure 4-5: The data used for application costing matures in both scope and quality over time based on your TBM roadmap and decision-making needs

As time goes on, IT leaders begin costing more of their applications and services, but often in a prioritized fashion. In the figure above, this process is shown by going from left (Corporate ERP) to right. First, the top 20 applications may represent approximately 80 percent of the application costs, for example. Then, workplace services, such as desktops, network connectivity, and user authentication, may represent a major controllable cost as well. By beginning with a narrow set of applications or services and expanding over time, you can minimize your up-front data requirements and still create highly actionable transparency early on. Attempting to cost all applications may be the last step or phase in your journey.

Notice the data quality dimension in Figure 4-5. It represents another dimension of your data roadmap. You might begin with good (or "good enough") data to begin your costing and improve it over time. The benefits of improving are more granular decision-making, usually focused on specific infrastructure used to support each application and service, and the labor to support and enhance each.

The People Needed for Transparency

The transparency of TBM empowers decision makers such as service owners, BRMs, portfolio managers, and business process owners; they are the consumers of transparency, responsible for improving cost for performance, business alignment, and other outcomes of TBM. However, what about the roles you need to create and sustain transparency?

The first three roles needed — your TBM administrator, TBM analyst and TBM program director — often exist within a dedicated TBM office (i.e., a small group focused on TBM). However, they may reside within a governance team, a strategy and planning team, IT finance, or even corporate finance. The other two roles — executive sponsor and corporate finance officer — are necessary to ensure organizational alignment, and these roles sit outside of the TBM office.

TBM System Administrator

The TBM system administrator manages your models and data, builds reports, administers TBM system user accounts, and trains those users. For most organizations, even large ones, it is not a full time job. If your TBM system is highly automated, integrated with your data sources, and provides for self-service analytics and reporting, a single analyst is often sufficient to get the job done even for large IT organizations. Indeed, some organizations outsource this role to a third-party provider who delivers the TBM system as a managed service.

TBM Analyst or TBM Architect

The TBM analyst, sometimes called a TBM architect, is pivotal to the success of the program. This professional understands the data and reports, works with data owners and report consumers to improve reporting, analyzes output, and guides decisions.

A good TBM analyst often has served in various IT roles prior to the current role and has learned many of the core disciplines of IT, such as systems administration, project management, service delivery, support, architecture, and application development. This experience not only provides a solid understanding of the data sources coming from IT, it means the analyst may have good relationships with data owners and IT decision makers.

The TBM analyst should understand both finance and enterprise technology and work closely with your TBM administrator to create meaningful reports, help all users understand those reports, and facilitate deeper dives into the data.

If possible, staff the TBM analyst or architect role from within your organization. Fortunately, the TBM analyst job is often seen as an exciting new role, key to improving value or reducing costs and therefore essential to the organization's success. It often appeals to employees who are looking for a new challenge and a way to expand their knowledge. For this reason, it can often be easy to find good candidates from within the organization.

TBM Program Director

Many times, the TBM program director is your IT finance leader (the CFO of IT, if you will). This makes sense when the IT finance leader reporting to the IT organization possesses the right leadership qualities and is thus able to build and manage relationships with key stakeholders. If not, another executive should be assigned or hired for the position within the technology organization.

The TBM program director should be included in the office of the CIO or be part of your IT governance organization. Elevating the TBM program at this level helps ensure that you continue to operate transparently and use data to drive important technology-business decisions at all levels of the organization.

Executive Sponsor

TBM is transformative and cannot be done well in a leaderless silo. The perspectives that TBM creates depend on data from too many parts of the business, and thus the value of these perspectives is wholly dependent on holding people accountable. Simply put, TBM success is not possible without executive sponsorship.

For most companies, the CIO should sponsor the TBM program. During its early stages, the CIO should be intimately involved in the TBM program to reinforce the importance of TBM to the success of his or her organization and to IT's business partners. The CIO should regularly address TBM during discussions with IT leaders, including any Office of the CIO staff. This will help ensure support for the program from those who must provide data and those who must act on the information that TBM provides.

The CIO should articulate the necessity of the program to the CEO, corporate COO, and other stakeholders and advertise early successes, such as cost reduction opportunities found or portfolio decisions made. Finally, the CIO should partner with the CFO to create and execute a roadmap for transparency that often includes changes to the corporate accounting model, such as how you charge back or hold business partners accountable for IT spending.

Corporate Finance Officer

A strong partnership with corporate finance is essential. It often helps to have a dedicated liaison within corporate finance to work with your TBM office. This person may be a corporate finance officer or analyst who is trained on IT. The finance liaison helps ensure that the TBM office has the financial data it needs (including data from any corporate sub-ledgers, like fixed assets or payroll), collaborates with the TBM office on the accounting policies that affect IT, helps resolve budget variances in a timely fashion, and ensures business unit incentives for IT consumption are in line with the TBM program.

Key Takeaways

- Use the TBM model to overcome the two-dimensional limitation of corporate accounting systems. Create perspectives for costs, consumption, and other facts needed by the different decision makers within your organization.

- Start with the corporate financial data as your source of financial truth, and include other data, such as asset lists, project data, tickets, and more to allocate and model your costs. Use the transparency afforded by TBM to fill in data gaps and improve data quality over time — a key part of any TBM journey.

- Use the model to translate between finance, corporate, and business unit on the perspectives of costs, resources, and consumption. Incorporate service performance, user satisfaction, or even business outcomes to balance those perspectives and thus enable fact-based tradeoff decisions.

- The data you need for better decision-making will evolve over time. You may begin with a smaller scope of data — say, for your ERP applications portfolio — and lesser data quality. Build from this simpler state in order to improve reporting and decision-making capabilities over time.

- Plan to employ at least a part-time TBM analyst or architect to manage data, run reports, perform analyses, and make recommendations. The TBM analyst is best hired from inside your team because she already knows your business, technology, and operations better than an external hire will. Leverage the fact that TBM is a valuable skill for any employee to learn and thus a fantastic step forward in the career of any senior staff member.

- Run your TBM program from within IT, but with proper partnership and collaboration with corporate finance. An IT finance leader can be a strong TBM office leader, but other planning or strategy professionals make good candidates as well.

- Be sure to provide the necessary executive sponsorship for your program. TBM is rarely successful when sponsored at low levels in an enterprise.

Chapter 5:
Delivering Value for the Money

Value is in the eye of the beholder. This facet has never been truer than with IT or business technology, as this value depends on the perception of your business partners. If your services provide them with something they want or need *and* have a positive impact on their ability to execute, then they might deem those services valuable (or even invaluable).

The catch, however, is even if your business partners view your services in a favorable light, they may still feel you're too expensive. That is why you must demonstrate that you can provide services and technologies cost-effectively; that your cost for performance is in line with industry peers and now, because of public cloud alternatives, third-party providers of similar services.

Delivering IT cost-effectively also means accounting for factors like security, disaster recovery, fault tolerance, compliance, and any unique capabilities you provide your business due to your embedded nature and deep understanding of your own business processes. This aspect is particularly true when comparing internally sourced services, such as application hosting or development, to third-party providers. External providers often do not bear the same level of responsibility for aspects like regulatory compliance or adherence to preferred-vendor purchasing policies that can indeed drive up costs.

As Richard Hunter and George Westerman point out in their 2009 book, *The Real Business of IT:*[39]

> *"Recognition of the business value of IT takes more than a change in viewpoint. In many enterprises, executives must overcome a long history of disappointment if they are to appreciate the value generated by IT. …*

---

[39] Hunter, Richard, and George Westerman. *The Real Business of IT: How CIOs Create and Communicate Business Value.* Boston, MA: Harvard Business, 2009. Print.

Successful CIOs begin to demonstrate and improve the value of IT by showing value for money. They make it clear — in word and deed — that the IT team earns its role as the company's preferred provider, every day. They report on IT's operational performance in terms of essential services and outcomes that are visible to the rest of the business. They link the cost of IT operations to the quality and volume of service. And they use unit costs and standard performance metrics to compare their services with those of other units or enterprises in an apples-to-apples way."

It is the final part of this statement that we will focus on in this chapter, namely how to use unit costs, standardized performance metrics, and benchmarking to demonstrate that IT is an efficient provider of technology and business services. In simple terms, this chapter describes how to manage and show that your cost-for-performance ratios are in line with competitors and other options (such as the cloud).

As Hunter and Westerman explain, business partner disappointment with IT is the norm. Cost transparency can change that perception, however, in ways that you and your business partners will find transformative. Transparency alone won't make up for missed deadlines, unplanned outages, security breaches, or the other table stakes of being a technology provider. Yet it can help right a misinformed perception that IT is either too expensive or fails to meet commitments.

Benchmarking is a powerful tool. Not only can it be used to defend your budget, it can tell you where you need to focus your analysis of spending to ensure dollars are allocated effectively. Benchmarking can highlight where you can increase or decrease spending to help meet business goals and influence positive project outcomes.

For example, at First American, a leading provider of real estate title insurance, CIO Larry Godec was charged by CEO Dennis Gilmore with figuring out just one thing: Were they spending too much on technology, too little, or just the right amount? That's what Dennis wanted to know. Finding out put Larry on a TBM journey that not only answered the question, but it also allowed the organization to rationalize spending in a way that continues to control costs even today while improving business unit P&Ls.

Before we get into the details of delivering value for money, we need to do a little housekeeping about terminology. It is true that the primary unit of measure in TBM is cost. However, cost is only used as a representation, a measure of resources — people, technologies, facilities, services — and an indicator of where these are being deployed and to what effect. Cost is also used because that is the one measure that everyone can agree on. Unlike value, a dollar is a dollar. It is unambiguous and universally convertible from geography to geography, country to country, and language to language. That makes it an ideal yardstick. But that is all it is — a yardstick. The cost of something is irrelevant without context.

So how do you know if you are delivering IT services cost-effectively? There are four techniques to use:

1. Benchmark by industry peers and business unit.

2. Perform per-unit cost trending to ensure continuous cost improvement.

3. Measure and manage the cost of spare capacity, unused assets, and vendor spending.

4. Closely monitor and manage your project spending.

Let's start with the first of these — benchmarking.

Benchmarking Your Costs

For many technology leaders, benchmarking often feels like a necessary evil. It is thrust upon them by their CFO who wants to ensure that they're getting sufficient value for the money they spend on technology (especially with shared IT service departments). While benchmarking is often maligned, it can be a very powerful tool for the technology leader to use to manage his or her own efficiency.

Benchmarking is the act of comparing your performance to that of a peer group (outside or inside the organization), a standard, or over time (from a baseline) using similar metrics with agreed-upon meanings. As we've discussed, benchmarking helps you identify where your spending is in or out of line with that of your peers.

Also, benchmarking allows you to spot the delta in your spending. TBM gives you the tools to zero in on why those costs are out of line by identifying the business and IT resource consumption patterns that are driving them. TBM thus reveals the *details* of your spending.

It is also important to remember that cheaper is not always better. If you are consistently spending more than a peer group benchmark, for example, then your organization is probably unique in some way compared to that other group, or your data could be off somehow. Either way, benchmarking will tell you whether something is amiss, and TBM will show you where to find it.

If you are well below the averages, then maybe you might be introducing more risk in some way, such as running tight on capacity or putting off much-needed hardware refreshes to save money. Regardless of where the data leads, your focus should always be on achieving the best cost-for-performance ratio for your organization, not just the best cost (or the best performance).

This is why finding and using the right metrics from comparable peers is so important. Would you compare your spending to a healthcare provider if you're an automaker? Probably not. So when looking for external benchmarking metrics, get them from similar companies. This is also why internal benchmarks can be so powerful!

When comparing internal business units, those metrics too must be viewed in context of what that unit of the organization is doing (e.g., Marketing vs. HR) and how it consumes technology. Consumption can make a difference. For example, if you're comparing the average cost of end-user computing, such as desktops, between an engineering department and corporate finance, the fact that engineers use much more powerful desktops, bigger monitors, and more storage than accountants do will make an obvious difference. Still, internal benchmarking can be very powerful because it highlights how your business units are consuming technology individually and how they compare to one another.

Benchmarking helps demonstrate to your business partners that you are serious about running IT efficiently. More importantly, benchmarking gives you an idea of where to start looking for improvements. As Forrester Research analysts Sophia Vargas and Dave Bartoletti, note in their September 2014 report, *Benchmark Your Enterprise Cloud Adoption*:

> *"However, keep in mind that industry benchmarks are based on averages and not best practices. While they inform you of the behaviors of your peers, they do not tell you what you should be doing — they tell what you should be thinking about. They are designed to trigger questions and areas of investigation that can lead to strategy changes."*

Instead of relying on raw comparisons with benchmarking data, you should analyze internal and external benchmarking to set achievable targets for your own organization to reach. These may be targets in terms of unit costs for key technologies or key spending ratios (e.g., run-the-business vs. change-the-business). For example, if you look at your own costs and consumption of storage and see them trending upward at a dangerous trajectory while your peers are consuming less storage on average, use this information to set a goal for reducing that trajectory over the next year.

Benchmarking is also useful in negotiating with vendors. Use benchmark comparisons to drive conversations within your IT organization on how cost-effective your vendors are. Then, use those comparisons to renegotiate with your vendors and bring their rates in line with industry peers.

The comparison that you then report to your business partners, the one that will show them how you're improving value, is to communicate:

a) we know where the market or industry is going in terms of cost and performance

b)   we've set a target in line with that direction, generally a reduced rate over the prior year

c)   here's what it means to our business both in terms of cost and performance

Without benchmarking, you have no idea how cost-effectively you are providing services. Because benchmarking helps you demonstrate cost-effectiveness, identify opportunities for improvement, hold your own people and vendors accountable for being cost-effective, and justify your budget to stakeholders, the benefits far outweigh any negatives that may arise as a result.

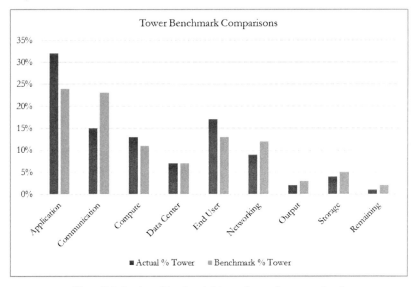

Figure 5-1: Benchmarking gives decision makers a clear perspective of variances between actuals and peer averages

Just as importantly, benchmarking can help you improve credibility, showing you as a good steward of your money. This facet was certainly true at Kaiser Permanente. "Our infrastructure benchmarking was very influential with our CFO," said IT Finance leader Steve Adams. "We were able to show her that the cost of running our infrastructure is in line with the industry, and we were benchmarking ourselves against the top quartile. In many areas we were doing well, and in other areas we could do better. But we had a plan on how to improve in those areas.

And that changed the discussion with the CFO from 'We're just spending money' to 'We really are managing what we're doing.'"[40]

Unit Cost Trending

Unit costs are simply your total costs on a per-unit basis for your services, technologies, people, and other inputs or outputs. These elements are defined by your TBM taxonomy. Measuring and tracking unit costs over time is highly insightful for commodity-like goods and services and also for highly customized ones too. This is because you're comparing the same thing over time, but with the needed perspective of *volumes (units)*.

There are two types of unit costs to understand and measure:

- **Input unit costs** are those for the resources and towers that you purchase, rent, pay, or subscribe to. For these, the cost of unused capacity is borne mostly by the provider. Generally, if you don't buy or use inputs, you don't pay for them. The main exceptions are contracts with guaranteed minimums.

- **Output unit costs** are those for what you deliver to your business partners, such as applications, services, or provisioned technologies. For these, you will bear the cost of unused capacity.

It's important to understand these two types of unit costs because they can vary over time for different reasons. Input unit costs vary when the price of something goes up or down, such as when a vendor raises prices or when employees get their annual pay raises. Output unit costs can vary because the input prices have changed *or* because you're operating at less than full capacity. Since the cost of unused capacity is included in the total cost (the numerator in your unit cost equation), but the units (the denominator) change with consumption, then the unit costs of outputs will be a bit more complicated than those for inputs.

---

[40] Adams, Steve. Interview for 2015 TBM Council awards program. August 2015.

Generally, the input unit costs of commodity-like goods and services should trend downward over time. This trend is especially true of the IT towers and sub-towers in the TBM taxonomy. When those unit costs rise, you know it is time to take action. This action may involve renegotiating with a supplier, finding new vendors, or reconsidering your sourcing model altogether (e.g., shifting from in-sourced to the cloud).

Evaluating your output unit costs will require you to consider your input prices, your consumption trends, anticipated capacity (including spare capacity), and other factors. The process also helps to understand your fixed and variable cost structure, which is important for communicating how the costs of consumption will change over time or change based on volumes. It also helps you set rates (prices) for your bill of IT (discussed in the next chapter).

Output unit costs also include gross measures, such as the cost of IT per employee. These costs serve as useful, high-level indicators of the spend on IT against broader business trends, such as employment growth and business volumes. However, like many such measures, they're only signals to tell you to look deeper. You'll still need to evaluate unit costs at a more granular level (e.g., by services and by major inputs, such as labor rates).

You can also use unit costing to call out areas of the business and IT that are not optimizing resources well. For example, online retailing giant eBay has a capacity allocation review board (CARB) that tracks fleet utilization, linking it back to the hardware acquisition teams who ensure what is purchased is used. Individuals and teams are held accountable for utilization minimums. Capacity is returned if not used and no new capacity is allocated until minimums are met. This prompts administrators and managers to take action, avoiding additional CapEx and driving OpEx costs — and therefore unit costs — down[41].

---

[41] Nelson, Dean. Phone interview. 16 Oct. 2013.

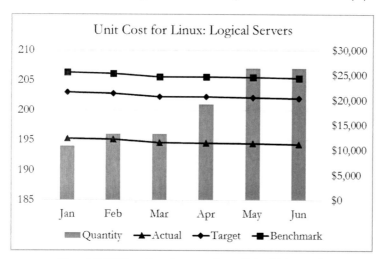

Figure 5-2: TBM enables unit cost trending to distinguish between the drivers of costs and efficiencies gained or lost over time

Unit costs that are rising *and* represent a significant portion of your overall budget should be targeted for further analysis and reduction if needed. Out-of-line unit costs that are not material, i.e., those that do not represent a significant cost to IT or the business, can be ignored.

Looking at per-unit costing avoids evaluating IT costs as a lump sum, which leads to poor decision-making regarding resource allocation and budgeting. Without transparency into what is actually driving costs, such as price increases for consumables like power, poor infrastructure utilization rates, or increases in demand (or all three), it is much more difficult to make informed decisions about where to cut spending, so the impact to the business is minimized.

Another good example comes from Kaiser Permanente. This firm compares its unit costs between regions and business units. "Comparing the costs of locations brings out differences and raises questions, like 'Why is the data center cost per server a lot more expensive in this location versus the other?'" said TBM Consultant Adi Israel. "Then we can explore that further with our system to see if it's driven by a higher cost for that data center overall or is it not as well utilized? Often the full answers aren't in the system but they drive the right questions, ones we wouldn't have otherwise known to ask or focus on."

Kaiser Permanente has also been able to take unit cost comparisons to the next level by calculating them on a per-member basis. "IT cost per member shows a distinct cost differential between regions that run hospitals and regions that don't," observed Israel.[42]

Costing Spare Capacity

Just because your unit costs are within the norms and are trending downward doesn't mean that you're being cost-effective. Another very important source of potential waste is excessive spare capacity. The cost of idle assets must be well managed in order to provide maximum value. This is a balancing effort: Too much capacity is wasteful, while too little capacity presents a performance risk except in the most predictable and stable environments.

Idle capacity comes in a couple of forms. The first is underutilized hardware assets, primarily servers and storage. The causes for this situation are many, but a big one is when application owners demand dedicated hardware without considering IT's long-term run-the-business burden. It is not until IT leaders can trace costs throughout the organization, putting the cost of idle capacity into monetary terms, that CIOs can confront their business partners with the realities of their own decision-making. IT leaders can then make changes, such as moving dedicated applications onto virtualized hardware to cut costs.

When your business partners finally see the total costs of the spare capacity that they drive, they're often shocked by how quickly those expenses add up. If you charge your business partners for the costs they drive, they will often quickly change their minds about the need for dedicated hardware.

Even without chargeback, showing how your business partners are driving costs can change behavior. The trick is to show how their consumption circles back to affect your capacity to take on projects or new services *they* consider to be critical. As an IT leader, you can

---

[42] Israel, Adi. Interview for 2015 TBM Council awards program. August 2015.

complain because of a business mandate to cut spending, but until you put that pain in terms your business partners understand, it will be harder to change their behavior in a positive way.

Assets supported by unnecessarily expensive infrastructure are just as problematic. Too often, for example, non-priority production data is sitting on the most expensive storage arrays instead of being relegated to a lower, more appropriate tier. Using TBM to trace storage costs back to an application and the business unit consuming it will highlight areas where cost and value are not aligned.

Another common source of waste is orphaned assets. These assets are installed and operating (powered on, licensed, managed, and supported) but are no longer providing demonstrable business value. This problem is addressed with the TBM model because assets are linked to their business purpose. If assets, such as servers or storage, have no business purpose, they can be decommissioned or repurposed with little to no effect on your quality of service.

Technology sprawl is a long-standing concern of CIOs that often leads to excessive idle capacity. What started with virtual machine sprawl, or the tendency to provision too many virtual machines due to the relative ease of doing so, is now becoming cloud sprawl. Public cloud obscures the problem because asset management tools often have limited visibility into cloud-based assets. As mentioned before, your vendor bills may not include the metrics you need to trace their costs to business outcomes.

Your TBM model should incorporate cloud costs, whether borne centrally by your technology organization or by your business partners directly. If those costs hit your general ledger and are captured consistently no matter who purchases them, TBM can provide the necessary visibility. In turn, you will know how big of a cost it is to your enterprise and take steps to better govern that spend and the capacity it represents.

Monitoring Project Spending

Project spending often accounts for 20 percent or more of an overall IT budget, including a large part of overall labor spending. Therefore, projects and project labor must be managed carefully. Most CIOs are delivering projects differently than in the past. They're employing Agile approaches to software development, which frustrates traditional project financial management practices. Agile employs the spiral-into-accuracy approach for measuring project goals and value over time. Because of this issue, project financials must be updated frequently and reviewed by not only project managers and the project management office, but also an executive steering committee and business unit leaders.

Project portfolio management as a discipline already includes a lot of oversight, including business case justification, steering committees, and CapEx spending controls. However, along with the changes Agile brings, more projects are spending OpEx dollars on cloud services. This trend is shifting the project portfolio management dynamic in a way that requires a much more holistic view of where dollars are being spent, by whom, and for what purpose.

Most technology projects are designed to either create new business services or wind down or enhance existing ones. These services consume resources from different IT towers and cost pools and are generally part of a run, grow, or transform business initiative that involves more than just a single stand-alone solution. This aspect means they need to be managed from a portfolio point of view; one that incorporates not only project financials (CapEx, OpEx, and labor), but also their overall impact on IT's long-term run-the-business costs.

Unfortunately, few businesses understand and manage their true overall project costs. They may attend to projects from a portfolio perspective as they relate to business needs, but rarely are they accounted for from an IT costs perspective. Nor does project management software solve this problem since most of these applications are focused on project milestones and tracking hours spent in the course of delivery of a project.

Project Name	Project Mgr	Stage	Pri	Status	CapEx Actual	CapEx Budget	CapEx Remain	% Contract
Project Apollo	Owensby	Design	2	Red	$761,721	$510,000	-49%	78%
Oracle Shop Floor	Hickethier	Build	1	Green	$547,083	$600,000	9%	7%
Server 2014 Upgrade	Guichard	Design	2	Green	$307,697	$550,000	44%	22%
Madrid DC Expansion	Lathem	Deliver	1	Yellow	$258,918	$217,000	-19%	15%
IT Service Management	Lemmonds	Build	2	Green	$247,056	$125,000	-98%	35%
Network Simplification	Hickethier	Deliver	3	Green	$165,296	$225,000	27%	40%
Workday HRM	Salines	Build	1	Yellow	$161,425	$315,000	49%	34%

Figure 5-3: TBM arms decision makers with multiple views of project costs and resources, including CapEx spend, budget, and variances

This situation ends up creating a lot of risk. When projects are not accounted for from a total cost perspective, it is difficult to calculate how much the resulting service or application will cost once it is in production. It also means your business partners will not understand why IT needs more budget just to keep doing what they were doing before (at least as the business sees it). Further, because technology is very difficult to take out of production once it is adopted, IT's run-the-business spending grows and will consume a greater percentage of the overall budget.

TBM provides both application- and services-centric points of view of your project spending. When you align projects to the services you deliver, you can reveal how necessary those projects really are. For example, if a service is performing well, will a new project enhance that performance in a way that adds net business value? If not, then the project should be reconsidered.

App Name	App Dev	Application Run Costs Total	Application Run Costs Fixed	Application Run Costs Variable	Application Run Costs Per User	App IT Owner	Stage	User Count	Opens	Tickets
SFXA	$761,721	$0	n/a	n/a	n/a	Larrosa	Build	65	-	-
Field Tech DB	$144,030	$70,403	$38,169	$32,234	$629	Lawrence	Operate	112	2,854	32
Key Doc Index	$124,021	$67,706	$35,879	$31,827	$927	Lawrence	Operate	73	586	66
LMS	$22,493	$66,292	$34,493	$31,799	$861	Reynolds	Operate	77	1,749	71
MyAccount	$13,782	$63,266	$31,873	$31,393	$2,531	Reynolds	Operate	25	639	11
ProCard	$115,321	$55,491	$33,019	$22,472	$1,290	Larrosa	Operate	43	777	40

Figure 5-4: TBM provides a view of application and service TCO, including run costs, development (project) costs, and resources consumed

This services-centric view of the portfolio is not entirely new. ITIL and other frameworks espouse a similar philosophy for managing projects from a portfolio perspective. TBM however puts a dollar value on new project spending that incorporates the total cost of your projects from the perspective of your delivered services. TBM does this by marrying the cost of supporting the new service to the IT towers and sub-towers it consumes, and also to the cost pools that support those towers.

TBM also helps control runaway projects before they get out of hand. Since most project management software is focused on managing project personnel and not finances, it can be difficult to understand when spending exceeds the value that a project will bring to the business.

TBM lifts this veil by mapping the number of hours spent on a project to the labor cost pool data. This process provides a clear view of project spending. Contractors are also included since they are accounted for in the External Labor cost pool. When Agile is employed, ongoing project spending updates become readily available, allowing leaders to keep a lid on costs as the projects progress.

Once costs are mapped into the TBM model, projects can be viewed from different perspectives: portfolio, services, business units, etc. This advantage gives you the ability to look at your project portfolio from an investment point of view: Are you investing enough in run-the-business vs. change-the-business initiatives? If not, why not? Are you balanced well enough to support your strategy going forward? How well is your project spending supporting run vs. grow vs. transform initiatives?

TBM's relentless focus on cost transparency ensures that project investments, once mapped to services, can be managed just like any other asset.

Key Takeaways

- Use TBM to manage and demonstrate cost-effectiveness ("value for the money"), an essential discipline for building trust and credibility between you and your business partners.

- Employ benchmarking to assess cost-effectiveness by comparing your actual costs and investments to relevant industry peers, third-party providers, such as public cloud, or internally between business units or locations. Use benchmarks primarily to set targets for unit costs, cost ratios, and other metrics, and then balance them against non-cost considerations, such as security, reliability, compliance, and performance.

- Unit costs reveal a lot about your cost-effectiveness. Measure and manage your unit costs to put your spending into the context of the volumes that you purchase and deliver. Trend important unit costs over time to identify and mitigate unwanted unit cost trajectories.

- Spare or idle capacity is a significant source of inefficiencies for many organizations. Measure and manage the cost of spare capacity, and give your business partners the opportunity to help you manage excess capacity by shaping their consumption.

- Measure and manage project spending in terms of both resources (e.g., headcount, hours) and costs. In addition, assess the impact of your projects on the ongoing costs of your services and operations to avoid a continuous increase in run-the-business spending.

ViewPoint: **New IT Demands**
New Approach to Benchmarking

Digital transformations and cloud strategies are changing the way organizations evaluate their technology spend. Because enterprises are integrating new technologies like cognitive computing, platform-based delivery, and the Internet of Things into their core business at such a rapid rate, they are finding the traditional measures of IT spending — percent of revenue or dollar per employee — no longer sufficient.

With digital and cloud, financial discipline and actionable insights are more important than ever as organizations shift from plan-build-run operating models to Agile methodologies to support their transformation. These disciplines and insights are available through TBM. Key among these is the ability to benchmark current spend to better understand opportunities for greater efficiency and smarter investment.

Benchmarking has traditionally been a passive activity, completed every several years to align IT costs with the market. In today's faster-paced world of digital, cloud, and Agile methodologies, benchmarking is becoming a more routine business process. As the practice of benchmarking integrates enhanced analytics, data visualization, and TBM processes, it is coming to the forefront as an important part of managing the digital transformation. But why?

Benchmarking increases visibility into costs, which leads to a more strategic approach to IT spending that supports negotiations with vendors and suppliers, identifies (re)investment opportunities and generates greater returns on investment. Never has benchmarking been more important than when enterprises are digitizing business processes. If poorly managed, the business risks of misspending those IT resources are enormous. Every technology resource is now a precious commodity for reaching corporate goals, and the tradeoffs must be clear.

Think of the impact of current technology trends on today's IT organization. The increased use of automation across the entire organization is reducing resource needs by as much as 40 to 50 percent in some areas; Agile development methodologies and DevOps are changing the rate at which software is produced; and advances in flash drives are slashing storage costs by up to 80 percent. Things are getting faster, better, and cheaper every day. CIOs need real-time insights into these trends to understand how and when they should capitalize on the changes. Benchmarking, when done properly and regularly, makes this possible.

Before the disciplines and tools of TBM existed, benchmarking was characterized by the challenges of manually collecting data, aggregating data into a common benchmarking taxonomy used for peer comparison, and providing a rearview picture of the landscape. Today, TBM provides a forward-looking view of IT costs. Imagine being able to identify opportunities on the horizon and model the impact of those opportunities through effective benchmarking, budgeting, and planning.

CIOs must help their people make better decisions faster. Disciplined processes address the traditional limitations of benchmarking, and the use of a common taxonomy and automation in data collection and aggregation means less time is needed for the collection process. As a result, more time can be spent on data analysis and strategic insight. This is known as decision agility, the increased pace at which difficult business decisions can be made.

Digital transformations often involve a change in delivery model as well. The comparison and benchmarking of those models is especially important in a digital strategy, to determine for example whether a cloud service is more cost-effective than a traditional (on-premises) service, or whether a public, private, or hybrid cloud approach best serves the business. With TBM, an enterprise can configure a fully loaded total cost of ownership (TCO) that goes beyond the mere subscription costs of cloud services to include retained costs as well. This allows for a much more refined cost analysis and an apples-to-apples comparison that is essential to creating a solid business case for change.

With a TBM-driven strategy that includes cost transparency, data validation, and benchmarking, organizations will find they are better positioned to leverage a hybrid IT environment. They no longer need to manage multiple cloud providers in silos. The integrated TBM approach ensures procurement, finance, legal, and operations all work from a single pane of glass. As businesses increasingly consume technology as services rather than products or assets, and as technology becomes a more significant part of business processes, its share of the corporate cost structure is sure to rise. And given the strategic nature of these technologies, benchmarking IT spending on a regular basis is fast becoming an essential business discipline.

Alex-Paul Manders
TBM Practice Leader, Americas
Information Services Group (ISG)

Chapter 6:
Shaping Business Demand

In our experience, misspent resources and misaligned portfolios in most organizations are the result of poorly managed demand — not a spend-happy or ineffective IT department. These IT organizations suffer because they are unable to change the conversation from using more technology to discussing the value of additional investment. This reinforces the more-for-less mentality of many business leaders when it comes to IT.

Look at IT from the eyes of your business partners. They see that consumer technologies — both hardware and "freemium" software — are dramatically cheaper than what they are getting from you. Also, as public cloud pricing continues to fall at the same time that capabilities continue to increase, they believe you should be able to do the same. Why is this so? Because they never see the total costs of supporting their applications and services over time, and they also fail to understand (or care about) their role in actual IT spending.

To be clear, IT departments that have had limited visibility into how their budget is being consumed, and by what assets or services, will find there are areas where costs can be reduced quickly when they employ TBM. Identifying and decommissioning orphaned servers or helping business units rein in application entitlements are good examples of these cost reduction opportunities. However, when business leaders are not held accountable for or at least informed of the costs they drive, no one (neither IT nor the business) can act effectively to reduce those costs — while still maintaining the desired service quality.

Because your business partners may be focused on next quarter's numbers, they may pay little attention to increased IT costs that are the result of last year's project investments. These leaders often have little visibility into how their behavior drives IT costs, and indeed, many still view technology as a tax that weighs on their profit margin. This isn't just a money problem. It's a matter of using IT resources wisely to create the most business value.

A 2014 McKinsey & Company study[43] demonstrated the connection between transparency and demand in improving efficiency. The firm's research revealed that cost transparency improved existing infrastructure efficiency by 15 to 20 percent over three years, with an immediate 10 to 15 percent improvement for new investments. These benefits are not possible with reshaping demand:

> *"These changes are tough to make. But if an organization can introduce a new model for demand and service management, it can usually realize 10 to 20 percent cost savings. While these changes are well aligned with deployment of next-generation infrastructure technologies such as private cloud platforms, several of the efficiency benefits, including shorter provisioning time, can be achieved with legacy infrastructure as well. The savings come, for example, from reduced tension between IT and business partners, leading to less costly service level agreements (SLAs), as well as from steering demand toward lower cost standard platforms and simplifying IT procurement."*

As the study points out, the benefits of managing demand to control costs are tremendous. When business leaders see the total costs, not just the project costs of the new technologies they desire, they will put less of an onus on IT to provide them with top-tier service levels, they will generate fewer pet projects and minor project changes, and they will work with IT to consume resources more efficiently. As one longtime TBM practitioner put it succinctly, "My business partners liked their projects a lot better when they were free."

Choosing What Demand to Shape

Before we talk about how to shape demand, it's important to discuss what demand you should try to shape. In most cases, it's not practical to

---

[43] Agarwal, Himanshu, Leandro Santos, and Irina Starikova. "Managing the Demand for IT Infrastructure." *McKinsey & Company*, Apr. 2014. Web.

use transparency to influence all IT consumption. Most likely, you have many services, applications, projects, and technologies (assets) that are consumed directly or indirectly by your business partners. Being transparent with everything, and providing choices for everything, would simply overwhelm your business partners. It could be counterproductive.

Shaping demand is in essence the act of providing informed choices. You are giving your business partners facts about their consumption, costs, quality, and other details so they can choose between several options. Should they authorize fewer users of an application? Should they ask for a less expensive tier of storage for their imaging files? Should they encourage their employees to choose cheaper desktop options? And so on.

As you can imagine, you can provide a lot of choices, but those choices can be overwhelming and detract from your goal of improving overall cost and value. So instead of trying to be transparent about all of your costs at a granular level, consider the following:

- **Controllability**: Which services, technologies, and projects can you change in response to changing business demand? For example, if your business partners choose to authorize fewer users of an application, can you alter the amount you deliver and the corresponding costs? (We'll talk about this more later in the chapter.)

- **Optionality**: Which services, technologies, and projects are optional and not optional? For example, many security services are mandatory and shouldn't be presented as options.[44]

- **Timeline**: If you alter delivery based on the choice of your business partners, over what time period will you and your business realize the benefits? Is it within the year? Is it beyond a year because costs are fixed? Long-term benefits should not be disregarded, but

---

[44] For this reason, security costs are often "baked into" the cost of services and technologies rather than presented as a choice of service.

you must set the expectations with your business partners accordingly.

- **Materiality**: Will changes in consumption make a significant difference in cost or business value? Providing a cheaper option that yields little overall cost improvement to your business is likely not worth the effort and potentially detracts from more impactful decisions.

Many IT leaders focus on influencing the consumption of a selected set of services, technologies, or projects at any given time. They assign rates to selected services in their service catalogs, but not every service (at least at the beginning). They report costs and consumption of that selected set, and report the remaining costs in less detail. Over time, they introduce rates for more services, technologies, or projects, based on current optimization goals. In this way, they take an evolving but priority-based approach to shaping demand.

Finally, consider the packaging of your services and technologies. Automakers provide option packages for the cars they sell rather than offering each feature as its own option. This not only simplifies production, it makes it easier for them to communicate value and price their cars, ultimately helping consumers make purchasing decisions. IT leaders can do the same thing: create packages of services that simplify the choices, and "price" those packages according to cost and value.

Shaping Demand with a Bill of IT

Even though shaping demand begins by providing transparency into how business consumption drives IT costs, this transparency does not automatically mean charging back IT costs to the business. It starts with delivering a bill of IT.

What's a bill of IT? It's like your monthly cell phone bill or cable bill, but it's for the services that your technology organization delivers to your business partners. An effective bill of IT contains the following elements:

- **services (or applications and technologies) consumed** by the business units, including the quantities (e.g., number of licensed users supported, project hours delivered, servers hosted)

- the **total and unit costs** of those services and how those costs were calculated, such as by published rates, budgeted amounts plus/minus adjustments, actual costs, or other key aspects to qualify

- drill-downs to show **who or what consumed the services**, such as the users or departments for which the amount is based

- clear instructions for **how to communicate errors or exceptions** or how to ask questions and get clarification

Typically, each business unit receives its own bill each month electronically. The business leader responsible for this expenditure reviews the bill, including all of its components, looking for anomalies or any glaring errors. Your BRM may sit down with the business leader to discuss the bill. What happens next depends on whether or not you charge back for your services.

Business Unit: Claims Processing		BU IT Cost/FTE:	$4,298				April 2016		
Bill Owner: Andrew Jones		Corporate Avg/FTE:	$2,325						
	Unit of	Unit	Financial		Budget-vs-Charges		Volumes		Plan-vs-Actual
Service Offering	Measure	Rate	Budget	Charges	$	%	Plan	Actual	Units	%
Business Applications										
Claim Central	Claim Processed	$22.14	$261,584	$272,831	($11,247)	-4%	11,815	12,323	(508)	-4%
Image Warehouse	Image Online	$1.32	$322,150	$306,417	$15,733	5%	244,053	232,134	11,919	5%
PolicyPro	User	$148.55	$182,419	$181,528	$891	0%	1,228	1,222	6	0%
	Subtotal:		$766,153	$760,776	$5,377					
Communications										
Office Comm Non-	Non-Sales HC	$154.83	$246,644	$243,702	$2,942	1%	1,593	1,574	19	1%
Email	Account	$30.09	$50,190	$47,362	$2,828	6%	1,668	1,574	94	6%
Lotus Notes	Account	$21.76	$9,422	$9,183	$239	3%	433	422	11	3%
	Subtotal:		$306,256	$300,247	$6,010					
Output Services										
Print - Cut Sheet	Impressions	$0.02	$25,750	$27,682	($1,931)	-7%	1,287,521	1,384,078	(96,557)	-7%
Print - Mail Other	Direct Charge	$1.00	$48,343	$45,227	$3,116	6%	48,343	45,227	3,116	6%
Print - Cont Feed	Impressions	$0.02	$23,466	$24,717	($1,251)	-5%	1,173,295	1,235,862	(62,567)	-5%
Dist Bulk Print	Impressions	$0.05	$12,135	$12,749	($615)	-5%	242,696	254,987	(12,291)	-5%
Print - Fiche/Film	Impressions	$0.02	$34	$32	$3	7%	1,714	1,588	126	7%
	Subtotal:		$109,728	$110,407	($679)					

Figure 6-1: The bill of IT gives technology consumers a clear picture of what they've consumed and how much it costs based on mutually agreed terms and rates

To really drive change, it is necessary for the business units to do more than just see and acknowledge how their own consumption drives costs. They often have to feel the impact to their P&Ls (or to the bottom line of their business) before those consumption patterns will change. That is why so many companies implement chargeback as a way to balance cost and consumption. Chargeback is a powerful tool *when done properly*.

This power to motivate change is what First American's VP of IT Chuck Niethold discovered. It was only when he made the shift to chargeback that the business really started to pay attention. "We could tell who really cared by how many logins there were into our TBM system [to see their bills for IT]. After we implemented chargeback, the logins skyrocketed," said Niethold. "There's no way we could get away from this now."[45]

Ultimately, chargeback creates *positive tension* that leads to cost-consciousness across the board. When done properly, (i.e., based on transparent, credible, and defensible cost data), the discussions are fact-based and result in tradeoffs that improve value.

Chargeback is powerful, but it's not always feasible. Fortunately, another way to shape demand without chargeback is to tackle costs at the executive level. By putting IT costs into business terms using the TBM taxonomy, such as the applications, services, and projects that are being delivered, and having conversations between the executive ranks about the total cost of those services, you can make top-down decisions. TBM gives you a prescriptive way to do this — complete with the taxonomy you will need to foster the right conversations with your business partners.

You can think of this process as a portfolio view of IT spending. While most businesses have a mature project portfolio practice complete with steering committees and clear go/no-go decision criteria, few approach IT costs in this manner. The reason is simple — it's because they can't. They do not have the types of insight that TBM brings to the table. With TBM, you will be able to look across IT spending in terms

---

[45] Niethold, Chuck. TBM Council CFO of IT workgroup presentation. 30 Apr. 2015.

of fixed, variable, discretionary, and non-discretionary spending that occurs in the business application services layer of the TBM model.

So, even without chargeback or a formal bill of IT, you can finally have an informed discussion with the business about where most of your budget is being spent and what applications and services consume the lion's share of that spending. That usually leads to eye-opening meetings about why that tiny little business unit or process "all the way over there" is consuming so many resources, or it can uncover lots of orphaned servers that were never shut down after a migration or an upgrade. From there, the conversations can finally turn to the value of all that spending, instead of just talking about dollars and cents in nonspecific ways or, worse, in bits and bytes.

With a bill of IT, you can even shape individual consumer behavior. The TBM model, if powered with the right data, can show who (literally) or what behavior (business units that demand incremental changes that drive up application development spending on the OpEx side of the ledger) is actually driving your costs. Or you can put costs into actual consumption terms, such as number of users per application, business-sponsored projects, or the systems and resources assigned to the services of each business unit.

Defining, Setting, and Communicating Rates

A different problem is created when the cost of something is communicated without any context — it becomes impossible to judge the value for the money. For example, $10 million spent on servers may seem like a lot of money, but if the cost per server is within industry norms, the value for that money appears more reasonable.

This why the TBM taxonomy defines the units of consumption for IT towers, applications, and services. Units may include physical and virtual servers, gigabytes of storage by tier, application users, transaction counts, and more. These are your cost drivers. While not a linear progression, in general, the more units you provide, the higher your total costs, but also the lower your unit costs.

During the budget planning cycle, you must estimate and communicate not only your total IT costs but the units of IT provided and the cost per unit. These are your unit costs. As described in the previous chapter, you should measure and manage unit costs to place spending into the context of volumes. However, they also serve another purpose as well: setting rates.

Rates are like prices.[46] They communicate the costs that will be charged to the business based on the volumes of services they consume. The advantage of using rates instead of using actual costs during each period is they provide better predictability of costs. Rates are typically set only once or maybe twice per year.

You can then use rates for your applications and services to more precisely communicate how IT cost is dependent on business volumes and help you change the conversation from "Why is IT so expensive?" to "Is this the right amount of IT, and the right quality of IT, for the business?", indeed a major outcome of using TBM.

Organizations with a mature rates management approach tend to define and set their rates during their annual planning cycle and hold them steady for the entire year. This means the rates are predictable for your business partners, so they can plan better. Organizations with a less mature process will need to revisit their rates more often.

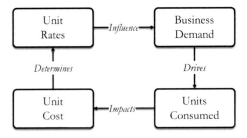

Figure 6-2: Rate setting is an iterative process with the business since unit rates impact business demand which, in turn, impacts unit cost

---

If standard rates are being used for chargeback, it is even more important to have a well-defined process for handling variances. Certain organizations recover variances differently based on the cause of the variance; for example, when the rate is inaccurate due to supplier price changes or budget overages, IT may cover those using a top-line adjustment or other finance mechanism. When the variance is due to volume differences, then the business units may be held accountable through adjustments to their P&Ls.

Ultimately, rates management depends on two sides of the same coin. Your team is responsible for the rate, and your business partner is responsible for the volume. Of course, those two measures are interrelated: A change in volume will obviously impact your rates. This is why rates and volumes must really be managed together through a close collaboration that is made possible with the facts from TBM.

Creating Effective Levers for Shaping Demand

Becoming demand-oriented and transparent means your business partners will want levers they can pull to manage the consumption, quality, and variability of the services they consume. In a perfect world, you would be able to provide those levers and act immediately on any decisions made by your business partners to change those factors. But it is not a perfect world.

With the cloud, the expectations of your business partners have changed. They expect you to provide an equally elastic infrastructure and cost structure. Just like Amazon or Salesforce.com, they want you to charge them for only what they consume each month — even if their consumption swings dramatically. This approach gives your business partners the power to control their costs.

Fortunately, there are two levers that can help you manage this expectation. The first lever, your variable cost ratio, reflects the degree to which total costs respond to volume changes. With a more variable cost structure, as volumes go up and down, so do your costs. Variable costs are the opposite of fixed costs, which don't change much (in the short term anyway) with volume fluctuations. The unfortunate reality for most CIOs today is that their cost structure is mostly fixed and non-discretionary — the complete opposite of elastic.

Fixed costs are not necessarily a bad thing when times are good and transaction volumes are rising (higher transaction volumes typically lead to lower unit costs). But when volumes fluctuate or are falling, fixed costs stand in the way of optimizing IT. Indeed, depreciation, amortization, data center costs, maintenance, and many other costs do not disappear without a write-off, which simply accelerates your OpEx spending.

To understand this aspect better, assume you have a major business application with costs that are 30 percent variable. The app's variable costs might include user license fees that can be reduced at your discretion and some cloud storage costs that increase or decrease with the number of users. If you cut the number of users, those variable costs decline, but the fixed costs remain. As a result of the fixed costs, the cost of that application will drop by only 30 percent if consumption *completely* stops.

While upping the variable-to-fixed cost ratio of this application will help you attain short-term cost benefits from reduced consumption, you and your business partners should recognize that it may also inflate your total costs because fixed assets can be leveraged, whereas variable cost structures cannot. If your costs are variablized and your volumes still rise, your total costs will rise as well.

The second lever you have is your discretionary costs. These are your costs or investments for services and projects that can be stopped at the discretion of the business. Doing so usually won't impact the short-term profitability of the business, increase risk, or result in non-compliance with regulations or policies. Discretionary costs are typically capital outlays or project spending, but not run-the-business expenditures.

You can cut out discretionary spending to save you money in the short term. Still, you should use TBM to identify those opportunities and tradeoffs that surgically reduce these costs without inadvertently cutting business capabilities or adding risk. The law of unintended consequences looms large over these decisions.

It's important to remember that fixed costs can be reduced too. Fixed does not mean immovable or immutable. Indeed, many CIOs find their greatest cost-saving opportunities in their fixed costs since this is where the greatest portion of the budget is spent. However, these savings depend on efficiency increases on the supply side (e.g., infrastructure consolidation, application rationalization, contract renegotiations, increasing use automation, and so on) and demand-side cost-for-performance tradeoffs (e.g., the business agrees to accept more application latency by switching to cheaper Tier 2 storage for certain production applications or cutting back on mean-time-to-repair and other support targets, etc.). These changes may reduce the quality-of-service levels, as applications are transitioned to lower infrastructure tiers, services are scaled back or eliminated, and the time it takes to complete projects and address new requests for service goes up.

Taken together then, cost ratios provide important levers to quantify and communicate value and control to your business partners. Without this knowledge, your business partners will never be able to help you help them. By introducing demand-side concepts and controls, you bring your business partners into the discussion in ways they never knew were possible. Without a financial model that provides transparency for total costs and the behaviors that drive them, you will never be able to significantly change the status quo.

Key Takeaways

- Use transparency to shape (influence) and manage business demand and consumption. Be careful when choosing what demand to shape, as it's not all-or-nothing. Sometimes being transparent about a subset of services, technologies, and projects yields better results by providing fewer, more impactful options from which your business partners can choose.

- Business transparency can be performed at several levels: portfolio-level for executive steering; business-unit level for business leader choices; and individual level for creating more informed consumers.

- If you're not using chargeback, reconsider your approach. Chargeback is a proven mechanism for creating accountability for IT consumption. Showback given to your executive business partners can be very effective, but it is still difficult to drive changes broadly without fiscal accountability.

- Shaping demand requires the creation of levers to manage consumption, costs, and value. Understand both your variable cost ratio and your discretionary costs, so you know how fast and how much you can shift costs to meet changing business demands successfully.

- Know that you can find a lot of room to cut your fixed costs by renegotiating contracts, consolidating infrastructure, automating processes, and taking other actions that don't depend on simply reducing your business volumes.

Chapter 7:
Planning and Governing for Value

The purpose of an IT budget is to govern IT spending and investments throughout the year. The budget also serves to communicate to line-of-business leaders and other stakeholders the anticipated cost of IT, so they factor it into their own budgets and their consolidated corporate budgets.

While ultimately a budget is about predictability, the budgeting process itself represents a terrific opportunity for the CIO to communicate value, collaborate on opportunities to improve the business, and fundamentally align his or her portfolio with the needs of the business. So why then in so many enterprises is IT planning simply viewed as ineffectual, or worse, just a barrier to being an effective business partner?

For businesses that view IT as an expense center organization or even a service provider, IT budgets and plans are treated as an afterthought of business planning. The result is a budget that is impractical to meet, misaligned with business plans, and inflexible. Contrast this situation with the value partner or business driver technology organizations that we discuss in Chapter 3 where IT planning is tightly integrated with business planning. Indeed, in business driver organizations, where IT is the business, business planning is also technology planning.

In value partner or business driver organizations, technology leaders follow a very different planning process. Because the P&L leaders own their technology functions, they clearly understand how the technologies they consume support their goals. They understand the consumption, capacity, and quality tradeoffs that must be made to meet these goals cost-effectively. Technology planning is part and parcel of such business planning.

In many IT organizations, the problem usually begins with the budgeting process itself. In these organizations, each line of business prepares its own fiscal plan, and the corporate CFO rolls these up into a consolidated plan for the business. Concurrently, the IT team creates its own plan that usually incorporates last year's numbers as well as requests for new applications and services, enhancements to existing applications and services, and additional capacity to support anticipated growth.

At some point during the process, the CFO hands the CIO a number (a top limit) for the IT budget. Usually, this number is lower than last year's or fails to grow at the same rate of the business. It is likely based on a top-down perspective about the costs of IT, such as a percentage of revenue or cost per employee, which poorly reflects the actual total spending of IT from the previous year. It is rarely based on the needs of the business (and, therefore, the needs for IT) for the coming year.

This approach fails to support a value-and fact-based conversation about what IT actually delivers, what the business consumes, how much it costs, and the value that IT spending brings to the business. It also creates numerous challenges for the CIO. First and foremost, it isolates IT from the business planning process. CIOs focus on their own plans instead of collaborating with their business partners to help their partners discover the art of the possible when it comes to technology.

Second, the CIO is forced to fit the needs of the business to the arbitrary IT budget limits set by the CFO. This demand severely restricts IT's ability to support the dual mandates of flexibility and agility that are increasingly the hallmarks of high-performing IT organizations.

Third, because finance owns the budgeting process, everyone is forced to translate their needs, plans, and expectations into general ledger and cost center terms. This demand makes it difficult to fully appreciate or explain to the CFO how new and existing consumption will actually drive costs on the ground. There is little or no connection between the terminology that explains a general ledger account and the actual business services that account supports.

This traditional planning approach sends IT leaders into a tailspin of "defensive budgeting," forcing them to creatively allocate the dollars they do have, so they can support the inevitable changes and variances that they know come with every business cycle. The result is a budget that impedes value creation, increases risk, and may even be impractical to execute because (a) it was developed in isolation from the rest of the business and (b) many of the assumptions the business units made about the coming year's spending are either lost in translation when numbers are put into financial terms or revised over and over again. Aside from quarterly budget reviews to look for variances and tweak forecast assumptions, at this point the business fiscal planning is typically done for the entire year.

This approach to budgeting-by-default wrongly assumes that business plans and conditions will remain stagnant (except for the few new investment proposals that arise here and there). Such a degree of stability is rare, so IT budgets then quickly become irrelevant, making IT rigid and inflexible in its ability to meet unanticipated needs or help the business seize new opportunities. By treating IT planning as a one-and-done event, the dialogue between IT, corporate finance, and the lines of business regarding IT overall spending and investment also becomes only an annual event.

Conversely, this conversation should be an ongoing one enabled by TBM. By improving transparency into IT's spending, IT leaders can show their business counterparts not only where current resources are being consumed but also where they can be shifted to support the unexpected — often without having to increase the overall IT budget.

This new, more iterative and interactive approach does not replace the existing corporate financial planning process. Instead, it augments that process by injecting IT into the business planning process throughout the year. This injection gives IT leaders the visibility they need to both better understand the business and suggest how new and existing technologies can help the business achieve its goals, take advantage of unanticipated moves in the market, and manage technology sprawl (i.e., shadow IT) throughout the organization.

Quickening the Cadence

Most IT leaders know that the annual cadence for IT financial planning is insufficient, but they lack the resources to do much about it.

A major factor that inhibits their efforts to change this frequency is IT budgeting, which is usually performed on spreadsheets. This approach not only makes it difficult to model and show costs per the TBM taxonomy, but it is a poor way to share updates, incorporate the input of others, summarize disparate budget submissions, find and fix errors, and so on.

Here is where an enterprise IT financial management system is essential to expediting collaboration, reducing errors, automating the aggregation, summarizing iterative budget submissions, managing feedback and approvals, and allocating budgeted amounts per the TBM model.

So, aside from automating as much of the process as possible, how can CIOs short-circuit the cycle of IT planning while still maintaining business alignment? Managing financial performance on a regular basis comprises several activities: identifying and acting on any budget-to-actual variances, updating the beginning of the year forecasts, and undertaking a quarterly review of the IT portfolio both internally with staff and with the business partners.

The first of these, managing budget-to-actual variances, is a standard financial management process used in nearly every organization. It is typically centered on general ledger accounts, cost centers, and authorizations-for-expenditures (AFEs) that track capital budgets. TBM augments this process by providing a new perspective of variances by the IT tower and sub-towers, applications, services, and even business units. These new perspectives help IT leaders understand the root causes of variances, such as consumption changes or supply inefficiencies.

For example, overspending on contractors is easy to spot in the general ledger; however, doing so does not answer the question of what actually drove the overage and what can be done about it. TBM provides the insights and facts to connect overage with the services or projects that drove it: Were there projects that required extra application development time or quality assurance? Did a business unit consume more of a third-party service to support an unexpected marketing campaign? Knowing the cause, not just the symptom, can help explain the variance and help you decide what to do about it.

Yet more important than the regular variance management process are the forecasting and business reviews. CIOs need to hold regular reviews with their business partners. These reviews (preferably held quarterly) are essentially mini-realignment sessions. Given the need for better alignment between IT spending and business needs, as well as the low value scores most IT organizations get, these sessions are also essential for improving IT's image as a provider of value. The transparency TBM provides is essential to making this yearly to quarterly transition successful.

Because TBM classifies and allocates resources according to the business goals that they support, this transparency will quickly highlight misalignments. So for example, if development dollars are being spent on a service or application that has been de-emphasized (e.g., classified as Eliminate), the CIO, IT leaders, and business partners can quickly spot the issue. It allows for a responsiveness not typically seen with a GL-based or project-portfolio approach. It is one of TBM's key value propositions, as it not only helps you understand the root cause of variances; it gives you the insights you need to devise better solutions and pursue them.

Forecasting for tomorrow's needs is much more difficult without understanding how your spending is being utilized to support business consumption today. By understanding the relationship between tomorrow's needs and today's spending — such as how service volumes are driving IT costs — IT leaders can more accurately forecast how much and where spending will need to change to meet new demand.

Finally, as discussed in Chapter 6, the very act of providing a bill of IT, ideally backed by a matching cost allocation approach (i.e., chargeback) drives a new level of alignment by encouraging a serious review of all major IT expenditures by their beneficiaries — and in terms they can understand.

When taken together — effective variance management, more business-aligned forecasting, regular business reviews, and the bill of IT — the result is that annual planning becomes less of a major undertaking. IT is more naturally forward-looking and business-aligned and can operate with a financial model that requires fewer adjustments.

A Hybrid Approach to IT Budgeting

For run-the-business spending, most IT shops utilize a baseline budgeting process that starts with the prior year's actual spending levels. From those levels, IT leaders adjust for headwinds, such as salary increases, additional employees, the OpEx impact of prior-year projects, and so on. They also look at tailwinds, such as depreciation roll-off, reduction-in-force, and other adjustments to determine the coming year's budget. Combined with the lack of transparency and planning problems we've just discussed, this approach creates a budget that fails to adequately reflect the needs of the business and, by default, also the needs of IT.

This is not to say that baseline budgeting is inherently bad. It is not. If the underlying data is accurate and extensive, baseline budgeting is an excellent way to account for run-the-business spending, since barring any major unforeseen events (like the 2008 financial collapse), your year-over-year costs will probably remain fairly consistent. Yet relying solely on baseline budgeting to account for all of a business's IT needs for the coming year usually leaves IT scrambling to make up for any funding shortfalls.

Zero-based budgeting is often cited as a panacea for this problem. Often mistaken for "starting from zero," zero-based budgeting is actually a repeatable process that organizations use to carefully review every dollar in the budget, manage financial performance on a monthly basis, and build a culture of cost management among employees.

According to McKinsey, [47] a "world-class zero-based-budgeting process is based on developing deep visibility into cost drivers and using that visibility to set aggressive yet credible budget targets." Setting credible budget targets is where TBM comes into the picture. Substitute "deep visibility into cost drivers" for "transparency" (or vice versa), and you immediately see how TBM improves any budgeting methodology. Of course, while zero-based budgeting is an effective tool for better aligning IT's budget with business priorities, most IT organizations lack the transparency needed to develop it.

So how do CIOs achieve the goals of zero-based budgeting — rigorously reviewing every dollar, managing financial performance on a monthly basis, and building a culture of active cost management — without radically changing their budgeting process?

Use TBM to adopt a hybrid approach. It is both practical and effective. Zero-based budgeting can be used for certain types of expenditures, while a baseline approach can be used for most others. Strong candidates for zero-based budgeting include capital expenditures, such as new projects, facilities and hardware, and OpEx spending on labor, depreciation and amortization, and your major contracts.

Since prior-year spending still remains a strong indicator of future spending, baseline budgeting is useful for calculating many of these costs. It is less useful when a new line of business opens, after a merger, acquisition, or divestiture, or after other events that make last year's spending largely irrelevant. In those situations, a zero-based budget likely will be needed.

Regardless of what approach you take — baseline, zero-based, or a hybrid approach — what really matters is rigorously evaluating your expenditures, so you can make informed decisions that benefit everyone. Ask how well do you understand the drivers of your expenditures? How

---

[47] Callaghan, Shaun, Kyle Hawke, and Carey Mignerey. "Five Myths (and Realities) about Zero-based Budgeting." *Five Myths (and Realities) about Zero-based Budgeting.* McKinsey & Company, Oct. 2014. Web.

will those drivers influence next year's costs and resource requirements? These are the types of questions your budget needs to address.

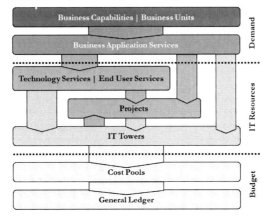

Figure 7-1: The TBM model helps you understand how business consumption impacts IT resources and the GL-based financial budget

What TBM adds is the ability to link the resources that you are expending, whether money, people, hardware, software, or otherwise, to the business consumption of your services. In turn, you can quantify and understand the relationship between them all.

Rigorously Reviewing Every IT Dollar

The fiscal planning cycle is a critical point for reviewing the prior year's actual spending, both internally and with your business partners. More specifically, the cycle is a critical point where you assess total cost, the utilization of your assets, the business consumption of your applications and services, and the overall business value and balance of the IT portfolio.

This supply-side, IT-focused review is necessary to form recommendations for improving value in the coming year. These recommendations should then be incorporated into the budget plan you present to the business. For example, you may decide to refresh desktops for a third of your workforce. This task will require not only a capital outlay but also has an impact on operating costs as well. The costs should be reflected in your draft IT budget.

One of the primary goals of this exercise is to foster communication by jointly evaluating the run-the-business portfolio in terms of existing business processes and needs *before* change-the-business investments are considered. Work with your senior IT leaders, BRMs, business partners, and other stakeholders to review the draft plans. At this point, the focus should be on assessing the business alignment of the technologies, services, applications, and projects that make up the current IT portfolio. Your discussions should focus on total costs, unit costs, business unit consumption trends, and value. With each review, seek new opportunities to optimize costs and improve value.

When complete, arm your IT leaders with the output by using TBM to translate your draft run-the-business budget into the cost of applications and services that each business unit expects to consume. A pro forma bill of IT is an effective way to accomplish this task, so the IT leaders can share the findings with their line-of-business leaders.

That's the beauty of TBM. Instead of going to your business partners with budget figures for hardware, software, developers, outsourcing, and so on, you give them budgeted costs and investments by services and applications. It will make sense to them. They may still ask why you need to spend what you do on those services and applications, but they'll understand that *they* are driving most of *your* costs and why.

Justifying IT4IT Investments

TBM also provides an excellent means for identifying and evaluating infrastructure and IT4IT investments, i.e., those investments designed to improve the cost-effectiveness or reliability of IT but having little or no direct business focus. You start by using the TBM taxonomy and the TBM model to map, define, explain, and understand any areas of inefficiencies.

For example, technologies with exorbitant support are easily spotted since you can trace where the money is being spent — in this case it would be flowing into maintenance and support instead of, say, application development. This not only makes root-cause analysis much easier; it also helps you justify IT4IT investments based on lower support costs for those technologies and services. If there is performance improvement, all the better, as that will improve the perception of overall IT value to the business.

Another challenge of IT4IT investment planning is that IT investments should be made for the sake of business outcomes, such as increasing revenue, reducing costs, or improving customer loyalty; IT4IT investments don't appear to meet those goals, but in reality they do. They're just not as directly connected to the goals as business-led IT investments are.

For this reason, it is imperative that CIOs put IT4IT investments into a business context, which means clarifying which services or lines of business the investment will enhance and what the impact will be on associated operating expenses — for both the business and IT.

Once again, the TBM taxonomy and TBM model are vital to use in this exercise. By translating the impact of IT4IT spending into the benefits for your services and applications, you can demonstrate business value. For example, imagine you're investing in a server refresh. While this might appear to be an IT-only investment, the benefits accrue to the applications and services those servers support. Over time, the business should receive lower TCO and improved reliability as a result of that investment.

This type of linkage between IT-led investments and business benefits not only makes your team's job easier, it helps you maintain a more cost-effective, reliable, and secure technology footprint.

Key Takeaways

- IT planning in many organizations fails to provide business value; it is a slow process too often disconnected from business plans and goals. Use TBM to enhance IT planning processes, conversations, and outcomes.

- Provide transparency in your budget proposal just as you would your actual costs, using the TBM model. In doing so, justify your budget in terms of services, applications, and projects instead of general ledger-based terms.

- Employ a hybrid approach to budgeting — a combination of baseline budgeting and zero-based budgeting — to provide greater fidelity to your fiscal plans. By revealing the connection between the apps and services that your business consumes and the costs and resources they drive, TBM gives you the facts that are needed to plan more accurately based on business demand.

- Leverage the transparency of your spending at budget time to rigorously review every dollar of IT spending. Find ways to improve efficiency or business alignment in the coming year and then incorporate them into your plans and metrics.

- Streamline your planning process, shifting from a long tedious annual process to a more frequent review of business goals, resource requirements, and the IT funds necessary to drive them.

Chapter 8:
Optimizing Your Business

Hopefully by this point in the book, you've begun to realize that TBM is a means to an end, not the end itself. The goal of TBM is to provide transparent information on costs and capability so that you and your business partners can make good decisions on how IT investments can drive value in your company.

Since TBM is particularly effective at managing your run-the-business spending, it is often the best place to start your journey. This flips the thinking in many organizations, where spend and value management efforts are overly focused on projects and change-the-business investments. Those efforts miss the majority of your total spending. Too often, the hangover from change-the-business spending (mostly in the form of increased OpEx spending as projects go live) is not factored into your business partners' thinking when they are considering next year's run-the-business budget. The result is spending simply grows unchecked year after year, but it feels like there isn't much to show for it.

This scenario only makes a bad situation worse by perpetuating a vicious cycle. First, growing run-the-business spending reduces IT financial and resource capacity for new investments and innovation. Yet, rather than forgoing these new investments, something else happens — a line of business takes it on, furthering the myth that IT cannot, will not, or does not innovate effectively.

In other cases, IT leaders make top-down budget cuts to make room for new investments by cutting other projects or delaying asset purchases. There is less money for IT to use to innovate. CIOs then have to resign themselves to doing more with less, spreading existing resources ever thinner in an attempt to meet business demands. This increases operational risk, frustrates employees, and jeopardizes end-user and customer satisfaction.

But there is hope.

Instead of flying blind when it comes to cost, capacity, and consumption only to recognize those issues after months, quarters, or even years of assumption-based decision-making, CIOs who adopt TBM reduce waste and misalignment on an ongoing basis, avoiding the "day of reckoning" that plagues many of those who do not. TBM provides continuous course corrections instead of waiting until a more massive correction is needed with all its complications.

Throughout the remainder of this chapter, we will discuss ways TBM helps you maximize the value of every run-the-business dollar.

Improving Cost for Performance

If we use the cost-for-performance ratio as the ultimate measure of IT efficiency, then ideally IT should deliver the right amount of security, availability, redundancy, responsiveness, and other qualities of service at the lowest possible cost. This focus does not mean that IT is done on the cheap. Indeed, if high quality is required, the costs will rise, but the cost-for-performance ratio still remains in check.

The problem is that most IT departments have no idea how efficient they are. Yes, metrics are everywhere, but they only paint a vague picture, one that is unconnected to how the business is actually consuming services and resources. Any CIO can communicate their total IT costs as a percentage of revenue or average cost per employee or some other gross measure benchmarked against industry peers. We've already discussed the fallacy of these measures.

Improving efficiency depends on addressing a variety of measures in the cost-for-performance equation. Ed Smith, CTO for Cox Automotive, has seen that too many IT leaders focus only on one measure — the rates or cost of the inputs — resulting in suboptimal results. He recommends[48] a balanced approach: "I've found that you should address the units, the efficiency of your delivery, and the rates or unit costs. The order you do this is important. Start by attacking the

---

[48] Smith, Ed. Phone interview. 29 Mar. 2016.

number of units that are driving your costs. For example, take a look at your support tickets; can you bring the volume of those tickets down by resolving the root problems?"

Smith didn't stop there. "Once you've tackled the units, and understand them better, you can go after efficiency. By efficiency I mean the number of units delivered per unit of input, such as hour of labor. In my support example, how can we process more tickets with the same staff? Can we automate more, such as providing self-service password resets?"

As a final consideration, Smith recommends going after the rate. "Focusing on the rate can yield some cost benefits, of course, but not as much as you might think. Renegotiating with a vendor on the rate or reducing your own employee costs can be counterproductive. If that's all you've got, you won't achieve much. It's the last step, not the first."

Below we discuss several areas where TBM can help technology leaders balance cost for performance by addressing a multitude of measures.

Infrastructure

For many if not most enterprises, infrastructure remains a common source of inefficiency, oftentimes the result of maintaining too much unused capacity. Too many IT departments purchase servers, storage, data center capacity, and other assets when the assets they already have are woefully underutilized. (By some estimates, even with virtualization, most servers still run at about 10 to 15 percent of their peak utilization rates.) Some CIOs choose this situation knowingly in order to lower risk. They don't want to run out of capacity, causing performance or availability problems. Excess capacity certainly mitigates this risk, but it also comes at a high cost.

The problem is that neither the business nor IT knows the dollar value of that cost, and most of the time there is no strong business case for owning this excessive capacity. Instead, IT departments purchase and provision dedicated assets because their business partners are afraid to run their applications or services on a shared infrastructure. CIOs can shift this mindset by providing their business partners with a precise picture of the costs that spare capacity does cost them.

The reality is most IT leaders know they have excess capacity; they just can't readily identify it. Even when they do know, however, they either lack the tools, processes, architecture, or perhaps most importantly, the political capital for redeploying excess capacity before they provision or purchase more assets. Fortunately, this situation can be rectified by adding capacity checks to the purchasing process. The dollar value of spare capacity should be part of these checkpoints and listed right alongside data on CPU utilization rates or spare terabytes of storage. TBM provides these facts.

Everyone within IT knows that the impact of spare capacity on resources is significant. However, over-provisioning is only part of the inefficiency problem. The other problem stems from poor decommissioning processes that are associated with the end of life for business applications. According to a 2015 research study[49] conducted by the Anthesis Group, Stanford University, and researcher Jonathan Koomey, 30 percent of all servers running today are "comatose." That's about 10 million servers powered on with nothing to do. This number equates to an estimated $30 billion in global data center capacity sitting idle (assuming an average server cost of $3,000 and ignoring infrastructure CapEx as well as ongoing OpEx).

Koomey concludes that "removing idle servers would result in gigawatt-scale reductions in global IT load, the displaced power use from which could then support new IT loads that actually deliver business value."

AOL used the transparency of TBM to identify and decommission 14,805 servers by convincing users and administrators that they needed

---

[49] Koomey, Jonathan, and Jon Taylor. "New Data Supports Finding That 30 Percent of Servers Are 'Comatose,' Indicating That Nearly a Third of Capital in Enterprise Data Centers Is Wasted." Rep. 3 June 2015. Web.

to increase server utilization rates.[50] They even established a "utilization czar" to enforce higher standards for that utilization. As a result, the efficiencies gained have been dramatic. The firm saved $4.3 million annually by reducing utility fees, maintenance costs, and even some software licenses.

Similar problems occur with storage. It is common to find excessive amounts of unused storage allocated to applications, business units, or development teams. Even with storage costs falling dramatically, this problem still gets very expensive very quickly.

In the case of storage however, it's not always unused capacity that drives inefficiency. Application owners and their business partners sometimes demand unnecessarily expensive storage for their applications. Many IT departments assign their top tier of storage (e.g., Tier-1 SAN) to applications and data that do not warrant this level of protection. In many cases, Tier-3 network attached storage (NAS) is more than sufficient (and at a fraction of the cost). In one medium-sized enterprise, the IT team found that simply re-tiering their application storage resulted in a $2.9 million savings over three years — with no loss of service quality to the business.

So, if these problems are so well known and obvious, why do they occur in the first place? Why hasn't IT reined in this excessive spending long ago? It's because IT leaders have little to no visibility into these total costs as they build over time. Small decisions to buy one or two servers or allocate a terabyte of storage here and there often add up massively over time. This leads to that day of reckoning we touched upon earlier.

These decisions are exacerbated by reports and metrics that fail to illustrate the total financial impact of IT on the business. A capacity manager staring at a server utilization report can see a potential problem. Without the ability that TBM provides to put a dollar figure on that spare capacity and how it impacts a service being consumed by your business

---

[50] Gates, Robert. "Purging Zombie Servers Saves AOL Money, Energy." *SearchDataCenter*. SearchDataCenter.com, 11 June 2015. Web.

partners, it is hard to judge cost for performance and decide what should be done.

Even CIOs who know their server utilization rates are low or that there is a lot of unused storage are shocked when they finally see the actual scope and total cost of the problem. This shock usually prompts them to take action, many indeed for the first time. It is not until IT leaders can trace costs throughout their organization, putting the cost of idle capacity into both monetary and business (service or application) terms that they can confront their business partners with the realities of the decisions that are being made.

Outsourcers

Another common source of inefficiency stems from poor governance of outsourcer contracts and performance. While there are many types of outsourcers, what they all have in common is that you pay them in return for a given level of service or output. Because many will deliver services to many different customers, they should have the economies of scale that guarantee efficiency. Unfortunately, these efficiencies are not always reflected in the bills you receive. Even if they are, you may not be *consuming* their services efficiently.

Many CIOs find that the cost of their outsourcing contracts continues to go up, but with little insight as to why. Yet, when CIOs challenge them to show cause, the outsourcer often agrees to a six- or seven-figure discount to appease the CIO. Similarly, they can't show how they came up with these discounted rates.

One CIO said he finally had it with his primary outsourcer. So instead of continuing this cycle of watching his costs climb and negotiating a new discount that saved the contract for the outsourcer, he decided to replace the single outsourcer with a multi-sourced model. This decision gave him greater clarity into the true cost of major towers of service.

However, breaking up a primary contract is not always a good idea. In doing so, you lose the benefit of a "single throat to choke" when things go wrong. He may also lose other benefits that come from having a single outsourcer, like trusted partner status or tight integration between the service provider's offerings and the company's portfolio of applications.

A better approach is to drive transparency into the cost, utilization, consumption, and quality of your outsourced services and use the TBM model. To do so means getting the right data from your outsourcers. This data often includes having the names, location, and other metadata for assets like servers, databases, and applications be provided by your outsourcer.

This approach also allows you to benchmark your outsourced services more effectively. As we discussed in Chapter 5, benchmarking should be a regular process to ensure performance and also that the price remains competitive. This process includes outsourcers. Hold them to the same cost-for-performance ratios to which you are accountable. It can even open the door to offering incentives for efficient service delivery, so that both you and your outsourcer benefit from better consumption decisions.

Labor

If you are like most IT departments, then labor is a majority of your costs. Employees, contractors, and consultants can comprise 60 percent or more of your OpEx spending and be a major component of your capital costs (depending on your mix of build, rent, or buy). As a result, it's imperative that you manage your labor efficiency (and also understand why people are always the first casualty of budget cuts).

Similar to the efficiency of your assets, you must also manage the cost for performance of your people. You do so by looking at their cost for output; things like servers administered, new users on-boarded, users helped, incidents closed, problems resolved, and lines of code written (or story points, function points, etc.). These are the basic units of output that your people deliver.

Managing the efficiency of IT labor is often easier said than done. On the plus side, many labor outputs are already measured. For example, most service desk suites track activities, such as incident resolution, password resets, new user setups, etc. Payroll systems and purchasing/payable systems tell you how much you've paid for employees and contractors. You need to begin measuring their costs on a per-unit basis (see Chapter 5).

Oftentimes your organization is structured to some degree according to the types of activities being performed. For example, Tier 1 support personnel are assigned to a specific cost center, different than Tier 2 or Tier 3. This means you can begin to understand the unit-cost-per-output for many of your activities. These rates in turn can be useful for benchmarking and trend analysis and can also be used to chargeback or showback the cost of these services.

More data is usually needed to improve labor efficiency. This data is usually supplied by time tracking. While time tracking is often unpopular, with TBM it conveys many decision-making benefits, such as:

- accurate costing of projects, including the capitalization of software development by clearly understanding who is working on what

- accurate costing of services by properly allocating support costs, such as incident resolution, change requests, and other tasks

- reconciling contractor and consultant invoices to ensure correct payment and accurate accruals for labor costs

- gathering justification to add, remove, or reposition resources, such as developers or administrators

This was the experience at First American. CIO Larry Godec was able to shift people over to high-priority projects with clear business benefits. He saved jobs and kept morale up, while simultaneously saving bottom line dollars — all the result of simply marrying time tracking data to better project financial reporting.

Services

Better managing the efficiency of inputs, such as infrastructure, outsourcers, and labor that make up your services is important. That effort still misses a key source of inefficiency in many organizations — the composition of your services and the consumption of them. Services can be inefficiently built and delivered using efficient resources, just like an inefficient manufacturing process can be built using cost-effective materials and cheap labor.

To illustrate, consider an application service, such as electronic health records (EHR). The infrastructure dedicated or allocated to the EHR system may be well utilized and in accordance with the guidelines of your capacity planners. The cost of development, support, and maintenance may be well managed, based on an appropriate mix of labor. Still, the total cost of the EHR application may continue to exceed its perceived value to the organization. How could this be?

This situation is common. It occurs when cumulative isolated decisions such as software design, infrastructure planning, and periodic enhancements, fail to keep the cost of a service or application within an acceptable range for a business. Gold-plating applications is common. A feature here and there, some top-tier storage, some high-speed networking, and a few dozen dedicated servers, and pretty soon the total cost is exorbitant. It's not uncommon for IT leaders and business partners to be shocked at the total cost of so many applications when they measure them for the first time.

One large enterprise CIO revealed how surprised they were by the total cost of their directory services. They had solid controls and efficient design over much of their network, including heavy server and network virtualization. However, a mistake in their technical design, which assumed server infrastructure requirements from a previous version of Microsoft Active Directory, resulted in a dramatic over-deployment of directory servers. Over time, the number of servers deployed and the resultant total cost to deliver, support, and maintain their directory services shocked even those who depended on them. Correcting that mistake saved millions of dollars a year.

The takeaway here is that your team must consistently manage your applications and services in terms of total cost. Over time, infrastructure changes, service enhancements, and other decisions erode cost-for-performance ratios. Because it is difficult to see the impact of individual decisions, monitoring total costs helps you spot opportunities to save money before a major system overhaul is needed to stop the bleeding.

Another way to keep a good check on service efficiency is to measure specific unit rates over time. For applications that process business transactions, consider modeling and tracking the cost per transaction. Normally, this is hard to do with any granularity, but because the TBM model allows you to see the component costs of a service (IT towers, applications, labor costs, storage costs, server, compute, etc.), that model enables you to understand not only your transaction unit costs, but also what is driving them.

It's not just application-based services that can be optimized. Labor-intensive services, such as a call center or help desk services, can be better optimized for significant gains as well. Many of those services can be automated, but building a business case for automation depends in large part on understanding the true cost of those services. How much does it cost to provision a new server, set up a new employee, reset a password, or resolve a PC issue?

Is automating those activities worth it? The answer depends on knowing the total cost for performing those services today. Otherwise, you will have to use some other metric, like wait times, which may or may not affect the true value of the service to the business. Is getting a new employee up and running in one day vs. three days really worth the expense of automating the process? Intuitively, the answer is "Of course!" Really, without knowing the true cost of the difference and the consumption you're having, it's hard to judge.

Aligning the IT Portfolio

Aligning the IT portfolio is the other supply-side pillar in the framework over which you can exercise much more control once TBM is in place. As in finance, where portfolios are used to manage investments from a holistic point of view, IT can also be managed as a portfolio or rather as a portfolio of portfolios, such as services, applications, technologies, platforms, vendors, and data centers. Unfortunately, too many CIOs focus too much of the time on just one portfolio — their programs[51] and projects. While programs and projects represents the bulk of your CapEx spending, they make up a relatively small part of your total costs. To increase the value of IT to the business, you have to manage the OpEx and CapEx of *all* of your portfolios well.

An easy way to think about this issue is that anything you can consolidate or rationalize is a portfolio. In the following sections we explore how you can use TBM to make portfolio-level decisions for each of these areas. However, in order to show how well aligned your IT portfolios are to the business, you need to know what your portfolios *should* look like. In other words, how do your CFO, CEO, and other business partners think IT should be spending its resources to help run, grow, and transform the business?[52]

Just like you, your business partners are unlikely to know the answer to this question either. To begin finding the answers, you and your business partners can use TBM to make informed decisions about what should be done to bring your portfolios into alignment with what the business needs and wants.

Services and Applications

Being service-oriented means you are driven by the needs of your business partners. Your service catalog is built intentionally to serve the needs of the business. While TBM gives you the tools and insights to deliver those services with ever-increasing efficiency, it also can help you optimize and rationalize your services and application portfolios in several ways.

First, TBM helps you shape business demand by providing your service owners, business relationship managers (BRMs), and business

---

[51] For our purposes, programs are defined as more than one project that shares a common business goal. For example, you may have one project to implement a data collection capability for customer devices and another for big data analytics that fall under a single program for predictive customer analytics.

[52] We don't include run/grow/transform metrics here; we use them for managing innovation, as discussed in Chapter 9.

partners with detailed insights into the total cost and unit costs of each of your services. When everyone can see how much the services really cost the business, they can make better-informed tradeoff decisions about where to spend their time and resources.

Better yet, if you hold your business partners accountable for their costs (via chargeback, for example), you further encourage them to be conscientious consumers. As discussed in Chapter 6 on shaping business demand, this approach is an organic way to reshape your portfolio based on the business value of services and applications.

Second, TBM gives your service owners the insights they need to provide better options to the business. Having options is a good thing. It gives your business partners choices, so they can consume services cost-effectively. Amazon Web Services (AWS) for example offers more than three dozen options for Windows server hosting. AWS customers get to choose from an dizzying array of menu options that include areas like processor types, cores, and clock speeds, networking speeds/bandwidth, memory types, storage types, and, of course, price.

Similarly, your service owners should be able to offer options to the business at a range of price points based on quality. This is not to suggest that you offer as many options as some of these cloud providers. (Amazon Web Services offers dozens of options for EC2 for each and every region!) But once you understand the cost implications of the choices you can offer and how they will be consumed, you can begin to piece together a manageable portfolio of tiered services that will meet the cost-for-performance tradeoffs your business partners can accept.

Third, TBM gives your service owners and business partners the information they need to rationalize the underlying applications. Oftentimes, services are supported by redundant applications. This is especially true after years of poor application portfolio management practices and after mergers and acquisitions. This aspect holds true even for enterprise applications, such as messaging platforms (email, instant messaging, voice, video, etc.) and even enterprise resource planning (ERP) software. This situation is a costly one.

Because TBM exposes the total cost and unit costs of each application, you quickly see how expensive it is to run multiple applications. But more importantly, you can now perform an accurate what-if scenario analysis. Just like using the TBM model for understanding your actual costs, you can use the same approach, along with your cost and consumption data, to model different options.

To illustrate, consider this example: a service that is currently supported by three different applications that each performs, more or less, the same function. Each has its own strengths and weaknesses, and the 200 users in each instance of those apps prefer to stay with the one they are currently using. So is it worth a switch? In the what-if scenario illustrated in Figure 8-1, the benefits are clearer.

	Current State	Scenario A	Scenario B	Scenario C
Application A				
Users	100	200	0	0
Fixed Costs	$75,000	$100,000	$0	$0
Variable Costs	$150,000	$300,000	$0	$0
Total Costs	**$225,000**	**$400,000**	**$0**	**$0**
Application B				
Users	25	0	200	0
Fixed Costs	$75,000	$0	$75,000	$0
Variable Costs	$35,000	$0	$280,000	$0
Total Costs	**$110,000**	**$0**	**$355,000**	**$0**
Application C				
Users	75	0	0	200
Fixed Costs	$150,000	$0	$0	$150,000
Variable Costs	$125,000	$0	$0	$333,333
Total Costs	**$275,000**	**$0**	**$0**	**$483,333**
Scenario Costs				
Total	**$610,000**	**$400,000**	**$355,000**	**$483,333**
Per User	**$3,050**	**$2,000**	**$1,775**	**$2,417**

Figure 8-1: A what-if scenario for applications reveals the best option for reducing the costs of supporting a service

All three scenarios are cheaper than keeping the status quo. However, by minimizing the impact of variable costs, Scenario B is the cheapest, saving $255,000 (42%) over the current state. Here, service owners, application portfolio owners, and your business partners can evaluate the three options and decide if consolidation is worth the hassle.

The fourth way that TBM helps you manage your service and application portfolios is using a top-down approach. Because TBM reveals your total spending, using dimensions like business outcomes and investment classes (e.g., invest more, invest less, stay the same, etc.), more and more CIOs are collaborating with their business partners so as to define the business capabilities IT supports and plan accordingly how to support them.

Godec did just this at First American. Early in his journey, he and his CEO, CFO, and business partners agreed to shift more spending into customer-facing technologies, so the business could pivot to a top-line growth strategy following the 2008 recession. Customer service capabilities led this list. Because of the portfolio view afforded by TBM, they were able to move budget from other areas that did not support this strategy to areas that did without adversely affecting their existing portfolio of customer-facing applications and services.

Similarly, many application portfolio managers choose to assess spending according to investment classes, such as Gartner's TIME model (tolerate, invest, migrate, and eliminate).[53] By labeling your applications within these investment classes, you can assess your costs (i.e., your spending) according to the importance of those assets to the business.

By properly labeling your project time, change tickets, and asset purchases, you need to add another important dimension to your

---

[53] We would advocate a fifth class, called Reduce, for those applications whose costs should be reduced, perhaps aggressively. These are applications that are still needed by the business, but also may offer cost reduction opportunities, such as reduced maintenance contracts, less developer time, or on-demand infrastructure via the cloud.

analysis: How much are you spending on new development vs. enhancements vs. maintenance in each investment category? In the following figure, you will see mostly maintenance in the tolerate class and a lot of new development or enhancements in the invest class. These proportions look reasonable but present opportunities for improvement, such as further cutting of enhancement dollars from applications classified as tolerate, migrate, or eliminate.

	New	Enhance	Maintain	Replace	Totals
Tolerate					
Hours (Dev/QA)	20	200	800	180	1200
Projects	$3,000	$26,000	$36,000	$22,000	$87,000
Tier 3 Support	$0	$4,000	$84,000	$5,000	$93,000
Purchased HW/SW	$0	$0	$4,800	$2,500	$7,300
Total Costs	**$3,000**	**$30,000**	**$124,800**	**$29,500**	**$187,300**
Invest					
Hours (Dev/QA)	1200	600	400	80	2280
Projects	$180,000	$85,000	$15,000	$11,000	$291,000
Tier 3 Support	$0	$5,000	$45,000	$1,000	$51,000
Purchased HW/SW	$49,000	$0	$0	$0	$49,000
Total Costs	**$229,000**	**$90,000**	**$60,000**	**$12,000**	**$391,000**
Migrate					
Hours (Dev/QA)	60	45	340	480	925
Projects	$9,000	$6,750	$12,000	$67,500	$95,250
Tier 3 Support	$0	$0	$39,000	$4,500	$43,500
Purchased HW/SW	$0	$0	$0	$1,200	$1,200
Total Costs	**$9,000**	**$6,750**	**$51,000**	**$73,200**	**$139,950**
Eliminate					
Hours (Dev/QA)	24	240	220	180	664
Projects	$0	$14,500	$0	$0	$14,500
Tier 3 Support	$3,600	$21,500	$33,000	$27,000	$85,100
Purchased HW/SW	$0	$0	$18,000	$0	$18,000
Total Costs	**$3,600**	**$36,000**	**$51,000**	**$27,000**	**$117,600**
Totals	**$244,600**	**$162,750**	**$286,800**	**$141,700**	**$835,850**

Figure 8-2: Reviewing app spending by investment class (TIME model) and investment type (new, enhance, maintain, replace) reveals potential misalignments in your portfolio

The power of TBM is that it allows you to go beyond simply monitoring these spending levels. Whenever you reassess your application portfolio, you can look to see if your overall spending levels by investment class should go up or down. Once you do that analysis, you can set targets for your application teams and service owners so as to meet these new investment levels.

The fifth way that TBM helps you rationalize your applications is by providing clearer insight into consumption. This focus works because TBM is a closed-loop system:

1. You use TBM to measure and manage the total and unit costs of your applications.

2. Your application, tower, and service owners help you "right-size" those costs because these owners don't want their costs to be unnecessarily bloated by the people, processes, and technologies they depend on.

3. You use TBM to communicate that cost and consumption to your application owners and business partners.

4. Your business partners help you get the consumption numbers right because they don't want to be charged (or held accountable) for what they don't consume.

When this system is in place, you can identify applications that are poorly consumed, then eliminate them or migrate users to corporate-standard applications on an ongoing basis.

Technologies and Platforms

Not only do you have choices to make about the services and applications you offer, you also have to choose between the different technologies and platforms on which they run. These choices can have a significant impact on your cost of doing business, both up-front and over the longer term.

TBM gives those who are responsible for making technical architecture decisions important facts about the technologies they already own. These technologies can include server hardware, storage systems, operating systems, middleware, desktops, mobile devices, networking, data center, mix of cloud vs. on-premises, and much more. Each carries a total cost of ownership that TBM can reveal, such as:

- total cost and unit cost (per server, per instance hour, per TB of storage, etc.) for each technology over a period of time

- cost and hours of labor spent on maintenance and support of each technology

- year-over-year cost trends

- cost by hardware platform, location, environment, purpose, and other breakouts

- average utilization rates[54]

- power consumption[55] of each technology

All are useful facts to have when comparing the cost-effectiveness of similar technologies or making purchasing decisions. But they're not perfect. They cannot tell you which technology or platform is truly the most cost-effective in complex scenarios. For example, a mainframe is undoubtedly more expensive to own than almost any Wintel-based server, but it may provide the most cost-effective compute power for a major application. On-premises infrastructure might be cheaper than public cloud infrastructure today, but it might not be over the long run. What you have to ask yourself then is, what is more cost-effective for your needs, both today and over time?

By arming your people to be able to make technology choices, both from the bottom up (looking at the technology portfolio) and the top down (based on application portfolio), TBM lets you shape the most cost-effective mix of platforms.

Vendors and Suppliers

TBM helps CIOs, vendor managers, and chief procurement officers get more value from their vendors by revealing the amount being spent

---

[54] This metric assumes you collect and use utilization data from systems management tools (e.g., server monitoring, storage management).

[55] This metric assumes you collect and use power data, such as power audits, power ratings of hardware, or power utilization data from power distribution units or monitoring solutions.

on each vendor. If your vendor managers classify vendors into strategic, preferred, and transactional categories, then, just as with investment classes (e.g., TIME), TBM allows you to see how much is being spent on each vendor type. This information helps to identify spending that should be shifted from tactical to strategic vendors, in turn reducing the number of vendors and consolidating spending on those you trust the most.

Further, just as it does for your internal resources, TBM reveals the unit costs of what your vendors provide. This data, combined with other vendor performance information, will help you understand which vendors are the most cost-effective. Your vendor managers can use this information to renegotiate contracts or eliminate less cost-effective providers.

More importantly, TBM reveals who and what are consuming those vendor-supplied goods and services. For example, TBM tells you which projects or services are consuming the hours of labor charged by your strategic development partner. It gives you the applications and services that are consuming the storage provided by a preferred hardware vendor, and so on.

Connecting vendors with the projects, services, and applications they support allows you to manage them better. First, you can ask the right people — project owners, application owners, business partners — how satisfied they are with each vendor's performance. Satisfaction surveys and reviews are an important tool to use for managing performance, but you need to know who is being served by each vendor first before you can survey them.

Second, you can better understand the risk that a vendor represents to your business. For example, if a transactional vendor is providing the storage that powers your most important business applications, you may want to reconsider that vendor's classification and reevaluate their contract and performance. For example, you may need to rebalance your vendor portfolio to mitigate the risk that one vendor represents.

Finally, TBM helps you understand vendor performance in more subtle ways. For example, TBM reveals the amount of support costs associated with the applications developed by a strategic partner. It shows how much you're spending to maintain hardware delivered by a preferred provider of servers and storage. When you know these facts, you will most likely find that some vendors cost more than you realized they do due to their poor quality.

Data Centers

Most enterprises maintain more than one data center. They may include everything from the most expensive, fault-tolerant (Tier IV) data centers to small server rooms (or closets). If you have more than one data center, you may need to manage them as a portfolio — knowing when to invest in one data center over another, when to migrate from one to another, when to close one, and how to make other data-center level tradeoffs.

TBM measures data center costs by rack units, square footage, location, region, purpose, tier, and any other factor for which you have data. Those costs include depreciation, leases, power, cooling, and other overhead. In other words, TBM measures the fully loaded costs of your data center on a total and a per-unit basis.

Using these metrics, you can compare the cost-effectiveness of one data center against another. Data centers can vary significantly in terms of cost-efficiency due to differences in power and cooling costs, lease or purchase prices, the degree of data center automation, age of the facility and equipment, labor rates by region (e.g., San Francisco vs. Bangalore), efficiency of installed hardware, and more. However, there are usually tradeoffs between these factors.

While a data center in one region might benefit from lower electricity rates, another might exist in a cooler climate. TBM clarifies those tradeoffs by showing the costs associated with each factor. You can then use these facts to decide where to host new applications or how to optimize data center costs.

Key Performance Indicators

So now that we've discussed how TBM can help you improve cost for performance by aligning your portfolios to the needs of the business, how do you know if you're doing these things well? How do you measure success? This is where the TBM key performance indicators (KPIs) come into play. There are many of them you can use that will be unique to your organization, so we'll just talk about the more common ones here.

Cost for Performance

The first cost-for-performance KPI is your **unit cost actuals vs. targets for your IT towers**. With infrastructure often consuming approximately 60 to 70 percent of overall IT spending,[56] this KPI is essential for cost efficiency. It is useful for both shops with in-sourced infrastructures and those with outsourced or cloud infrastructures. In almost any case, you should still set goals for cost reduction to take advantage of price/performance improvements over time.

As explained in Chapter 5, you should use a combination of your actual prior-period costs and industry peer benchmarks to set achievable targets for your tower teams based on a variety of factors. Many CIOs and their TBM leaders set spending reduction targets for towers on an annual basis, often cutting 3 to 5 percent each year for key towers like server/compute, storage, networking, and end users (e.g., workspaces).

The second KPI is similar to the first. It is your **unit cost actuals vs. targets for business-facing services or applications**. Per-unit cost targets for services or apps (inclusive of the towers that support them) should be set annually during planning. Those targets are based on budgets, expected units consumed (from capacity planning), and industry benchmarks (where available). Actual costs per unit should be reviewed monthly or quarterly.

---

[56] This figure includes all cost pools, including internal labor.

This KPI is essential because it relates to the costs that your business partners see and really care about. If you use rates to charge back or communicate their costs, this KPI helps you ensure you're meeting or beating your established rates and doing it on an ongoing basis.

These two cost KPIs are important, but they do need to be balanced against performance. To do so, use two other KPIs, the first of which is your **percentage of business-facing services meeting SLAs**. To add a useful weighting factor to this measure, use the cost of those applications. For example, if your total service costs in a given month are $1 million, $900,000 of which are meeting or beating your SLAs, then your attainment is 90 percent. In this way, more expensive applications or services are weighted more heavily, thus better reflecting the value delivered.[57]

The second of the performance KPIs is **satisfaction scores for business-facing services**. This measure helps you understand performance from the perspective of your business partners. The measure reflects the outcome of user surveys or similar practices. You can use Net Promoter Score[58] or some other mechanisms. Be sure to assess satisfaction for all major services, however. You can then use cost as a weighting factor for this KPI.

By measuring, managing, and reporting on these four KPIs, you can help your team achieve and demonstrate the best cost-for-performance scenario.

---

[57] Whether total costs are commensurate with value may be debatable. Given TBM's emphasis on aligning cost and value of your portfolios, we assume the correlation here and therefore advocating weighting certain KPIs (e.g., SLA attainment, satisfaction) according to cost.

[58] NPS is a management tool developed by Baan Consulting for measuring and managing customer loyalty. Net Promoter Scores range from +100 (all customers are promoters) to -100 (all customers are detractors). Learn more at https://www.netpromoter.com/know/.

Metric	Implications for Value
Unit Cost Actuals vs. Targets for IT Towers Unit cost targets for towers should be set annually during planning based on budgets, expected units consumed (from capacity planning), and industry benchmarks (where available). Actual cost per unit should be compared monthly or quarterly. These should be set for the majority of your tower spending.	With infrastructure consuming approximately 60% to 70% of overall IT spending, this holds tower owners responsible for cost efficiency and can dramatically improve overall value for the money spent on IT.
Unit Cost Actuals vs. Targets for Business-Facing IT Services or Apps Unit cost targets for services or apps (inclusive of towers that support them) should be set annually during planning based on budgets, expected units consumed (from capacity planning), and industry benchmarks (where available). Actual costs per unit should be compared monthly or quarterly.	Business leaders only understand costs in terms of the services or applications they consume, not towers or infrastructure technologies. Managing the unit costs of services or apps helps you shape business demand.
Business-Facing IT Services or Apps Meeting SLAs Based on total cost of the portfolio, this percentage reveals how much of your applications or services that are delivered to business unit customers are meeting service-level agreements.	Meeting service level agreements with your business partners is essential to delivering value for the money. This helps you balance cost optimization with service quality.
Customer Satisfaction Scores for Business-Facing Services This measure reflects the outcome of surveys of the users of business-facing services. This may include Net Promoter Score or other mechanisms, but should not be limited to the service or help desk. Instead, all major services should be included in the survey.	Performance should be viewed from the perspective of the business users. While SLA attainment is an important, subjective measurements of performance can be very useful.

Business-Aligned Portfolio

Oftentimes, CIOs use the business capabilities they've defined as part of their business architecture planning, e.g., market and sell, design and build, customer support, etc. Others use service lines or lines of business as a close proxy for outcomes. The first KPI relies on these categories to show **actual spending against targets for corporate outcomes**. It helps to answer the question: How are all of your IT resources supporting your business goals? It should also reflect total spending — OpEx and CapEx — although those amounts may be shown separately.

The next portfolio KPI is your **actual spending against targets for business-facing applications and services**. This information is highly valuable for executive-level discussions with business partners on where resources are being spent, including with your CEO and CFO. As with the first KPI, this portfolio should include total spending.

Another KPI is the **total spending against targets for each vendor category** — strategic, preferred, and transactional. Vendor spending may seem inappropriate for a KPI, but many of your business partners have a lot of influence over the technology solutions they purchase and therefore which vendors are employed. Also, this KPI is different than outsourcing, managed by assigning spending to your labor cost pools and allocating it up through the model to those that consume it. Having a fact-based conversation about how your dollars are spent on vendors, however, and comparing that information to the vendor strategy you have in place will help you gain business support and improve positive execution of your plan.

The final KPI is app or service **spending targets for TIME categories** (Tolerate, Invest or Innovate, Migrate, and Eliminate), Gartner's model for application portfolio management. It assumes you've worked with your business partners to classify your applications based on TIME or some similar methodology, for managing application lifecycles. If so, you can use TBM to demonstrate alignment to the decisions you've made together. Here, both usage and resource consumption trends, transaction volumes, and dollar values are useful.

Metric	Implications for Value
Actual Spending (TCO) against Targets for Corporate Outcomes (or Categories) A portfolio-based view of TCO (OpEx and CapEx, including projects) by corporate business outcomes (e.g., capabilities, service lines, lines of business) should be produced monthly or quarterly for executive steering committee or governance reviews.	Since IT is often provided as a set of shared services, facilitating governance conversations with corporate executives is important to ensure business alignment. These conversations should drive top-level mandates for change, such as changes in spending for specific areas of the business.
Actual Spending (TCO) against Targets for Business-Facing Services or Apps A portfolio-based view of TCO (CapEx, including projects, and OpEx) by the services and/or apps that the lines of business consumes should be produced monthly or quarterly and presented to the LOB owners.	In concert with top-level mandates, line of business discussions about spending provides additional insights about where consumption and costs can be optimized or where additional investments are needed.
TCO by Vendor Category A view of CapEx and OpEx by vendor category (e.g., strategic, preferred, transactional) should be produced and reviewed quarterly.	The right vendors can bring tremendous value to your business. Therefore it's important to ensure spending is being focused on the right vendors and according to business priorities.
TCO by TIME A view of app and/or service TCO (CapEx and OpEx) by TIME (tolerate, invest, migrate and eliminate) or another rationalization model should be produced quarterly. This should include trends (up or down from prior period) to identify anomalies (e.g., increased development spending on apps marked for elimination).	Having a plan for rationalizing applications or services is vital to simplifying the IT estate. However, it must be governed by carefully monitoring resources (via dollars) against each category.

Key Takeaways

- Leverage TBM to stop the vicious cycle often associated with project spending: Projects continue to add burden to your operations. Left unchecked, your run-the-business spending will continue to grow, crowding out your resources, increasing enterprise risk or limiting agility.

- Use the facts of TBM to have fact-based discussions about your infrastructure, outsources, labor, and services. Find sources of inefficiency, such as poorly utilized assets, unmanaged outsourcing costs, misallocated people, and bloated software solutions.

- Evaluate your resource consumption to ensure solid alignment to business priorities. Manage your services and applications, technologies and platforms, vendors and suppliers, and data centers as portfolios, allowing both for tradeoffs and tough decisions.

- Use a combination of cost metrics and performance metrics to assess cost for performance.

- Use portfolio-related metrics to measure business alignment based on corporate goals.

Chapter 9:
Transforming Your Business

It wasn't that long ago that business executives viewed technology not as an engine of growth or an enabler of change, but simply as a way to streamline processes and cut costs. While that vision still holds true in many organizations today, it is becoming increasingly clear that those businesses that embrace technology as a way to fundamentally transform how they operate and exploit new opportunities will be the market leaders of tomorrow.

Consider this example. GE, the world's largest producer of jet engines, no longer sells engines to airplane manufacturers like Boeing and Airbus. Instead, it rents them to the airlines in a "power by the hour" business model. In this paradigm, GE takes over the burden of financing the engines, each of which can cost tens of millions of dollars. But it also monitors and services them, providing a predictable revenue stream for GE.

This model has significant benefits for GE's customers, too. Because GE owns the engines, provides maintenance and earns revenue based on uptime, it is incentivized to invest in reliability to reduce maintenance, costly repairs, and downtime. This focus means the airlines benefit from improved reliability, resulting in fewer flight delays and cancellations. It might even reduce airline liability when there is an engine-related accident.

This sample type of shift is happening in IT as well. Through public cloud models, technology providers are shifting from selling on-premises products to delivering their products as services, like Microsoft has done with most of its Server and Office product lines. Like GE's engine customers, cloud provider customers benefit from a more complete solution that is maintained and managed by the provider at a very predictable cost.

Despite these compelling examples, many CIOs continue to employ a more traditional approach for delivering IT to their businesses. In turn, this impairs the ability of the business to be transformed.

This chapter is largely about transforming the business of IT so IT becomes an enabler of that broader business transformation. A transformed IT department enables business agility, greater innovation, growth, and competitiveness. A legacy approach to delivering IT gets in the way of the business.

What does a transformed IT department look like? It is one that runs IT as a business. The following table illustrates the differences between the legacy IT model and this new model.

Legacy IT	IT as a Business
New services and shared investments are funded by the business as capital outlays. The business, in effect, buys new stuff.	New services and shared investments are funded by IT and/or corporate, and expenses are recovered through chargebacks over time based on consumption.
Projects are the center of portfolio management programs. Project resources are viewed as fungible and moved around as needed. Waterfall-based planning and management is common.	Services, not projects, are the center of portfolio management programs. Investment levels are dictated by service needs. Service delivery teams are more stable. Agile and DevOps are the norm.
IT cost structure is heavily fixed. Changes in consumption have little impact on IT cost structure in the short term.	IT cost structure is more variable. Changes in consumption directly affect IT cost structure.
IT provides few service level choices to their business partners.	IT provides many service level choices — tiers, price, performance, etc.

Legacy IT	IT as a Business
IT tends to build and capitalize its services, utilizing corporate-captive resources and CapEx funding or contractors and integrators.	IT serves as a broker, sourcing new services or service components externally. Many services and components are acquired as services using OpEx dollars.
IT governs its own spending and performance, and not that of other business units. Shadow IT is not embraced and is poorly governed at an enterprise level.	IT governs the technology strategy and execution for the entire firm, including the technology services that are owned by its business partners.

The optimizations made possible by TBM allow you to transform your enterprise by adopting an IT-as-a-Business model and mindset. For example, you lighten your day-to-day management load, so you can make changes more easily and faster; you free up budget for innovation; and you rationalize your services portfolio to focus your innovation resources on what's most important to the business.

Yet simply optimizing the delivery of IT isn't sufficient to empower the level of innovation and agility needed by today's enterprises. In this chapter, we'll talk about how you can use the data and tools of TBM to drive more value from your innovation investments and improve your ability to respond to new opportunities and challenges.

Investing in Innovation

The tools of TBM, especially the TBM taxonomy and the TBM model, give you a business lens for reviewing, sharing, and discussing innovation spending. It shows how much you're spending to run and improve your IT services. In essence, it flips your portfolio view from project-centric to a business-centric perspective.

The following sections explore how TBM helps invest in innovation by providing more comprehensive oversight of project costs, shifting to a service-oriented approach for managing investments, funding an innovation program, and driving shared investments.

Project TCO

Project spending often accounts for 20 percent or more of your IT budget, including a large portion of your overall labor spending. That spending can represent a big risk for your business as runaway technology projects continue to plague modern enterprises. A 2011 global study[59] of 1,471 IT projects concluded that project failures not only waste money but often also jeopardize the very companies they were intended to improve.

The study's authors, Bent Flyvbjerg at Oxford University's Saïd Business School and Alexander Budzier at McKinsey, found that most projects come in 27 percent over budget. The more alarming finding was that one in six projects actually had cost overruns of 200 percent and schedule overruns of 70 percent! They referred to these massive failures as *black swans*.

It's obvious from these statistics that projects and their associated project labor must be managed carefully. Yet many CIOs are delivering projects differently than in the past, often using Agile development methodologies. These approaches promise to improve the success rate of technology projects by improving business collaboration, allowing for more course corrections, and delivering software sooner with a precise emphasis on continuous improvement. However, Agile frustrates many traditional project governance techniques, especially financial management.

Here's why. In contrast to waterfall approaches which begin with a well-defined project plan and budget,[60] Agile employs a spiral-into-accuracy methodology for delivering a new software package or service. It takes a more flexible view of project funding and milestones, getting more accurate as the project progresses. Agile teams don't prepare a

---

[59] Flyvbjerg, Bent, and Alexander Budzier. "Why Your IT Project May Be Riskier than You Think." *Harvard Business Review* 89.9 (2011): 601-03. Print.

[60] Please do not confuse well-defined with accurate. Waterfall-based approaches commonly suffer from major cost overruns and missed deadlines.

soup-to-nuts project plan like they used to, so holistic project budgets rarely exist. This doesn't mean project spending can't be managed. Instead, the spending on Agile projects must be continuously reviewed.

Despite the changes brought about by Agile, many IT leaders continue to focus on projects as the primary object of monitoring and management. Projects are proposed, along with a business case (or cost-benefit analysis) that considers its expected benefits and expected costs. IT leaders and their business partners then monitor the projects for their execution against these plans and proposals.

TBM helps IT leaders and their business partners manage the cost of their projects and portfolio by clarifying the *total* cost of each project, as opposed to just the labor hours and capital outlays. This management includes hardware and software purchases, non-contractor services, and other invoiced costs such as public cloud services. TBM makes this possible by driving accountability. When service and application owners have visibility into project costs (which will drive up their operating costs later) they can and will govern their investments better. Not only will they understand the capital costs incurred today; they can model the future costs once the projects enter production. In turn, they can take the necessary steps today to prepare for tomorrow's burden.

Furthermore, by providing business owners with transparency in their project spending, TBM involves the business in shaping the services portfolio. As Chuck Niethold of First American said, "Now the business is not only less resistant to cutting projects, they're actually *helping* us cut them."[61]

Business accountability leads to better oversight of minor enhancements as well. As we've discussed, these incremental enhancements add up to a significant part of the overall budget over time. They do little to change your business while robbing strategic priorities of much-needed resources. To change the business's mindset, Niethold provides his project and business leaders with reports that

---

[61] Niethold, Chuck. TBM Council CFO of IT workgroup presentation. 30 Apr. 2015.

quantify the cost of these minor enhancements. Their response? They now defer enhancements by adding them to the punch list of larger projects and releases. This change has saved both money and resources.

Services Not Projects

In addition to clarifying project TCO, TBM also provides two new perspectives for your project portfolio: better estimates of future operating burdens and improved accountability through better transparency and reporting. Still, many IT leaders are managing change-the-business spending differently than before by focusing on levels of investment in their services. In other words, they're shifting from *project* (or input) management to *service* (or output) management.

This change makes sense in an Agile environment, where many services are implemented quickly as a minimum viable product and then continuously improved over time. Because a project implies a fixed time horizon, whereas services live on indefinitely, with Agile it can make more sense to invest in a *service* portfolio instead of a *project* portfolio.

Managing your innovation portfolio as services instead of projects also conveys a number of benefits. First, CIOs tend to establish a stable team for each of their services. Team members learn to work better with one another and have time to become experts in their services. A stable team roster for each service also improves productivity.[62]

Second, CIOs and their business partners match investment levels to the *business value* of their services. Those levels reflect both capital and operating costs, spanning run-the-business and change-the-business resources. In managing service spending levels in this way, you create a more business-aligned portfolio.

---

[62] According to a 2013 study of more than 50,000 Agile teams, those whose members were 95% dedicated were almost twice as productive (in throughput per team size) as teams whose members were 50% dedicated or less. See: "The Impact of Agile Quantified" at https://www.rallydev.com/resource/impact-agile-quantified-sdpi-whitepaper.

Ed Smith, CTO for Cox Automotive, employs this model of services portfolio funding. "The project model works great if you're a consultant!" he said. [63] "But in software companies or complex enterprises with portfolios, we have to set our investment levels based on where they'll have the biggest business benefit over longer time horizons. We've acquired several development teams over the years and this way we can right-size based on value to the business. You have a semi-permanent team — of at least a year — and you incentivize them based on business metrics."

Smith pairs this funding model with other techniques as well. "We focus a lot on team productivity vs. project performance. For example, we look closely at team yield, or the amount of development vs. non-development time for each team. We want our developers coding, and fewer people watching them code. We also watch velocity of execution, which should be going up or holding steady over time. If it's going down, we look at software complexity, team skills, team management, and other factors. But the emphasis is on the team, not projects."

This approach is generally how SaaS companies and independent software vendors work. They establish product teams based on investment levels determined by a variety of factors: product strategy, product line revenue, competitiveness in the marketplace, cost to maintain and support the product, planned/desired features, and so on. While few CIOs will want to forsake project-oriented financial management entirely, augmenting those approaches with TBM and emphasizing a service portfolio construct provides the following benefits:

- You have more flexibility and are able to make tradeoffs between operating resources and capital ones. For example, you choose to spend more today on service quality to reduce operating costs later.

- You can address the cost of public cloud services, usually classified as operating costs, when using public cloud services as part of your

---

[63] Smith, Ed. Phone interview. 29 Mar. 2016.

innovation approach; in this way, you trade up-front (project) costs for ongoing (subscription) ones.

- Your business partners will better understand how future operating costs will impact their P&Ls, since their technology operating costs depend on the total cost of the service, not just recent capital or project costs.

- You can focus on the value of the service to the business rather than the value of individual investments (i.e., projects). Sometimes multiple projects can enhance a single service. While there are methods of dealing with these situations when assessing benefits, it's a good practice to continuously evaluate the service total cost of ownership against business outcomes, such as revenue generated or costs saved.

To illustrate, consider this extreme case: You rely entirely on the offerings of commercial cloud providers to innovate for your business. There are companies today who do so; they no longer build or own any technology, they cobble together and integrate cloud offerings. In essence, everything is rented, and there are no assets on the books.[64] In this scenario, a traditional governance program focused on managing projects would have little to do as labor hours and CapEx spending are either minimized or eliminated completely. There may be some project resources associated with sourcing, integrating, and configuring cloud services. But those resources are tiny compared to traditional application development and systems integration work.

In taking a traditional, project-centric governance approach to a project-*less* reality, you would fail to adequately govern your innovation dollars. Furthermore, your business partners wouldn't be able to see how your service changes or introductions will impact their P&Ls next year. While this example may seem a little farfetched, most CIOs are moving

---

[64] Companies who take this approach should still record and track their public cloud assets even though they are rented. For example, they should have an inventory of public cloud servers in their IT asset database. Cloud-sourcing is not a substitute for proper IT management.

more in this direction, leveraging the cloud wherever they can to accelerate innovation.

By presenting your labor, hardware, software, and project investments (both CapEx and OpEx) in the context of your services, TBM allows you to balance your innovation portfolio better. TBM shows you how much you're spending by service, service category, program category (i.e., run vs. grow/transform), *and* by project. This focus enables you to:

- identify any over-investment in services by considering all spending: CapEx and OpEx, both project and non-project;

- evaluate how much you're investing for each business unit, including the impact of shared investments (projects or spending on services that can benefit multiple business units); and

- assess current project investments by business initiatives and business capabilities.

These capabilities are what differentiate *service* portfolio management from *project* portfolio management.

Funding Your Innovation Program

Many CIOs and even CEOs fund innovation programs through pure research, experimentation, and prototyping. These are not the same as R&D programs, which are normally focused on application development in a more structured and stage-gated approach. Innovation programs rarely fit into a service or project construct, because their focus is on "ideation," not development. Further, in distinguishing these programs, they often use resources from both IT and the business. In many enterprises, they are even set up as distinct business units or departments to better isolate them from the whims and rigors of day-to-day operational funding and tradeoffs.

Regardless of the program's constructs, too many enterprises fail to adequately fund IT's part in innovation. A recent CIO survey[65] revealed that the top challenge in delivering innovation is "budget constraints." CIOs also said there were too many resources dedicated to running the business and too much difficulty in finding the right people; both were barriers to innovation. In other words, CIOs too often lack the resources for their innovation programs — even when business leaders cite digital innovation as a high priority. Given that CIOs often sponsor digital innovation programs,[66] it is surprising that so many businesses fail to adequately fund IT's role in these efforts. So why are CIOs struggling to fund something so important to their businesses?

Innovation funding suffers when CFOs and other business leaders evaluate the IT budget as a percentage of revenue and then conclude that the IT department is adequately funded. If CIOs commingle their run-the-business and change-the-business resources with their innovation resources, innovation funding will always suffer because it has no immediate business benefit.

Innovation programs should not be evaluated using the same short-term metrics as those used for services or projects. They're not about running the business, developing the next release of software or even adding a new service in an existing line of business. They're bets you are placing on the future of your business. Like all bets they are speculative, so they should be funded separately from run/grow/transform spending (see below).

---

[65] The CSC survey represents the opinions of 590 IT leaders from firms with an average of 697 IT employees. To read the survey results, find it online at http://www.csc.com/cio_survey_2014_2015

[66] A September 2015 McKinsey report found that CIOs are the sponsors of digital initiatives 35% of the time, second only to CEOs (46%). Source: Bughin, Jacques, Andy Holley, and Anette Mellbye. "Cracking the Digital Code: McKinsey Global Survey Results." McKinsey.com. McKinsey & Company, Sep. 2015. Web.

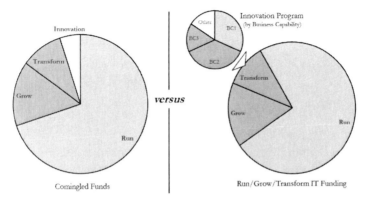

*Figure 9-1: Commingling innovation funds with the rest of IT funding puts them at risk; they should
be funded separately from IT and jointly with non-IT innovation funding*

Figure 9-1 illustrates the danger of commingling funds. On the left, innovation funds come from general run/grow/transform spending. The problem is this spending is evaluated as a percentage of revenue or some other gross measure. It will put downward pressure on innovation funding since it shrinks in proportion with the budget.

The right-hand side of this model presents a different view. Here, the innovation program is treated as a separate fund. That fund might be evaluated based on business capability or some other set of categories, but it's not lumped in with the rest of IT spending. This model should include the line-of-business resources, so the business understands the total investment it is making in innovation. When the innovation program yields a new IT service prototype, only then does it become part of IT's transform (or grow) spending (as a project, for example).

Innovation programs should not be structured as projects either, because the project paradigm places a drag on this type of innovation. Mike Benson of DIRECTV realized this issue and took a different approach.

"We took 10 ideas, brought them in, and then we funded two of them. They have six months to come back with a capability. We're tracking them with TBM, because they're not a project. I don't want to use the word project because then, all of a sudden, they want a project manager, they want to add overhead. Innovate doesn't mean 'I've got to put the timeline together, and I have to do waterfall now.' It's really, 'Let's try this, see if that works. If it doesn't work, try this, try this, try this,' anything to try to get to a mission or an idea."

CIOs can use TBM to address this funding challenge by clarifying the existing run-the-business burden and separating innovation funding from the usual operating and capital budgets. Those budgets, when built using the hybrid-based budgeting described in Chapter 7 (zero-based and prior year), demonstrate business necessity and efficiency. They show how IT resources are being used wisely to deliver on the commitments IT leaders have made to the business, but no more.

The innovation program should be set aside with its own resources above and beyond the costs that you've agreed are right for running your business and the other investments you've agreed to make. Like DIRECTV, you can use TBM to keep tabs on your innovation program.

Shared Investments in Towers

Shared investments come in a few flavors. There are those that are tower-level investments (technologies and infrastructure) and support more than one service that your business partners consume, such as a database management system or directory services that support multiple applications. Also, there are investments in shared services, such as your ERP system and your network services. What they all have in common is they present challenges for prioritizing and funding: Who pays for (or approves) a shared investment? And how do you estimate, measure, and assess the business benefits from it?

Let's consider the first example, the tower-level shared investment which benefits multiple services. These IT4IT investments often compete for funds with business-facing projects. Even though these IT4IT investments are not "nice to haves," it is still difficult to get funding for them because their benefits are indirect and potentially difficult to measure. They also compete with non-IT4IT investment options.

The TBM model helps you gain the dollars you need by changing how you justify the shared investment. Instead of asking your business partners to fund a shared investment based on technical merits, your service owners justify the investment based on shared business benefits. Your service owners can use TBM to translate the technical benefits into business ones. This approach is illustrated in the following figure.

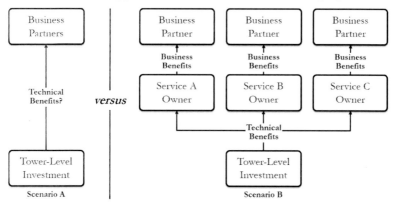

Figure 9-2: TBM relies on your application or service owners to justify tower-level investments

Consider how this spending would appear in a bill of IT. In Scenario A above, technical benefits are communicated to your business partners, and your business partners receive a bill that shows the cost of a database upgrade. They see server hardware, database software, and staff hours, for example. The bill speaks in bits and bytes, not business benefits.

In Scenario B, using TBM, your business partners don't see the tower-level investment in their bill of IT. Instead, your service owners, who benefit directly from the shared investment, make the business case for it. They are able to describe the benefits in business terms, such as improvements in application transaction times, improved security and reliability, and faster resolution times from supporting vendors. In this scenario, your business partners see a bill that reflects the additional investment in the services they consume. As far as they're concerned, their services just got better for the money they spent.

Not only should you use this approach to build your business case for tower-level investments, you should track the performance of your investments at the service level: How well have those services served your lines of business? Have they reduced business costs or enhanced customer service? What revenue has been generated or enabled? This type of business analysis can only be done at the service level.

Shared Investments in Services

Investing in shared services suffers from a slightly different challenge than investing in towers. Here the business benefits should be easy to see. Yet who these investments benefit, and therefore who should pay for them, may be harder to articulate. By revealing who consumes your services and in what kind of volume, TBM helps solve this conundrum. In enterprises that price their IT services and charge for them, IT leaders can disclose the impact of any new investments on their service rates (prices) and thus have informed discussions about the impacts to the business.

Consider this example: You have decided to migrate your document management solution to a new platform. Your legal department however needs features that are not in the standard edition of the new service. With TBM, you can create two different service-level packages: one with the features that legal needs and another that serves the rest of your users. Even if the added features aren't licensable from the vendor on a user-by-user basis, you can still rely on internal pricing to fund them fairly.

TBM goes further in helping you justify shared investments to your business partners. With TBM, you can build comprehensive, long-term business cases that reveal the TCO impact of new investments. This impact may include cost efficiencies that are realized over time. But to get to this point you have to understand your TCO for the existing platforms and the expected impact on this TCO in the future. TBM gives you the data to build this business case successfully.

Enterprise Agility

IT departments often steer like an oil tanker — slowly and cautiously. Many CIOs struggle with tremendous momentum in the form of cost structures, staff, skills, and methodologies that prevent them from reacting quickly to new demands. To improve their ability to respond faster, many CIOs are adopting Agile development methodologies and embracing the public cloud.

The following sections explore how TBM helps improve agility by allowing you to change your cost structures, leverage the cloud, exploit decentralized IT decision-making, and use data to make better decisions faster.

Fixed Investments vs. Variable Costs

One of the biggest barriers to making the shift to an IT-as-a-Business model is the IT cost structure that exists in most enterprises. These cost structures tend to be heavily burdened by fixed costs. You incur fixed costs from applications that you build or buy, hardware that you install, facilities that you purchase or lease, and even from most of the people you employ. These assets and resources will cost you money even if your business doesn't use them.

Fixed costs inhibit financial agility. They don't go down just because your business is in a down cycle or when it reduces headcount. Instead, fixed costs just eat at your P&L month after month. These costs frustrate your business partners, but they often tie up capital and operating funds when your business needs them most. But it's not just business cycles that heighten the pain of fixed costs; they also get in the way of giving your business partners choices in the services they consume.

This doesn't mean fixed costs aren't controllable. Don't confuse fixed and variable with controllable and non-controllable (or even discretionary and mandatory) costs. In fact, as pointed out in Chapter 5, many fixed costs are controllable. For example, much of your travel and expense budget is considered a fixed cost. You've set aside budget for training, meetings, and other activities that have little to do with the volume of services you deliver; yet when times are tight, those expenses are often the first to be cut.

While transparency makes cutting fixed costs easier, over the years, many firms have already cut controllable expenses. They've renegotiated contracts, rationalized portfolios, cut support staff, and offshored or nearshored development work. The IT costs that remain are stubbornly *fixed*, and often less controllable than before. Because of this fact, many CIOs are now working to "variablize" their costs. Some do so because they want to cut budget without laying off employees, cancelling important projects, or taking other measures which impair their ability to innovate.

Others are variablizing costs to improve how they manage demand. Fixed costs often create a disincentive for your business partners to conserve. They know that if they consume less, their costs won't go down. It's like dieting without losing weight. Few conversations are more painful than when you tell your business partners that their IT costs didn't go down just because they used less.

To variablize costs properly requires a new perspective. For starters, you must first understand how the consumption volumes of your services vary with your business volumes. For example, if you're a hospital CIO, you need to know how outpatient services (your business volume) drives the volumes of your electronic health records (your EHR service). Some service volumes vary directly with your business volumes; others do not.

When variablizing your costs, you should first focus on the services most affected by use. You'll almost never see a perfect correlation between the two; instead, it's a matter of degree. TBM helps you figure this degree out by giving you the facts about service consumption over time. With this data in hand, you can compare historical service volumes to historical business volumes.

For the next step, you need to know what percentage of your service costs are variable — also on a service-by-service basis. It's not good enough to know that your overall IT costs are 60 percent fixed and 40 percent variable; it's the consumption of each service that drives your costs either up or down.

When you know these two factors — business volume dynamics and service cost structure — you can determine where variablizing your services will help you link IT costs to business volumes. This focus is illustrated in the following figure:

| Services | Business Relationship | | | Cost Structure | | | |
	Business Service	Biz Trend	IT Product Units of Measure	Correlation: IT Units to Biz Service Volume	Fixed	Var.	Recommended Action
e-Health Records	Patient Services		Records Stored	Strong	70%	30%	Variablize costs
Surgery IS	Surgeries		Surgeries	Strong	70%	30%	None
PACS	Patient Services		Images Stored	Medium	60%	40%	Variablize costs
Teleservices	Patient Services		Visits	Medium	55%	45%	Variablize costs
Claims Processing	Patient Claims		Claims Filed	Strong	75%	25%	Cut costs
Lab Management	Laboratory		Lab Tests	Strong	25%	75%	None
Corporate Email	All		Users	Weak	50%	50%	None
Pay Processing	Payroll		Paychecks	Strong	10%	90%	None

Figure 9-3: Analyzing variable costs by services can help you understand where to change your cost composition based on consumption patterns

In Figure 9-3, EHR consumption volumes strongly correlate with business service volumes. In other words, when the hospital delivers more patient services, EHR volumes increase by roughly the same degree. However, the corporate messaging IT volumes correlate very little with any business volumes. Knowing these relationships helps you understand how your volumes will vary based on business trends.

For many IT departments, the hard part of this analysis is knowing the variable cost percentage of each service. If you've been managing your costs at the cost pool or tower levels, but not allocating these costs up through the tower and service layers to the business units that consume them, it will be hard to determine the necessary variable cost ratios. You need to use the TBM model to understand your service cost dynamics. You may then find that the ratios differ significantly from service to service.

When variablizing service costs, there are a number of approaches you can take. First among these is cloud-sourcing whole services or the components of your services. For example, you can switch to a cloud provider for an entire service like CRM or to a development platform, or you can cloud-source components, such as storage or computing. In either case, the TBM model will help you understand the degree to which the public cloud will variablize your service costs.

Outsourcing is another approach. It is highly dependent on the contract and nature of the services. Most outsourcing contracts include minimum service levels (at which point the prices are renegotiated), a "deadband" within which contract charges remain fixed, and predefined methods (additional resource credits and reduced resource credits, or ARCs and RRCs) for adjusting charges when volumes fall outside the deadband limits. This scenario means outsourcing contracts are variable, but only to an extent.

These approaches help you variablize your costs, which then make it easier for you to charge your business based on their consumption. But there is another way to provide this benefit to your business partners. You assume the risk of the capacity you carry.

In other words, someone must assume the risk associated with carrying capacity, no matter what is being delivered. Retailers assume the risk of carrying inventory. Banks assume the risk of carrying loans on their books. Telecom companies carry the risk of network capacity. If these firms don't somehow monetize this risk, they eat the costs of carrying it. IT is no different.

Even cloud providers like Microsoft and Amazon have to carry capacity. Ironically, cloud providers have mostly fixed-cost infrastructures. The public cloud business model assumes the risk of carrying excess capacity. To pay for that risk, they include a profit margin in the prices they charge.

Few CIOs can price their services to include a profit margin. Indeed, the majority of IT departments that charge back for their services are required to recover 100 percent of their costs, no more and no less. Then you have a choice to make. Continue to charge for your total capacity, which discourages your business partners from consuming less, or charge a fair price for only what is consumed and thus encourage conservation.

The cloud — private, public, and hybrid — gives you the technical capability to provide capacity on demand. Indeed, your business partners are learning to love this model. The tools of TBM also enable you to charge based on consumption, but only if you can make that change in your financial model. It includes how you're funded and how business unit P&Ls are charged for what they consume. You have to work with your corporate CFO and business partners to make this change. However, in the end, you will have variablized the IT costs for your business partners by assuming the risk of your capacity.

Variablizing costs for your business partners is a major step in running IT as a business. It helps you transform the way you deliver IT services and the way your business partners consume them. In doing so, you improve the agility of your business.

Discretionary Investments

A major facet of business agility is your ability to make change-the-business investments and react to new opportunities, threats, or business conditions. Unfortunately, many CIOs find they have little spare capacity for truly spur-of-the-moment project spending. As one healthcare CIO told us a couple of years ago, her department was known as the "Department of No!" Upon analysis, she found that even without considering new requests from her business for new projects, she was already overcommitted, at 107 percent of her project capacity.

Situations like hers are not uncommon. Mandatory spending like adding capacity, meeting compliance requirements, and maintaining platforms takes its toll on your capital budget and project resources.

The first step in addressing this challenge is getting a better handle on your investment portfolio (per Chapters 5 and 8). You may need to improve project transparency, which should include evaluating whether or not your mandatory investments are truly mandatory. Project sponsors have a nasty habit of labeling projects as regulatory or compliance investments when they are not (not entirely, at least). Consider creating additional oversight for any *mandatory* investments that cannot be justified on other merits.

If you've shifted to a service-oriented funding model as described earlier in this chapter, you have an important decision to make regarding your agility. What is the right amount of discretionary spending? In other words, should you increase funding for your services to increase discretionary spending, or find ways to decrease mandatory spending?

Discretionary spending is a direct measure of agility. Having few resources to dedicate to discretionary investments means your resources are spent on mandatory (non-optional) needs. If an opportunity arises that requires new investment, you won't have the resources at the ready to take advantage of it. Spinning up new resources takes time in a service-oriented model that clearly emphasizes team stability.

Public and Private Cloud

CIOs and business leaders alike often cite agility as their reason for embracing the cloud. But for most, cloud adoption is happening only in pockets. Market figures certainly demonstrate this situation. According to Gartner, despite double-digit growth, cloud computing accounts for less than 5 percent of overall IT spending.[67]

Too many business and technology leaders embrace certain public cloud services (e.g., point SaaS applications) while avoiding others (e.g., cloud compute and storage for their mission-critical applications). If given the choice between public cloud and on-premises infrastructure, many decision makers choose the latter because they lack the facts to justify either option. Instead, on-premises just feels like the safer choice.

Sometimes the facts do justify the on-premises choice. Yet many times the differences in cost and quality clearly favor public cloud services. The TBM model clarifies these differences so you and your business partners can make more informed choices.

The power of transparency to shape business consumption can be instrumental in adopting a more cost-effective technology, even when the business perceives risks in doing so. Indeed, this was the experience

---

[67] Gregor Petri. "Three Factors Will Continue to Impact Enterprise Cloud Playbooks." *Gartner.* Gartner, Inc., 30 Sep. 2015.

at First American, first with virtualized servers and then with public cloud, as reported[68] by VP of IT Chuck Niethold:

Some departments were skeptical of virtualization at the start. But after documenting savings in implementation, Niethold was able to go to another with a projection of what its savings would be.

"I could say, 'Hey, I can lower your costs by 40 percent.' Without that data, it was harder to get people to move," he recalled.

Over the past year, First American's use of Azure has mushroomed from $500 a month to $300,000, and he expects to have similar conversations with business managers in 2015 about the potential of cloud use. His staff knows the expense for a certain application running in a virtual machine on-premises. When it makes sense to, he can point out to his counterpart in the line of business what the potential savings might be on Azure.

By providing accountability for costs, TBM helps IT leaders foster the right discussion about the tradeoffs of cost, risk and performance — *given the facts*. In this way, TBM provides a powerful incentive for the adoption of new technologies, such as public cloud services.

Shadow IT

Shadow IT is one of those buzzwords that has struck a chord with IT leaders over the last decade. It's defined as the purchasing and deployment of information technology performed outside the auspices of the IT department. Therefore, it also implies a loss of control for CIOs, many of whom struggle to articulate the value of what their teams do.

Many IT leaders have learned that shadow IT is nothing to be feared, and since it is here to stay, it has to be embraced so it can be managed. Many have recognized that their business partners not only have the right to buy the third-party products and services they need, but they are often

---

[68] Babcock, Charles. "First American: Cloud Analysis Points to Savings." *InformationWeek*. UBM, 10 Feb. 2015. Web.

best situated to do exactly that. For example, many CMOs are more adept at choosing marketing automation tools than their IT departments are. Shadow IT is not only inevitable; it is essential to business agility.

Still, shadow IT carries risks for the enterprise. Any new IT service introduces security risks and vendor risks to a business. Business leaders sometimes overextend themselves with new technologies, then find themselves unprepared to integrate or support something they've just purchased. Businesses lose their negotiating power over vendors when they purchase the same services from multiple buying centers.

Creating transparency for your enterprise's technology spending will help address these risks. The TBM model helps you do this by using your general ledger as the source of all spending, modeling it against towers and services to reveal gaps in your data. Your business partners may purchase IT outside your IT procurement processes, but these costs will still come through your TBM model.

Shadow spending is part of your business's IT costs, and the technologies acquired by your business partners often impact your centralized IT costs for support, security, and integration. With enterprise-level transparency in place, you can perform more meaningful benchmarking for your total IT spending and value.

Data-Driven IT Business

The business benefits of data-driven decision-making have long been touted by management gurus and academia. But it wasn't until 2012 that these benefits were rigorously examined. Then, Andrew McAfee and Erik Brynjolfsson at the MIT Center for Digital Business led a team to test the hypothesis that data-driven companies are better performers.[69]

After interviewing executives at 330 public companies and analyzing data from annual reports and other sources, the team found that being data-driven did indeed improve the results. After controlling for a variety of factors such as labor, capital, and IT investment, the most data-driven

---

[69] McAfee, Andrew, & Erik Brynjolfsson. "Big Data: The Management Revolution." *Harvard Business Review*. 1 Oct. 2012. Web.

companies were 5 percent more productive and 6 percent more profitable than their competitors.

If businesses perform better when they employ data-driven decision-making, wouldn't IT departments also perform better if they did the same? There are many anecdotes where the data provided by TBM helped an enterprise move more quickly and improve results. eBay's corporate split with PayPal is one such example.[70]

In September of 2014, after 15 months of standardizing and integrating eBay and PayPal infrastructure, eBay announced it was splitting into two separate companies. This meant that eBay's technology division would have less than a year to separate into two independent entities while continuing to power a $260 billion e-commerce engine through a record-breaking holiday shopping season.

According to Dean Nelson, VP of Global Foundation Services at eBay, "Most people didn't believe we could actually do [the split] in that timeframe. I didn't know if we could do it in that timeframe! How do we size, price, plan, organize, and execute this separation with such an aggressive timeline and an expectation that we will not interrupt the business?"

With the TBM model in place, making the split proved to be easier than Nelson imagined because they'd already structured the data into modular cost elements. He and his team then used the model to design, plan, split, and manage the two infrastructures.

"Even though this is a hugely complex project, it was easier with the TBM model. We knew what we had, we knew where it was allocated, we knew who owned what, we knew what the cost structures were, and we could establish a budget that rolled back up into our split committee. This model produced a surprisingly accurate budget and timeline to enable these companies to operate independently."

---

[70] Vignette built from public sources and from 2015 TBM Awards interviews and video case study. eBay was a winner of the 2015 TBM Council Infrastructure Trailblazer award. See video: https://youtu.be/eAURUmd4G_Q

The team successfully split the commerce engine into two independent, highly efficient engines, each a hybrid containing parts of the other's TBM-optimized infrastructure. On July 20, 2015, PayPal began trading *and operating* as a separate company.

Nelson acknowledged that the split is just the tip of the iceberg in how they used TBM to make decisions: "Looking back over our TBM journey, we have increased rack density four-fold; we've reduced the cost per megawatt delivered by 53 percent; we reduced the watts per core in our servers by 69 percent — all while supporting a doubling in commerce volume. We could make these data-driven decisions because we had the taxonomy and data flowing through it, month after month, year after year."

Having the data provided by TBM empowers faster decision-making. It also helps IT leaders improve the quality of the data they have about their assets, consumption, users, and more. By putting their data into the context of a TBM model, revealing gaps in that data, and adding a financial dimension to data quality, TBM provides the transparency *and the incentives* for IT employees and business partners to get the data right.

This improved decision-making has benefits beyond standard TBM use cases, just as the eBay split shows. According to one energy industry CIO, TBM helped his company improve the quality of their user entitlements data, i.e., the people who have access to a given application. Before they had implemented TBM, nobody in the business seemed to care if user entitlements were wrong, even though it had led to audit findings and security risks. When the business units were charged back to their users based on their entitlements, the business unit leaders started paying attention. The entitlements were quickly cleaned up, improving security and compliance. This entitlement cleanup had one other benefit: They were able to reduce the number of user licenses for many of the applications, resulting in additional cost savings.

As a data-driven approach, TBM speeds up decisions. It also helps IT leaders connect what they do to their business goals in a way that wasn't possible earlier. In turn, TBM also helps improve business performance and the value of IT. Improved value, after all, is the primary goal of TBM.

Key Performance Indicators

To help you measure innovation and agility, the TBM model augments your existing metrics via the following KPIs that emphasize business and financial perspectives.

Investment in Innovation

The first TBM KPI for innovation — your **run-the-business vs. change-the-business ratio** — is hardly new to many IT leaders. Since the run/grow/transform model was first introduced by the META Group[71] in the early 2000s, many CIOs have been measuring run vs. change (grow and transform combined). Since then, many CIOs have found their change spending inadequate and are working hard to increase it as a percentage of overall spending. Some have set goals for this shift, such as Rebecca Jacoby's goal of shifting from two-thirds run-the-business spending to two-thirds change-the-business spending at Cisco.

Run/grow/transform spending should be measured on a total basis — OpEx and CapEx. Note that not all OpEx is run-the-business and not all CapEx is grow- or transform-the-business. For example, non-capitalized R&D costs (such as those incurred before the capitalization period begins) for a new service that will help the business enter a new market might be classified as transform; the capital costs of a server refresh might then be classified as run. Instead, they should be classified based on their value or outcome for the business. This is hard to do without the TBM taxonomy.

Another useful KPI is examining your **investment by value categories**. It is a measure of your investments by dimensions like replacement, maintenance, enhancements, and new. CIOs can measure

---

[71] Later acquired by Gartner, which continues to promote the run/grow/transform model. More recently, Gartner has proposed a new model for bimodal IT organizations which stratifies funding into fear-based, fact-based, and faith-based investments.

these categories and focus project resources on enhanced and new capabilities, thereby improving business value. As with run/grow/transform, CIOs should baseline their spending for these categories, set practical goals for improvement on at least an annual basis, and monitor their progress at least quarterly.

Another KPI is **on-track projects by spending and headcount**. On-track means on-time, on-budget, and on-performance. This KPI demonstrates how well IT is delivering on its project-related commitments. By using dollar values, as opposed to the raw number of projects, this KPI focuses your conversations on those larger projects that likely will have a bigger impact on your business. For organizations that fund based on services instead of by projects, this KPI might be replaced by team productivity metrics.

The last KPI is the total **economic value added (EVA)** of your investment portfolio. Similarly, net present value (NPV) may be used. Many IT organizations are beginning to use EVA to determine and communicate the value they deliver. While not without its flaws, EVA provides an effective measure of operating profitability of a business unit *from the perspective of the shareholder*. It does so by essentially reducing the net operating profit (after taxes) by the average cost of capital for the business unit.

The major differences between EVA and NPV are the time horizons for each. EVA considers only the current time period (e.g., current fiscal year) while NPV is based on the expected long-term cash flows of an investment. Therefore, EVA promises to provide an accurate measure of profit contribution for a period of activity, while NPV is subject to errors in future cash flow estimations. This is why it is so important that the NPV of projects or investments be adjusted from time to time to reflect the most current understanding of future cash flows.

EVA is not a measure to be undertaken by IT alone, as it relies on assumptions about the amount of capital invested in IT that is not traditionally available to IT decision makers. Instead, employ EVA if the rest of your business is also applying EVA valuations. If that is the case, corporate finance should have a well-defined method of allocating capital and determining average capital costs, both of which are required for EVA calculations. If EVA is not employed by your business, instead rely on NPV and your IT spend ratio to determine, manage, and communicate the business value of IT.

Because EVA and NPV both consider the benefits of any investment, TBM helps by connecting IT investments to the business benefits they provide through services to the business. The transparency of TBM enables IT leaders and their finance partners to understand the revenue improvements or cost reductions associated with a new investment both over the short term (i.e., current period) and the longer term. In supporting these metrics (of which EVA is preferred), TBM helps IT leaders keep shareholder returns in mind when making decisions.

Metric	Implications for Value
Run-the-Business vs. Change-the-Business Run-the-business (RtB) spending includes both capital and operating expenditures needed to operate and sustain business operations. RtB activities are vital to your business but there is a tendency for them to increase year-over-year as previous change-the-business investments impact ongoing operations. RtB vs. Change-the-business (CtB) spending should be reported each quarter.	If cost for performance and business alignment are managed well, those efforts should help free up investment for innovation (change-the-business). Therefore, this KPI not only helps ensure RtB is being optimized, but it puts additional emphasis on the business managing its demand and understanding the tradeoff of existing consumption vs. new capabilities.
Investments against Targets by Value Category A view of investments by category (e.g., replace, maintain, enhance, or new) against targets should be produced quarterly.	This KPI helps IT and business executives understand the impact of technical debt or modernization requirements that might be crowding out new or better capabilities.

Metric	Implications for Value
Projects On Time, On Budget, On Spec A view of total project spending and headcount split by those that are tracking to scope, budget and deadline should be produced quarterly. It should be split by executive (BU) sponsors and reviewed during the quarterly business review.	This KPI demonstrates how well IT is delivering on its project-related commitments. By using dollar value of projects, as opposed to the raw number of projects, this KPI focuses the discussion on the larger projects that likely have a bigger impact on the business.
Economic Value Added (EVA) of the IT Investment Portfolio EVA of the IT portfolio should be calculated quarterly or annually based on the business benefits of new or enhanced services that drive revenue or productivity.	EVA provides an effective measure of the operating profitability of a business unit from the perspective of the shareholder. It does so by essentially reducing the net operating profit (after taxes) by the average cost of capital for the business unit.

Enterprise Agility

Agility KPIs show you and your business partners how much you've shifted your resources to a more IT-as-a-Business model. This shift is not a binary one, as few IT organizations are fully delivering everything as services; instead, they focus on a spectrum.

The first KPI here is the percentage of your **OpEx spending that is funded by BU consumption**. In other words, of your total operating costs, how much do you recover via chargeback (or nominally via showback) methods that rely on consumption factors, such as seats or usage by your business partners. Charging for what is consumed is a strong indicator that you're providing the services your business needs. It implies a more market-like orientation to your service delivery, a setup that fosters conversations between IT providers and consumers about value delivered for the money.

The next KPI is the **IT delivered by the cloud**. This measures how much of your IT (as a percentage of your total OpEx) is delivered as public *or private* cloud services to the business. The more you deliver via cloud, the more agility you create for your business. However, since agility often comes at a cost, this measure should be balanced against the cost-for-performance KPIs described in Chapter 8.

Another KPI here is the **variable cost ratio of your services**. This KPI measures how much of your business-facing service costs (i.e., apps or services delivered to the business) are fixed (i.e., static, regardless of consumption) or variable (i.e., vary in line with the volumes of consumption). Since a variable cost structure also comes at a price, this KPI should also be balanced against cost for performance.

The last *financial* KPI for agility is the **percentage of your project or investment spending that is discretionary**. As noted above, discretionary investments are those that are made to enhance services or introduce new ones, as opposed to mandatory investments, such as compliance, capacity upgrades, reducing technical debt, and maintenance. The more you've allocated to discretionary spending, the more you can shift when necessary without adding any new investment.

A final KPI for agility is non-financial but nonetheless essential: the **TBM data quality index** is a measure of the overall state of your data quality. It reflects how much of your TBM model is driven by data and measures other facets of data quality, such as completeness and referential integrity. Organizations with high-quality data are able to make data-driven decisions, and in turn, they make these decisions better and faster.

Metric	Implications for Value
IT OpEx Funded by BU Consumption This measures how much of OpEx is funded (via chargeback, or nominally via showback) by consumption factors such as seats or usage.	When delivering IT as services for which the business can choose to consume (or not) means holding them accountable for their consumption. The greater the share of IT OpEx funded through consumption, the more IT is being delivered in this way.

Metric	Implications for Value
IT Delivered by Cloud against Targets This measures how much of IT (as a percent of Opex) is delivered as private or public cloud services to the business. Clear criteria for which services are designated cloud services are needed for this KPI to be meaningful.	Public and private cloud services are, by definition, rapidly elastic and on-demand, and its consumption is measured to provide a basis for allocating costs. Cloud enables the business to use IT services as needed, providing agility and connecting business consumption and the costs incurred.
Variable Cost Ratio by Business-Facing Service against Targets This KPI measures how much of the business-facing IT costs (i.e., apps or services delivered to the business) are fixed (i.e., static regardless of consumption) or variable (i.e., vary in line with volumes of consumption). Targets should be set while considering implications for short- and long-term total costs.	A more variable cost structure is beneficial in situations where business volumes are falling or are expected to rise and fall. A variable cost structure helps match IT costs with business revenues. However, targets for variable costs should be set based on tradeoff considerations.
Discretionary Project Spending against Targets Discretionary projects are those designed to enhance services or introduce new ones, as opposed to mandatory investments such as compliance, capacity upgrades, reducing technical debt and maintenance.	When mandatory spending consumes a high percentage of project spending, the business has little ability to innovate or respond to new threats or opportunities. Greater discretionary spending as a percentage of the total indicates a greater capacity to innovate, as funds can be shifted more easily.
TBM Data Quality Index This measures the overall state of data quality for TBM. It measures missing data sets, gaps in data, breakage between data sets, and the use of assumptive data in driving allocations. It should trend in a positive direction, although setbacks may occur after major changes in the model or data sources.	As IT leaders become data-driven in their decision making, better data quality for TBM means they can make better decisions for improving business value. Better data also improves operational maturity, making it possible to run more efficiently and reliably.

Key Takeaways

- TBM has become a core part of how many technology organizations are becoming service providers to their business partners.

- Use TBM to change the way you invest in innovation. Shift your focus from discrete projects to funding and governing service investments, including setting funding levels based on need and value.

- Separate innovation program spending from the rest of your IT spending to isolate it from short-term considerations. Innovation spending is like venture capital; it's a bet on your company's future.

- Rely on your service owners to justify shared investments in towers. TBM provides a model for doing so.

- Leverage TBM to improve the levers you have for agility. For example, manage your variable cost ratio and oversee mandatory investments and projects, as these can rob you of important resources for discretionary spending.

- Embrace shadow IT by using TBM to provide enterprise-level transparency and visibility of technology spending. Use this awareness to better manage the risks associated with distributed IT decisions.

- Improve the quality of your IT management data to build a more data-driven IT organization. Leverage the transparency and incentives that TBM provides to improve your data quality continuously.

Chapter 10:
Continuously Improving Value

A commonly overheard refrain at the annual Technology Business Management Conference is that TBM is a journey. That any transformation in the way you manage the business of IT takes time should be no surprise. Just don't assume that there is no value from TBM until you reach your destination. With each step in TBM, you achieve greater value.

From the very start, TBM gets your people talking about how IT impacts the company's bottom line and its part in creating value. Imagine the power of having system administrators understand better how what they do fits into the grand scheme of your business. They start thinking about what they consume that delivers their part of the value chain; and they know who consumes what they deliver and how it impacts their business partners' costs and value. By leveraging the TBM model, every part of your IT organization will see the bigger picture.

The TBM model and its associated taxonomy also can begin to resolve issues about what is or is not a service. People see how services are delivered to and consumed by the lines of business. They can be technical like hosting services, and they can be application and end-user services as well. By seeing the components of your services along with their costs and resource consumption, those services become more concrete and measurable.

The TBM journey begins with this mental shift, but it depends on making continuous improvement to the way you manage the business of IT to be ultimately successful. Much of this improvement will come in the form of more accurate data, but it also comes from integrating TBM into your day-to-day processes and thinking and using TBM to drive value conversations with your peers.

In this chapter, we'll apply the lessons that were garnered (sometimes the hard way) from hundreds of TBM transformations and tool deployments. In particular, we will discuss requirements that, when met, dramatically improve the odds of success with TBM. They include:

- **measured business goals** based on the key TBM metrics or related ones, often combined on a balanced scorecard with non-TBM metrics;

- **governance** that includes the proper sponsorship, administration, communication, and oversight of TBM within the enterprise;

- **routine processes** for TBM integrated with other existing management processes or implemented as new ones;

- a **roadmap** for TBM communicated to IT and finance stakeholders and to your business partners;

- **shared ownership** between IT, finance, and the lines of business;

- **evolution of data, modeling, and analytics** that takes advantage of improvements made using the roadmap; and

- **insights, actions, and value tracking** to ensure the improvements are made and then communicated to the stakeholders.

In the following sections, we'll discuss each of these.

Measured Business Goals

In Chapters 8 and 9, we discussed the value conversations and associated KPIs made possible by TBM. These include elements like meeting or beating unit cost targets for your services, alignment of your spending (TCO) to business goals, percentage of investment spending that is discretionary, and your variable cost ratios for your services. The question you need to ask now is which metrics are most important to your business, and what targets (goals) should you set for them.

For example, Cisco's Jacoby defined the one metric and goal that ruled: Her team would shift from two-thirds run-the-business spending to two-thirds change-the-business spending. Why was this ratio so important? In working with her business partners, Jacoby knew that the top goal for Cisco was to grow its business and find new ways of generating revenue. That meant their current spending levels on innovation were insufficient, so she needed to significantly shift her budget to do what the business needed to do.

It didn't mean the run vs. change metric was the only one. She employed others, such as IT spend-by-business capability and TCO by service. These were important for driving change and ensuring that spend shifts at the macro level were not made by sacrificing other important goals or priorities. They were monitored in service of the larger end-game, but not in place of it.

The goals empowered by TBM will likely change over time. For many enterprises, the journey starts with the goal to save money, i.e., improved cost for performance. Those CIOs begin by baselining their costs and setting targets for them, as described in Chapter 8. The overarching KPI for them would be the percentage of IT costs that meet or beat unit cost targets.

After hitting those goals and deciding that straight cost reduction is less important, those CIOs might start emphasizing other TBM-based metrics, such as IT delivered by the cloud or investment by value category.

In setting targets, such as reduced unit costs of services that are in your "tolerate" category, you should also set targets or limits for other ratios that provide a balanced perspective. In other words, choose metrics for managing the risk associated with the behaviors that you're encouraging for your primary goal. Unit cost targets that are balanced against SLA measures are a good example.

You might also ask, how do you set the target *values*? For example, if you're setting targets for unit cost reduction, how aggressive should you be? There are a few ways to do this task, depending how confident you are in your data. If you have good data to use, you can model changes to your unit costs based on the actions you plan to take. For example, if you plan to renegotiate an outsourcing contract for several towers, how will the reduced rates impact the unit costs for providing services to your business partners? This is something you can model using a what-if scenario, carefully planning to estimate your achievable targets and choose the best mix of providers and towers to achieve your goals.

Sometimes this plan isn't feasible; perhaps the data isn't there yet. In that case, you can set targets that you believe are reasonable. It is what Nelson did at eBay. He set 10 percent unit cost reductions and similar goals for their teams — even though they weren't sure these goals were attainable. While this approach means you may fail to meet your goal, it still creates the proper incentives for your team. Let's face it. Many business goals are set this way, applying gut instinct as much as data analysis.

Regardless of the way you set goals, it's important to have them. They are how you drive behavior, accountability, and progress. They're also what you should be communicating to your stakeholders to demonstrate that business improvements can continuously be made.

Program Governance

Governance is about ensuring the success of the program. It refers to the people and processes for overseeing and administering the program. It starts with proper executive sponsorship and extends to the processes executed by the TBM office for the cross-functional oversight of the program itself.

Executive sponsorship, which we discussed briefly in Chapter 3, is essential for TBM. This essentiality is due to the strategic nature of TBM and its impact on incentives and your decision-making model. The TBM program must be sponsored first by the CIO or CTO, i.e., the head of the technology department. Sponsorship should not be in name only; the executive should engage with the team on a regular basis to ensure progress is made.

The need for sponsorship cannot be overstated. Without it, your people will pay scant attention to the numbers and the analysis provided by TBM. Your technologists won't act on financial information because it hasn't become a normal part of their jobs. They won't help improve the data needed for TBM, because they fear the transparency of what they're doing or are embarrassed by the poor quality of their numbers. Proper sponsorship, however, will light the TBM fire under the feet of your team, and you should use both carrots and sticks to ensure that fire moves forward.

A great example of sponsorship is Larry Godec of First American. As the CIO, he is actively engaged in the TBM program. When his VP of TBM struggled with getting some development teams to submit their hours on a timely basis, Godec intervened. He asked his VP to send him a list of the people who had failed to report their time; he then sent each one of them an email "encouraging" them to submit on time. It worked. Within just a few reporting periods, Godec no longer needed to ask development teams to submit their time. It had become a habit. This 'habit' now provides him and his team with the essential details needed for managing their investments.

Having a TBM office is also essential to a successful program. In many cases, the TBM office is a formal, distinct team within the office of the CIO. Headed by a TBM director, the office also includes the necessary support for running reports, including ad hoc reports and their analyses for maintaining the models and the data. Many TBM offices, even for Fortune 500 companies, are just two to three people (including the Director). Larger TBM offices are found when duties are extended to such functions as IT planning, business relationship management, and other duties.

The TBM office is sometimes also built into other functions. The most common of these occurrences are:

- IT finance, usually within IT, but sometimes within corporate finance

- the program management office (PMO), especially when it owns service portfolio management duties, not just projects

- an IT governance team that might also include handling roles for performance management and reporting

Many times, the TBM office is established as a shared service within IT, providing analytics and reports to other functions. These might include the PMO (for project costs and consumption), business relationship management, and IT strategy and planning.

Carefully consider the skills needed for your TBM office. The program director should be someone who has a proven track record of driving something strategic and building strong relationships with both IT and non-IT business leaders. This individual will need to evangelize the program, communicate a vision for TBM, and collaborate with IT leaders on defining a roadmap that integrates with IT and the business roadmaps.

The TBM administrators will need to fulfill the roles of solution architect (i.e., requirements, design, modeling, reporting, etc.), together with ongoing report development, ad hoc analysis, and data management. Sometimes this is a single person; sometimes the effort is split into two roles (usually no more than two). Third parties, including your TBM solution vendor, may be able to provide you some of these services for a fee (as a managed service).

Your TBM team should understand your business (e.g., your business applications, BU leaders, how people are incentivized) and your IT operations (e.g., your systems, data, administration teams, and practices), or spend the time to learn them. This information will prove to be invaluable as you work to improve your TBM capabilities (and data), gain acceptance of the program, and make the decisions.

A final and necessary part of TBM governance is cross-functional oversight. You should establish a steering committee that is comprised of senior representatives from IT operations, applications, change management, governance (if separate from the TBM office), and IT finance (including corporate finance, if needed). If you have a separate function for data governance, it should also be represented on the TBM steering committee.

Routine Processes

TBM is only as effective as the processes it implements or supports. Formalizing those processes (i.e., making them routine and repeatable) will help you standardize reviews and analysis, ensure better accuracy and timeliness of the information, identify and resolve issues in a more timely fashion, and ease the burden of performing those processes on a regular basis.

TBM processes are of two types: those that are a core part of TBM, and those that are augmented by TBM. The former are new to the enterprise that is adopting TBM, but are few in number. Processes being augmented should already exist, but they may include new elements or involve different people because of TBM.

Core processes that are introduced with TBM include:

- a **TBM month-end close** that consists of importing updated data sets, performing initial reviews with IT finance and data owners, resolving any data quality problems, and producing the necessary reports for distribution;

- producing a **monthly or quarterly bill of IT** for distribution to your application owners, line-of-business leaders, and other stakeholders;

- performing **ad hoc analysis** at the request of the decision makers in IT, finance, or even the lines of business;

- **setting service rates (prices)**, usually on an annual basis (during annual planning) or semi-annually or quarterly; and

- **monthly or quarterly data quality reviews**, focused on identifying data deficiencies and managing improvements against the plan.

TBM augments many other processes, including:

- **monthly budget variance analysis** by IT finance, cost center owners, and tower/app/service owners;[72]

- **monthly operational reviews** by tower, app, and service owners that incorporate financial reviews against budget and targets (e.g., unit cost targets, SLA attainment, etc.);

- **vendor performance reviews** that include financial reviews against vendor-related targets, such as unit costs, consumption of vendor services, and spending by vendor categories;

- **capacity planning and procurement processes** to ensure that capacity costs are properly considered and to evaluate options, such as public cloud services;

- **problem management procedures** whereby analysts consider the cost impact of problems that are causing incidents and tickets;

- **service portfolio management,** including the definition, analysis, and approval of the services at all stages (e.g., pipeline, catalog, retired, etc.);

- **demand management,** including the use of incentive-based rates (prices) and packaging; and

- **asset and configuration management** incorporating data quality metrics from TBM along with asset-related financial metrics.

The list could go on. What's most important is to ensure that the core TBM processes are implemented, managed, and governed (measured, monitored, and improved). No less important, the non-core processes should be implemented or augmented with TBM based on the goals you set for your organization.

For example, if your goals include improving cost for performance, you should ensure that the TBM metrics and data are provided to your

---

[72] In many cases, having tower, app, and service owners review their variances is only possible with the reporting provided by TBM, so this type of variance analysis is a new process for those functions.

application, tower, and service owners and that these areas are held accountable for meeting their targets. In turn, they should review their own targets as part of any standard management review processes.

TBM Roadmap

A TBM roadmap is essential. It is the plan for your TBM journey. It outlines the phases you'll go through with TBM and shows you how each step builds on the ones taken before it. The order and timing of these steps are determined by the following factors:

- **Your business strategy and imperatives.** The choices you make about transparency, data, decision-making, roles and responsibilities, and other TBM elements should well align with what's important to your business. For example, if you're undertaking an ERP-enabled business transformation, your roadmap might begin with a transparency that focuses on ERP applications and projects.

- **Your IT strategy and initiatives.** Whatever is going on — adopting public cloud, implementing chargeback, integrating an acquired company after a merger — your roadmap should align with and support these initiatives.

- **Your data availability and quality.** Because data determines what you can do with the TBM model, your roadmap depends on good data. As such, TBM will influence your investment in data quality. The good news, as described in Chapter 4, is that TBM helps you improve data quality simply by sourcing it and using it.

- **Your IT processes and maturity.** Since TBM augments and depends on existing IT processes, such as service level management (service catalog), asset management (CMDB), and others, it is necessary to align your roadmap to the processes that exist or will exist, according to the plan.

Fully implementing a roadmap typically takes 12 to 18 months and often includes three phases, similar to the following:

Phase 1 – Build the Foundation: The first phase, which can be executed in as little as 90 days, creates a foundation of cost transparency wherein your team gets a better handle on costs and consumption by cost pools, general ledger accounts, cost centers, towers, vendors (including cloud providers), projects, and people (labor). At this stage, you begin to benchmark your costs and consumption by towers and other key ratios, as described in Chapter 5.

Some organizations use this phase to begin changing their IT planning process; using the clarity they get into their spending to accelerate IT budgeting and forecasting processes, as described in Chapter 7.

The business value of this foundation is enormous. It sets up a cadence for using financial information better while helping your people demonstrate a grasp of your costs. It is instrumental in demonstrating cost for performance on the supply side. And as the word "foundation" implies, it sets you up for the second and third phases.

Phase 2 – Move Up the Stack: Here, you focus on application TCO and service costing. Having metrics at this level of your model will allow you to discuss the business value of your spending, possibly for the first time, with your business partners. These metrics support application rationalization initiatives and help you plan better based on business demand (e.g., zero-based budgeting).

During this phase you may begin to dive deeper into your tower costs as well. This action involves getting better asset data than you might have today. You might also incorporate cloud billing data into the model. By taking these steps, you will understand why your costs deviate from infrastructure benchmarks and identify areas of waste, such as underutilized and orphaned assets, as described in Chapter 5.

Phase 3 – Connect with the Business: During this phase you create visibility into consumption and costs at the business unit and business capability level. This action sets you up to deliver a bill of IT and start shaping demand, as described in Chapter 6.

At this point, you've connected the standard TBM model from the bottom to the top. This is a sensitive time, as support from your business partners can be lost at this point. You may want to roll out business unit reporting (your bill of IT) in a phased approach, starting with a friendly business partner or two.

Shared Ownership

As you've probably figured out by this point, TBM cannot be implemented in a silo. By definition, TBM depends on the support and accountability of IT leaders, corporate and IT finance officers, and your line-of-business leaders. These stakeholders should be represented on a TBM steering committee that meets regularly to discuss the TBM program's success, its barriers, a roadmap, and the value created. Each stakeholder needs to understand his or her role in TBM. Let's take a look at the most common roles:

Infrastructure and operations (I&O) is on the hook for much of the data needed for your program. They should take solace in the fact that few I&O organizations possess good data from the beginning; instead, successful I&O shops shine a light on their data with TBM and use its transparency to improve data quality. Their teams, such as asset management, incident management, and systems administration, may be concerned about the impact of transparency and the TBM decisions on what they do. You can show them how they'll benefit — such as gaining better governance of business demand for their people and assets — but you should also identify and address the concerns they may have as data owners.

Furthermore, many I&O organizations are going through their own transformation because of TBM. Many are building their own private clouds, learning how to use the public cloud, and improving the way they deliver infrastructure services.

This also means they may be rolling out other tools, such as IT service management software. While TBM can help with this transformation, I&O leaders will have a lot on their hands and must thus understand all the synergies that are possible.

Corporate finance provides the financial data used for TBM. But more importantly, it provides legitimacy and provenance for this data. As a result, they need to understand how TBM-based cost reporting compares to their own, where it complements it, and where it may conflict. For example, many finance teams allocate IT costs based on rules that may have little to do with how IT is actually consumed. Incentives such as performance bonuses may be based on historic allocation rules. Because your TBM program will improve the way that costs are allocated and reported to your lines of business, you need the support and endorsement of corporate finance to keep value conversations from devolving into arguments over the veracity of your numbers.

If you have a dedicated IT finance function or IT liaisons in corporate finance, they must be directly involved in the TBM program. Because they will probably be asked to support new processes (even as TBM streamlines other processes), such as reconciling the bill of IT with accounting, they must understand the TBM impact on their jobs and the benefits of the change.

Your **line-of-business leaders** will also be impacted directly by TBM. First, the way you disclose IT costs and consumption data will change, giving these leaders new reports to review each month or quarter. They must understand what's expected of them, and how to take actions based on that reporting.

For example, how do they reduce consumption of a service you provide if they believe its value does not justify the cost? When will they see the benefit of the reduction? This last question is an important one since the biggest impact of TBM to line-of-business leaders may be how their P&Ls are impacted by changes in IT cost allocations. If you shift to a consumption-based chargeback approach, for example, there will be winners and losers. Some business leaders do benefit under the old models — consuming more IT resources than their peers without the corresponding payback. Correcting this aspect will hurt their profitability. Extreme care must thus be exercised during this period.

Many CFOs implement a grace period for the change, whereby "two books" are maintained during the transition in order to give P&L owners (and IT providers) enough time to adjust to any changes.

Evolution of Data, Modeling, and Analytics

As described above, your roadmap depends in part on the data you have gathered and its quality. While assumptions about consumption and supply aren't a bad way to start many allocations, their power is limited. Real data overcomes these limitations. This makes sense. If your roadmap calls for optimizing asset utilization based on the consumption of infrastructure by application, you'll need a good asset database, utilization data, and application mappings to complete the task.

Improving the power and value of TBM means improving your data and vice versa. This virtuous circle will not only improve your TBM model and the reports you generate, but having real data behind your model means that changes you make to your technology estate will be reflected in your actual costs.

A successful TBM program includes a focus on data quality that aligns to the roadmap. You should improve data quality to improve the model and improve reporting so you can create new value. TBM provides the transparency of data quality (see Figure 10-1 below) needed to do so. Be sure to focus on data quality metrics and your reporting roadmap as part of your governance program.

Figure 10-1: Data quality report shows the status of specific data sources (Source: Apptio)

Insights, Actions, and Value Tracking

TBM provides value by being incorporated into the processes you use to manage your assets, people, vendors, and so forth, as described above. It does this largely by allowing you to set meaningful targets for your leaders to hit, using total costs to shape business demand, and providing for regular reviews by your executives and managers. Yet at the beginning of your TBM journey, these aspects may not be enough.

When you're just starting out, many of your people won't really understand the power of what they can do with the right information. So, rather than telling them how to use TBM, show them. This sounds rather basic, but TBM leaders often take a "build it and they will come" approach: deliver reports to decision makers and hope they will do great things with them. In truth, they don't know how to use the reports yet.

To fix this situation, tell your TBM team to go "insight hunting" as soon as possible during your journey. What is insight hunting? It's a short project where a small team (often just one or two people) use TBM to find potential cost reductions, efficiency gains, ways to improve agility, and other improvements. Insight hunting does two things: First, it helps the TBM team understand and address the limitations of their data and reports. Second, it empowers them to teach others by example.

You should encourage insight hunting on a regular basis, even well after you have established the program. Be sure to create shared incentives for your TBM team, data owners, and those others who are responsible for the systems or people that will be optimized. Set goals and establish ground rules (such as insights that cannot reduce service quality or increase risk). Set a deadline by which time the findings will need to be reported back to the TBM steering committee or the office of the CIO.

Lance Warner, First American's TBM architect, found that you have to partner with decision makers if you want to capitalize on optimization opportunities. "You make the insights a feather in their cap, not yours," he said. "You want to give them something that they can feel proud of, and maybe get rewarded for, because that's how you build support among the people who you depend on."[73]

Taking action on your own insights is also essential to program success. Too often however, TBM programs fail to track the value they create. To remedy this problem, TBM leaders must do two things: track progress against the selected value metrics discussed in Chapters 8 and 9, and establish value realization tracking for the TBM program.

Value tracking should be centered on *business* metrics, such as increased revenues, reduced business costs, improved customer satisfaction (e.g., Net Promoter Score), and so on. The primary metrics used by your company should be your North Star. If your CEO has put lower costs to serve customers or greater revenue from new markets on the list of corporate goals for the year, they should be on your short list, too. Your TBM team should understand these metrics and link the actions of TBM to your corporate goals. For example, how has the TBM program helped reduce the cost to serve customers, for example, by reducing the cost of online support transactions? How did they shift spending and resources to projects or innovations that help tap into new revenue sources?

By initiating insight hunting on a regular basis and tracking the value realized from TBM, you will kick-start your TBM program and better incorporate it into how you manage IT. Over time, you can even make insight hunting a broader team effort, with small groups using the data from TBM to find new value and sharing those insights across the larger teams, creating a cycle of continuous improvement.

Hopefully, your team already tracks business value realization, so it can measure and articulate the benefits of IT to your business partners. This will reflect IT's contribution to new business capabilities, for example. It should also include the value of projects that are initiated as the result of TBM. However, since many CIOs don't yet measure value

---

[73] Warner, Lance. Phone interview. 5 Aug. 2015.

realization, you should use TBM as an impetus to start just such a program.[74]

Key Takeaways

- Recognize that TBM is a journey, not a destination. Emphasizing continuous improvement is essential. Emphasizing perfection from the start is a recipe for inaction.

- Focus on the TBM hallmarks of maturity. These are critical success factors that have been identified from the hundreds of TBM programs established in the last five years.

- Begin with defining very clear business goals for your TBM program. These should map well to the value conversations of the TBM framework: *Cost of Performance, Business-Aligned Portfolio, Investment in Innovation* and *Enterprise Agility*. These will give you the metrics or KPIs that can be stated as measurable goals for your team.

- Establish proper governance or oversight of your TBM program, including executive sponsorship. If your TBM program is not worth sponsoring at the executive level, it may not be worth doing at all.

- Build the right processes for TBM that are based on TBM. Ensure they are repeatable and also staffed properly.

- Define and communicate a roadmap for your TBM program. Ensure that it aligns with the broader roadmap for your organization.

- Foster shared ownership of TBM that is based on a partnership between IT, corporate finance, and your line-of-business partners.

---

[74] Value realization tracking has been described elsewhere and a full treatment is beyond the scope of this book. In particular, read Chapter 8 ("Measure the Value Delivered") of *Real Business of IT: How CIOs Create and Communicate Value* by Richard Hunter and George Westerman.

- Focus on continuous improvement of your data, modeling, and analytics. In so doing, you will be able to produce ever more impactful analyses and decisions.

- Document the insights and decisions made using TBM and track them over time. Doing so helps ensure you realize the value of the decisions you make. Much of this focus should be inherent to your TBM processes and program.

Chapter 11:
Expanding the Business Partnership

Let's revisit the technology business models we explored in Chapter 3. Think about your model today and how you want it to evolve. Then ask yourself: Are you a true partner with your line-of-business leaders? Do you and your people collaborate with those leaders on business decisions? Do you jointly define your business strategy and infuse your knowledge of digital business, analytics, and security? Do you plan together, or is it a "they plan the business and then we plan the IT" approach?

Today, not having the technology leader at the business table puts any business at a disadvantage. If nothing else, a firm's digital strategy depends too much on a strong business-IT partnership. The authors of *Leading Digital* emphasize this point: "Many executives told us that, given their IT units' poor performance, they were going to find a different way to conduct their digital transformations. The business executives were going to move forward despite their IT units, not with them. We did not find this to be true with Digital Masters, which have much stronger IT-business relationships than non-masters do. . . . When the relationship is strong, the IT-business partnership merges customer and product knowledge, technical knowledge, organizational change capabilities, and IT capabilities into a single, continuous collaboration."[75]

Up to this point, we've discussed how TBM empowers a collaboration between IT leaders and their business partners whenever they've taken either a service provider or a value partner role, in which decisions are largely or entirely about IT-related tradeoffs (via the value conversations). These models are based on trust and facts, and they optimize the overall value of the investment in technology. However,

---

[75] Westerman, George, Didier Bonnet, and Andrew McAfee. Chapter 8. "Building Technology Leadership Capabilities." *Leading Digital: Turning Technology Into Business Transformation*. Boston: Harvard Business Review, 2014. Kindle ed.

business capabilities are comprised of more than just technology. They include labor and other resources that create revenue or collect cash for your firm. A true partnership means you jointly collaborate on your entire value chain, not just the IT resources and its tradeoffs.

What would TBM look like if you applied it to the entire value chain, including non-technology costs and resources? How would this new model impact the business partnership you have (or want to have) with your line-of-business leaders? Most importantly, how would TBM help you and your business partners improve your overall business, not just the business value of your IT investments?

CIOs are beginning to move in this direction with TBM. They're going beyond IT to help their executive teams understand their broader business portfolios (beyond just IT). They're using the same principles that we've discussed earlier in this book and applying them to answer business questions and make tradeoff decisions, sometimes those between technology and non-technology costs and resources.

In this chapter, we'll look at three examples. The first is AOL, which has used TBM to move from a foundation of efficiency to true collaboration on strategic business decisions, such as taking over Microsoft's display advertising business on Xbox, Skype, and other products. The second is Cox Enterprises, which uses TBM to make enterprise-wide decisions across a federated IT model that spans a corporate shared service IT department and three major business units. The third is Cisco, which has grown beyond its IT-as-a-Service strategy to an "everything-as-a-service" strategy.

From Technology Operations to
True Business Partnership

AOL[76] has been through its fair share of transformations, from the pre-internet pioneer America Online to a media/online hybrid known as AOL Time Warner, to independent digital media company AOL. In the summer of 2015, AOL was purchased by Verizon, setting the stage for its next transformation into a global-scale advertising and media platform. Its strategy includes among other things the use of Verizon's mobile data as a strategic advantage to compete alongside Google's search data and Facebook's social data assets.

To fuel AOL's business reinvention, CIO James LaPlaine is employing TBM to help lead a technology transformation that includes a shift from captive data centers to a public cloud-first strategy, rationalizing technology investments from acquisitions, and optimizing both infrastructure and applications to process business transactions more efficiently. What most separates LaPlaine and his team from many other technology departments is the way he partners with his business leaders on the big decisions.

Like so many CIOs who have embraced TBM, this partnership began with a focus on increased efficiency. LaPlaine has been able to reduce costs of AOL's central technology services by 23 percent year after year while supporting 127 percent growth in its business transaction volume. This not only enables greater scalability, it has positioned LaPlaine to collaborate with his business partners. It helped bolster LaPlaine's credibility as a business leader on top of his already proven technology leadership skills.

This collaboration started small by focusing on what types of information LaPlaine's business partners needed most to make the decisions. "We first rolled out TBM [reporting] to a friendly property

---

[76] Vignette built from public sources and from 2015 TBM Awards interviews and video case study. AOL was a winner of the 2015 TBM Council Business Innovation award. See video: https://youtu.be/McS_JDp2XgA

that we thought would be willing to go through an iterative process with us, one that had already been asking financial questions," LaPlaine recounts. "We showed them our portfolio of services, and then we showed them the data and said, 'This is what you consume out of central infrastructure each month.'"

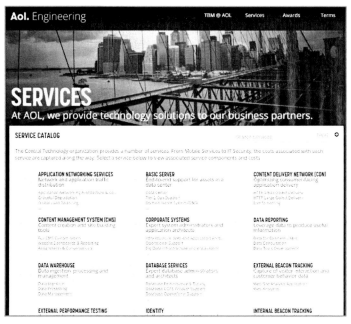

Figure 11-1: AOL's central technology organization delivers a well-defined catalog of services and invoices business units monthly using TBM[77]

"Complete transparency is the goal, including the data behind the metrics, so that folks have no question whether these costs are made up based on arbitrary rules," LaPlaine explains. "TBM helps us tie dollars to decisions. One month we say if we do this, that cost will go up, or it will go down. When we revisit that decision we can look at the data to see, was our analysis right? As they see not just costs but services we provide, what drives their cost, and that their decisions and consumption actually impact the cost structure, it builds these secure, safe places to have all kinds of dialogues and move the transformation agenda forward."

---

[77] Source: AOL Engineering web site (http://engineering.aol.com/tbm), visited 9 Nov. 2015.

What began as a technology optimization focus has since become a focus for optimizing *business transactions*, such as advertisements served. To help cut through complexity and drive decisions, LaPlaine uses business transactions as a way to compare service options which defy a useful comparison at the level of their individual parts. This is necessary because AOL's revenue and competitive advantage depends in part on its ability to summon computing power for real-time bidding on advertisements. "We're participating in high-volume transactions, kind of like high-frequency trading in the marketplace," LaPlaine explains. "So we need to look at the cost of architecture and geographic options to get closer to the consumer, for example."

As part of its strategy to compete more equally with Facebook and Google, AOL acquired Microsoft's non-search advertising business in nine key markets in the summer of 2015. As part of the deal, AOL took over responsibility for sales of display, mobile, and video ads on Microsoft properties in the U.S. and eight other markets, thereby adding new assets and new demand to AOL's portfolio of services. This move, in addition to being acquired by Verizon, gives AOL an enviable portfolio of digital business assets for advertising.

"We play in the supply and demand side of advertising. We participate in advertising exchanges. We have real-time bidding systems," says LaPlaine. "And our view is that AOL is now in that portfolio of advertising, equivalent to Facebook, and Google, and the big players that are in that space. And with the addition of Verizon's data set, we now have new information to do better targeting, which makes content that people read and the advertising they see more relevant and more interesting to consumers."

With an increased volume of transactions, the cost dynamics, technical architecture, and other elements were crucial to the decision. "While we were doing the acquisition, we needed to validate that the revenue we'd gain wouldn't be offset by additional cost in our infrastructure," explains LaPlaine. "We're adding all that traffic into our portfolio, so we needed to see if this looked like it would be healthy new business for the company."

LaPlaine used monthly data already in his TBM system for available capacity, transaction volumes, and current costs and then modeled the expected difference in costs to support the added number of transactions from Microsoft.

"We modeled what it would cost to support this new business," LaPlaine recounts. "We wouldn't have been able to do that, had we not first started with the transparency model. We wouldn't have had the foundation. We would have done a ton of guesswork, probably by percentage. Someone would have said, 'Well, today our cost for IT is 5 percent so let's assume 5 percent for Microsoft.' If we had done that, the math wouldn't support the deal and it wouldn't have happened. Maybe we would have been right, maybe we would have been wrong," he added. "I'm just glad we don't live in that world today at AOL."

LaPlaine credits the TBM methodology and the model they built in their TBM system with helping IT cement its position as a business partner. "We are an equal partner with the business. We are not a subservient IT organization. Having command of the facts about the technology costs to run and grow the business has built credibility. What we've done at the company is moved from IT transparency to IT value."

Governing Enterprise Value

Cox Enterprises[78] is a unique business. As a group of privately held companies, Cox provides a diversified portfolio of communications, media, and automotive services. The company's major operating subsidiaries include Cox Communications (cable television, high-speed internet access, telephone, home security and automation, commercial telecommunications and advertising solutions), Cox Automotive

---

[78] Vignette built from public sources and from 2015 TBM Awards interviews and video case study. Cox Enterprises was a winner of the 2015 TBM Council TBM Champion award. See video: https://youtu.be/72g8Y939UyE

(automotive-related auctions, financial services, media and software solutions), and Cox Media Group (television and radio stations, digital media, newspapers and advertising sales rep firms). The firm's major brands include Autotrader, Kelley Blue Book, Manheim, Savings.com, and Valpak.

To cost-effectively serve the core infrastructure needs of their distinct business units, Cox Enterprises hired Greg Morrison as CIO in 2002 and put him in charge of all corporate IT functions, such as infrastructure, messaging, ERP, and other services. Morrison's background leading a shared service organization at Prudential Financial in the 1990s positioned him well for success at Cox. Upon arriving, Morrison began shifting the culture of his IT organization to a more business-centric one.

"Moving to a shared services model, or any model that is more business-centric, means you have to think about your organization more like a business. In particular, you must manage the business performance of your services, as product managers do for their product lines," explains Morrison. "You need to manage the relationships with your business partners, as account managers do with their clients. In a product-oriented organization, these roles exist naturally; in a traditional IT organization, they often have to be created."

Like most acquisitive companies, Cox Enterprises began consolidating and operating more technology capabilities for its subsidiaries, and its corporate IT expenses began to rise. The CFO determined that to control costs, Cox Enterprises would charge expenses back to the various business units in its subsidiaries while providing cost transparency to enlist them in decision-making on how they would use the shared resources. Without knowing it at the time, this decision marked the start of their TBM journey.

Lisa Stalter, Senior Director of IT planning and governance at Cox Enterprises, remembers their first steps. "We had to pull something together quickly, and we didn't have systems and processes in place," she recalls. "We introduced some very high-level service catalog taxonomy, and some very high-level cost allocations. That initial transparency raised more questions, like 'Which applications are you supporting for me?' and 'What do each of those cost?'"

To address these new questions, Stalter began to create transparency at a more granular level and then link charges to business consumption. She created a view into the TCO of each application service and the costs driven by technical services that were supporting each application. Chargebacks were now based on this granular view, which allowed each business unit to see what applications it was consuming, how much those applications cost, and what was driving those costs. "We went from clumsy conversations about whether we had the right numbers to value conversations about what services they needed and which they didn't," explains Stalter. This choice helped Cox Enterprises get a grip on its shared service IT costs and value.

Around this same time, one of Cox's subsidiaries was pursuing its own services transformation. Based on his experience at two previous companies, Mark Satterfield, Vice President of IT for Cox Automotive, understood the value of TBM to a service-delivery organization. "When architects plan a building they need multiple blueprints such as engineering, mechanical, and civil. We also needed different blueprints, or different lenses, for how we organized, how we designed, how we deployed, and how we delivered services," Satterfield relates.

Satterfield's team began adopting TBM within the subsidiary alongside the implementation at Cox Enterprises. In doing so, both the shared service provider (Cox Enterprises) and the shared services consumer (Cox Automotive) were using TBM to understand consumption and costs to make informed tradeoff decisions. Within Cox Automotive, business leaders began to better understand what they were getting from the shared services organization as well as what their own services and applications were costing the business.

This parallel path of Cox Enterprises and Cox Automotive served as a foundation for governing enterprise value. After a couple of years, the other two subsidiaries — Cox Communications and Cox Media Group — were using TBM as well. By adopting the standard TBM taxonomy, all four Cox technology organizations were thus able to speak the same language.

"Our services are different," Stalter admits, "but the building blocks underneath them really aren't. There's really nothing valuable or strategic about defining towers and cost pools a different way." In other words, they could use the TBM taxonomy to be able to speak the same language without sacrificing the nuances of their own unique service portfolios.

To help further optimize enterprise value, the Cox companies began feeding the data from their individual models into an overarching corporate model that was maintained by Stalter. These choices empowered new analysis across the enterprise. "We do internal benchmarking now," Satterfield says. "We can compare and contrast each of our organizations, which leads to conversations about what we might be doing differently from each other. We can see, 'Hmm, that seems like this vendor or that tower is running hot, or running cold. Let's see what we can do together.' So together as a Cox family of companies, using a standard model helps us gain efficiencies."

In a matter of only a few short years, Cox has gone from a highly distributed IT organizational model where each business unit maintained most of its own technologies and services to a federated model supported by a common taxonomy, shared data, and internal benchmarking. This progress not only positioned their leaders to optimize costs and value, but it also helped accelerate even bigger business decisions, such as corporate acquisitions.

Take Cox Automotive, for example. Over the past several years, the firm has acquired over a dozen companies to assemble an enviable collection of brands that include Autotrader, HomeNet Automotive, Kelley Blue Book, Manheim, and vAuto. The company's recent $4 billion acquisition of Dealertrack is expected to put Cox Automotive in the range of $8 billion in revenue. This rapid growth also means more diversity and complexity with business models ranging from a digital marketplace platform (Autotrader.com) to SaaS solutions for dealers (Dealertrack) to a wholesaler and auctioneer with inventory (Manheim).

Cox Automotive's distinct business units have grown from 8 to 23 and employees from 3,500 to more than 24,000.

The time required to go from acquisition to integrated operational view was also accelerated by the TBM model and the analytical skills of the TBM Office. "When we added Manheim to the Autotrader group of companies to form Cox Automotive, the hardest part of integrating financial models was learning the structure of an unfamiliar general ledger," explains Satterfield. "After that, the standard TBM taxonomy had already given us an industry-standard set of categories and compositions, and we already knew how to map GL cost centers and accounts into the model. This used to be something we'd need outside consultants to come in and do, but we were able to onboard millions of dollars in spend and normalize it into our TBM model in just 72 hours."

Cox Automotive CTO Ed Smith emphasizes the impact of TBM on his team's ability to make fast decisions. "We had planned on months of work to integrate Manheim into our overall operating model," says Smith. "The TBM team put it together in just a few days. It gave us a consolidated view so we could start comparing and finding opportunities to better leverage our spend. It was a huge win."

Smith further adds, "TBM is a necessary business competency for our strategy. The automotive industry is changing tremendously. We are going to wind up acquiring companies and we're going to have things that don't necessarily fit together naturally on their own. So one of the underlying capabilities that you have to be really good at is how you manage your technology spend to build and integrate products the right way."

Cox Enterprises demonstrates that TBM can be used to manage value beyond a single IT organization. They've optimized costs for IT across the enterprise by collaborating more closely, while still being able to make business decisions faster. In a multifaceted, technology-powered company, this capability will prove to be essential.

Empowering Everything-as-a-Service

As almost anyone who works in IT knows, Cisco[79] is the world's largest provider of networking technology and services. While the firm's long-held leadership in backbone technologies, such as routers and switches, is the core of its strategy, Cisco's growth is dependent on extending the role of networking to new markets. The company is constantly delivering new products and solutions — even new communications paradigms — in order to better serve customers and grow its business.

Executing this strategy is no trivial matter. Cisco faces strong competitors in its core markets as well as in new ones. Cisco must continue to operate more efficiently, innovate faster, and serve its customers better than its competitors. Cisco's IT organization is essential to doing these tasks successfully.

In 2006, then-CEO John Chambers knew that Cisco needed more than its IT department at that time could deliver. More money and more resources weren't the answer. So he named Rebecca Jacoby SVP and CIO for a very simple reason. Jacoby had managed a successful transformation of the company's global supply chain (no trivial feat) and he needed her to similarly transform its IT organization. He knew she didn't come from IT; she was a business person and a manufacturing executive, but these credentials would work in their favor.

As CIO, Jacoby made a decision to focus very heavily on IT, becoming a world-class provider of services. She called it their IT-as-a-Service transformation. By delivering everything as services, IT would be better aligned to Cisco's lines of business and more adept at supporting innovation and improving operations. They defined a service taxonomy that included technical services, such as a network and infrastructure, up to business services and capabilities. This taxonomy provided for a

---

[79] Vignette built from public sources and from various interviews with the author between 2013 and 2016.

comprehensive, business-connected view of services, not just an IT-centric one.

Jacoby would also change the conversations that IT was having with their business partners. Instead of talking about technologies, they would talk about value and business tradeoffs in a common language. They went so far as to define these tradeoff conversations for several aspects of their services:

- **Scope, source, and architecture.** Where do they want to source a service? Do they want to build it internally? Do they want to purchase it as a cloud service? Do they want to outsource the whole shop, or just part of it? How do they architect it?

- **Cost.** How much are they willing to spend on the service? How will they determine the *cost of goods sold*? What price should they charge the business?

- **Quality.** What level of service do they need to provide? Do they need to provide different tiers of service at different price points?

- **Time to Capability.** How quickly do they need to have the service in place? What's the business impact or lost opportunity of waiting?

- **Risk.** What level and types of risks are they willing to accept? How much are they willing to spend to reduce the risks?

These conversations would lead to good decisions for Cisco. "These decisions are not just good for IT; they are good for the business," said Jacoby. "They are instrumental in our ability to shift spending from run-the-business to change-the-business investments, in turn helping us execute on our business strategy. My goal is to reduce the cost of running IT services 5 to 10 percent per year on a sustainable basis — funds that Cisco can choose to deploy to strategically change the business."

These fact-based conversations were so important that Cisco's IT leaders decided to make sure everyone in IT consistently described the tradeoffs associated with their services. "What we found, however, is that not everybody in IT had the skill set to deal with this," said Jacoby.

"So we set out to help everyone in IT be extremely competent in discussing them."

These tradeoffs were incorporated into a variety of conversations. They were part of the quarterly service reviews that became an essential component to how her organization improved value. They were also used in discussions with their business partners, such as annual strategy alignments. In turn, these conversations were instrumental in the way that Jacoby's team came to think and communicate, but they are as much the outcome of her transformation as they are a part of it.

This change in conversation and in culture was powerful. Jacoby had made service owners the cornerstone of their IT-as-a-Service transformation. The service owners — as "general managers" of their services — became responsible for thoroughly understanding what they were delivering and deciding how to better deliver their services while lowering costs. In general, service owners are expected to reduce their run-the-business costs by 5 percent a year, savings that are then reinvested into the change-the-business portfolio (to meet the goal also set forth by Jacoby). In turn, these savings eventually led to the dramatic shift in spending from run-the-business to change-the-business.

The transformation of IT to a service provider is just the first part of the story. When Chuck Robbins succeeded John Chambers as CEO, he promoted Jacoby to SVP of Operations for Cisco. She now oversees the global supply chain, global business services, security and trust, and IT organizations. This means Jacoby is responsible for what Cisco calls business operations and more generally what Cisco calls operational excellence.

At the same time, Cisco veteran Guillermo Diaz has been promoted to SVP and CIO of Cisco, reporting to Jacoby. Diaz was a key architect of Cisco's IT-as-a-Service transformation. Now, Diaz's focus is on transforming their overall IT experience by strengthening foundational business capabilities while enabling new business models, such as service, software, and SaaS. This task will take a whole new level of partnership and collaboration between IT, the business operations, and the broader business.

To meet this new challenge, Jacoby and Diaz are now applying the disciplines of TBM to business operations. It includes critical business capabilities such as quote-to-cash, supply chain management, and human resources processes. These, too, are delivered as services (Operations as a Service), as part of their "services everything" approach to creating value.

"It's really the extension of how we've leveraged IT as a Service into really helping the business accelerate the policy and process changes or transformation that we have to do as you move, not just as you build up the architecture, but as you transform," says Diaz. In other words, this transformation to "services everything" goes beyond IT.

This services-everything approach for business operations mirrors what was done for IT and supply chain, including service ownership and service reviews. "We just did the joint service review, having launched those about a quarter ago," says Diaz. "So taking the same concepts [from IT as a Service] and the same mindset around service, and now we're doing these joint reviews with the business, especially business operations, to show what the total cost of the operation is versus just the IT component. Now you're able to start to look at the total end-to-end cost of the operation."

Cisco now employs two interrelated and connected TBM models: their model for IT and another model for business operations. In doing so, they can see how IT costs and consumption are driven by IT services and in turn how they are consumed when delivering business capabilities. They also understand the total cost of delivering those capabilities out of the business operations group under Jacoby. In essence, TBM has been extended all the way up through their entire business model.

This bottom-up approach to TBM may at first seem anachronistic, but it was born out of the leadership that IT is well positioned to demonstrate.

"In the perfect world, you start working your way down from the business model and [business] offer to the business architecture to the operational flows that have to be there, to the systems needed to support that, and to the technology," says Diaz. "But we actually led with a lot of the systems and the technology to put a stake in the ground. It really helped the business understand that you do need to come from that business down, versus the technology up."

Cisco IT has established its path forward with IT as a Service and TBM. Now with its everything-as-a-service approach, Cisco will begin to realize the broader benefits of TBM's overall principles and disciplines.

ATMs, Cable Boxes, and More...

There are many other stories about applying the disciplines and tools of TBM to other areas of the business. These stories feature business leaders (IT or non-IT) who married a services approach to a data-driven perspective of total costs and business insights (e.g., consumption, quality, reliability, and revenue). But instead of applying the approach to traditional information technologies and services, they've applied them to other business technologies.

Consider the Nationwide Building Society,[80] the largest building society in the world. In addition to the delivery of more traditional IT services, Nationwide is responsible for managing nearly 1,400 ATMs in the United Kingdom. Nationwide manages these ATMs as a service, including property management, maintenance, cash inventory, and more. They have extended TBM, which it employs to manage all of its services, to include optimizing its ATM services as well.

This effort means more than just managing ATM costs. By combining property data, property costs (rental cost for where the ATMs are located), usage data, how many people carry out transactions on the

---

[80] Vignette built from public sources and from 2014 TBM Awards interviews and video case study. Nationwide Building Society was a winner of the 2014 TBM Council IT Services Transformation award. See video: https://youtu.be/4Q80R-wJJUo

machine, and profiles of who transacts on the machine (customers vs. non-customers), the group can assess the business performance of the ATMs. They now make data-driven decisions based on how quickly they should fix an ATM if it breaks, whether it's profitable, or whether it should be removed. "We've made some big decisions recently around this area which has resulted in quite significant changes to the ATM footprint," explains Mike Pighills, Head of Business Management. "We're talking multi-millions of dollars."

Another example is from a large provider of cable TV,[81] internet access, and phone services in the United States. With tens of millions of subscribers in a highly competitive market that hinges on both cost and customer satisfaction, the TCO, quality, and reliability of set-top boxes can make a big difference to the success of this overall business.

The SVP of quality decided to quietly pursue a project to see if a total cost of ownership analysis was not only feasible but could also help them optimize quality and reliability. He gathered a small team of data analysts who met with business process owners to better understand the data that was available. This data included data for purchase, testing, returns and repairs, and customer support (such as in-home visits, phone calls, and online chat sessions).

Armed with this data, they configured automated data and modeling rules to drive an operational rhythm that spanned more than 200 video, cable modem, and phone device configurations. Interactive dashboards allowed users involved in supply chain, procurement, testing, and other business functions to analyze and understand cost and quality metrics and their details from many different angles.

An early insight that emerged from the data was how much cost had been hidden. Procurement accounted for less than 30 percent of the total cost of a device. The other 70 percent was now exposed, revealing a difference in lifetime costs per device of $20 to $50, depending on the device and its configuration. This insight has had a significant business

---

[81] Vignette built from interviews with the author. Interviewees have chosen to remain anonymous.

impact. By adjusting their mix across millions of devices purchased each year, and tens of millions of devices supported on an annual basis, future cost savings will be substantial.

However, the real impact will be the improvement in actual customer experience. Each service call avoided is a happier customer. The data from TBM is helping the company select vendors with better reliability. They've also started to influence the way their vendors design their products, as they know they're no longer being evaluated on purchase cost alone.

With the increase in digital and the integration of business technology (BT), operational technology (OT), and more traditional information technology, expect to see an increase in the use of TBM software and its disciplines to optimize not only costs but also quality, risk, and value. TBM is fast becoming the ERP of the digital supply chain.

Key Takeaways

- By employing TBM, technology leaders demonstrate business savvy, technology prowess, and data-driven decision-making. As a result, technology executives can apply TBM to broader business challenges.

- By linking technology with business outcomes, TBM helps technology-centric businesses make major business decisions, such as taking on new business opportunities. In this way, TBM puts technology leaders at the decision-making table along with their group of business leaders.

- TBM can provide the glue to hold together the federated IT organizations of large, distributed enterprises. It provides a common language for them to collaborate, and it provides useful tools such as benchmarking costs to use between business units to find and realize synergies.

- IT leaders are born to lead other "as-a-service" transformations for their organizations. They understand the technical aspects of delivering everything as a service and are prone to systematic thinking. TBM gives those leaders a new way to manage the entire stack of a service from technology all the way up through current and future business capabilities.

- TBM disciplines and their tools can be used to manage technologies that sit outside the normal realm of IT departments. Anything for which the true total cost is a mystery and for which data can reveal the drivers of those costs can be made transparent using TBM. In doing so, business leaders can improve not only their costs but achieve other business goals, such as improved customer satisfaction.

Chapter 12:
The Best Time to Start

Entrepreneurs sometimes struggle with the question of *when* to do rather than *what* to do. They know what they want to do and sell; but they wonder when the right time is to start their business. Is it best to take the plunge when the economy is hot? Or start a venture during a recession? Try a Google search for "is now a good time to start a business" and you'll find articles from every year and every economic cycle touting that "now" is the best time ever.

There may be some truth in this pattern of advice. According to a 2009 study[82] by the Ewing Kauffman Foundation, well over half of Fortune 500 companies and just under half of the Inc. list were started during a recession or a bear market. These successful, enduring companies started when the economy was weak. Of course, this means the other half of these successful, enduring companies started when the economy was strong. It appears that anytime during an economic cycle is equally ripe for starting a business.

Similarly, now is a good time to be the CEO of your new technology business, no matter the current state of your own business cycle. TBM programs have been started in both good times and in bad. Several large, integrated oil companies got their TBM program going when the price of oil was over $100 per barrel. Many big banks began right after the Great Recession, but when earnings were much softer than the year before. As you read earlier in the book, First American started theirs when the real estate market was just about to rebound. And many CIOs embraced TBM as a way to optimize costs when business was tough. TBM helps whether times are good, bad, or even ugly.

---

[82] Stangler, Dane. "The Economic Future Just Happened." Kauffman.org. Ewing Marion Kauffman Foundation, 9 June 2009. Web.

But are you and your people ready? To answer this question, let's look at the data. Our first version of the TBM Index, reflecting data from more than 300 global enterprises, shows a familiar bell curve of TBM maturity along the dimensions that relate to service orientation, data quality, management processes, and more.[83] At one end of the spectrum, many had not defined their services in a very meaningful way; they had very poor data about their assets, projects, and people; they hadn't defined roles for service owners or business relationship management. At the other end, Cisco had been on their IT-as-a-Service transformation for a few years, leveraging TBM to drive accountability and aggressively shift resources from run-the-business to change-the-business. Most other organizations fell somewhere in between these two ends of the spectrum.

Is there a right time in a fiscal year to start TBM? TBM does not depend on your fiscal cycle. It provides for a historical analysis and transparency of your IT resource spending, utilization, and consumption that is useful at any time. Transparency can be used in the latter part of the year to improve, accelerate, and justify your budget and throughout the year to better understand and manage variances.

The lesson here is that waiting for the "right time" to start TBM is a mistake. Now is the right time to start because your business needs a cost-effective technology partner that is well aligned to both its needs and its strategy. It needs business innovation and the agility to respond to new opportunities and challenges. These are the outcomes that can be facilitated by TBM.

So know that it's a good time to start. Now where do you start?

Assess Your Current State

It's hard to plot a route on a map if you don't know where you currently are. The same is true for TBM. Most CIOs who began the journey with their teams discovered that they weren't at step one; instead,

---

[83] Version 2 of the *TBM Index*, done in partnership with McKinsey & Company, reflects a similar curve of maturity in most areas.

they had taken many of the steps forward toward TBM maturity without even calling it TBM. For example, most had started to define their services and service levels, implemented performance measurements, and developed at least a modicum of cost reporting and analytics; some had taken strides in improving asset management, project management, and time/resource tracking; a few had established formal service owner roles. These steps provide an excellent foundation for TBM, but TBM also will help accelerate maturity in each of these areas.

Where are you?

To get a good handle on your current state, you have a few options. First, you can participate in the TBM Council's TBM Index,[84] a survey-based assessment and benchmark of your service orientation, operating model and organization, tools, and management capabilities. The survey takes about 30 minutes and will give you a good idea of your maturity in these areas. The TBM Council and our knowledge partner, McKinsey & Company, can provide you with comparisons to norms and recommendations for improvement based on your own situation and needs. In other words, use the TBM Index to see where you are.

The TBM Council's technical advisor and partners can also help. The technical advisor, Apptio, can help you understand the tools, capabilities, data requirements, and models behind an enterprise-class TBM system, along with how its other customers have used these to drive outcomes and improve maturity. The TBM Council's partners and sponsors include firms like KPMG, Information Services Group (ISG), Deloitte, EY, Cask, Maryville Technologies, and McKinsey & Company. These and other firms have built consulting practices that focus on TBM and are capable of quickly assessing your maturity.

---

[84] Take the survey at http://tbmcouncil.org/learn-tbm/tbm-index.html

Understand Your Business Case for TBM

TBM improves your ability to create value. Yet make no mistake. It takes an investment of time, talent, and money to adopt TBM disciplines and tools. How do you justify such an investment?

Many CIOs have justified their investment in TBM qualitatively. They knew they needed TBM to run an efficient, business-aligned, value-maximizing technology organization. They felt the pain of not having the facts to make the right decisions. They also knew the importance of having a business management system: They've delivered such systems to their business partners for many years, without having one of their own.

For others, a quantifiable business case was needed. If that's your situation, don't limit your business case to cost reduction. Instead, think about what your team needs to improve, set measurable goals for those things, and estimate the business benefits of each. To illustrate, consider the following examples:

- Are you too expensive, or perceived as being so? If so, set goals for achieving and then beating unit-cost targets or cost ratios that are based on industry benchmarks or cloud prices. Plan to do this year after year.

- Are you too inflexible, unable to respond quickly to business opportunities or threats? If so, set measurable goals for cloud adoption and for variablizing your costs and goals for discretionary project spending as well.

- Do you need to innovate more? If so, measure your innovation investments and your run-vs.-change ratio. Set targets for distinctive improvement. Measure progress toward these goals along with your backlog of business requests, the business value realized from your investments (e.g., revenue from new technology-enabled business services), and other factors such as on-time/on-budget project performance.

- Do you need to align your portfolio better to your precise business needs? If so, set goals for portfolio rationalization, such as a reduction in the number of business applications supported.

You may have noticed that these examples come from the value conversations (and KPIs) defined by the TBM framework. More importantly, each one can be assessed in terms of business value, usually in monetary terms. How much will you save by meeting or beating the unit cost targets that you set? How much faster can you respond to business demand by variablizing your costs and adopting the cloud, and what's that change worth to your business? How much more revenue can your business expect to earn by investing more in innovation? How much will it save your business to reduce your application footprint, and how much can you improve performance by focusing more resources on strategic applications or vendors?

Instead of asking how much *can* TBM help you save or improve, ask yourself how much you *need* to save or improve and what's reasonable. The answer is different for every company, and it often depends on relative TBM maturity. Recent findings from the TBM Index research[85] show that the top quartile of organizations, in terms of TBM maturity, achieved a 15 to 25 percent improvement in quality of service, up to 20 percent in IT cost reduction, and a 15 to 25 percent increase in on-time delivery. These results were about 10 to 15 points higher than those benefits achieved by companies whose TBM maturity was average. In other words, as you mature your TBM capabilities, you'll be able to deliver better quality services, faster and more cost-efficiently.

The beauty of this approach — starting with the practical outcomes you need to achieve and can achieve — is that the TBM approach defines measurable goals for your program. Use these not only to justify your

---

[85] Santos, Leandro, and Himanshu Agarwal. "Archetypes of Adoption: Driving TBM Practices to Business Impact." *Technology Business Management Conference 2015*. Hyatt Regency Chicago, Chicago, IL, USA. 29 Oct. 2015. Speech. Slides at https://tbmcouncil.jiveon.com/docs/DOC-3101.

investment, but also to make them part of your team's annual business goals. Also use the TBM model to transform them into measurable objectives for individual teams.

Finally, know that you're not alone. If you need help with your business case, the TBM Council's partners will help you build one.

Learn From Your Peers

If there is one thing that distinguishes TBM from many IT management frameworks, it is that TBM has been developed through a community effort and by applying data, tools, and processes to real-world problems. The TBM Council is at the heart of this development. Founded as a non-profit in 2012, the TBM Council actually began back in 2007 as a series of CIO telepresence meetings hosted by Apptio founder Sunny Gupta. It has since grown into an organization with thousands of members, an annual conference that attracts over 1,000 executives, and CIO and CTO board members from the United States, United Kingdom, Germany, and Australia.

The mission of the TBM Council is to develop and promote global standards for managing the business of technology. It is the only CIO-led organization dedicated to this purpose. This book is a big part of the TBM Council's mandate, and it was written largely based on the stories, lessons, and standards shared in this community. The Council provides many opportunities — globally, regionally, and virtually — for CIOs, CTOs, IT finance leaders, IT planning and strategy professionals, and others to discuss challenges, share ideas, and learn from one another.

To join the TBM Council and learn from many others about TBM, learn more and register at www.TBMCouncil.org.

Appendix A:
Technology Business Model Archetypes

The following tables present the characteristics of each technology business model archetype in a comparative format. The characteristics are the same as those described in Chapter 3, but are presented in a way that allows you to compare each one. In doing so, the following tables can be used to understand your own technology business model characteristics.

Business Value

Business Driver	■ Business services are delivered by technology organization to external customers based on an intimate knowledge of the market and its customers ■ Value is measured through the P&L for the business service
Value Partner	■ Business services are delivered based on an intimate knowledge of the business and close collaboration between business owners and technology owners ■ Value is measured based on true business impact (e.g., more revenue, higher win rate, faster sales cycles)
Service Provider	■ Value is based on the quality of services and their impact on the organization ■ Business partners more easily balance the cost of IT with its value ■ Business partners can compare your services with those of third-party providers, such as public cloud options
Expense Center	■ Value is difficult to articulate, resulting in a top-down emphasis on cost cutting ■ Business unit leaders often drive technology decisions in their own silos

Service Portfolio

Business Driver	▪ Service portfolio includes revenue generating business services advertised to external customers
Value Partner	▪ Service portfolio includes business-specific services and applications, backed by an efficient and integrated enterprise technology platform
Service Provider	▪ Services are well defined, costed, priced, and advertised through a catalog
Expense Center	▪ Services are not well-defined ▪ Instead, the organization focuses on the management of assets, projects, and costs

Business Alignment

Business Driver	▪ Product managers own and manage their product lines, including their technology resources
Value Partner	▪ Business process owners partner with service owners to build and optimize digital processes and business applications
Service Provider	▪ Service owners and BRMs exist ▪ Service owners work with BRMs to balance costs, service levels, risk ▪ BRMs help partners understand technology choices, levels of consumption, and impact to cost allocations
Expense Center	▪ No service ownership or business relationship management functions exist, at least formally

Creating Transparency

Business Driver	▪ Business leaders know the total cost of delivering business capabilities, including on a per unit basis ▪ They understand their business cost dynamics, how all costs are shaped by changing business conditions and demand
Value Partner	▪ Tech leaders know total cost and per unit costs of delivering app services ▪ They often understand the costs of the business capabilities they support ▪ Service owners understand how services enable business outcomes and at what cost
Service Provider	▪ Tech leaders know the TCO of services, including TCO per unit ▪ Asset owners know how assets are consumed by providing services ▪ Service owners know how services are consumed by partners and at what cost
Expense Center	▪ IT leaders see costs through a financial reporting model (GL accounts, cost centers) ▪ They have few meaningful metrics to discuss cost and performance tradeoffs with their business partners

Delivering Value for Money

Business Driver	▪ Business leaders monitor tech and non-tech costs ▪ They manage unit costs of business capabilities (e.g., cost per trade, cost to serve a subscriber) ▪ They aggressively seek cost efficiencies by trading labor costs for technology costs (via process automation) or by improving reliability

Delivering Value for Money

Value Partner	▪ Tech leaders monitor the unit costs of business application services ▪ They balance tech spending across their portfolio and make tradeoffs to improve value ▪ They measure and manage investment levels in their services as a portfolio over time
Service Provider	▪ Tech leaders monitor the unit costs of their services and towers ▪ They benchmark costs & cost ratios regularly to identify variances ▪ They regularly set targets for improving cost for performance and measure attainment
Expense Center	▪ Cost efficiency depends on systems management practices (e.g., capacity planning) w/little insight into financial tradeoffs ▪ Benchmarking, if performed, is done once every one or two years ▪ Spending cuts are driven top down without understanding impact on service levels or risk

Shaping Business Demand

Business Driver	▪ The cost of technology is baked into the firm's product prices ▪ Demand is shaped through the market in which the firm participates
Value Partner	▪ Technology costs are evaluated as business costs ▪ Investments in technology are based on the business impact to product-line P&Ls
Service Provider	▪ Business partners are allocated costs based on consumption of services using rates (prices) ▪ They receive a bill of IT w/consumption details ▪ Business partners are incentivized to balance consumption and service value

Shaping Business Demand

Expense Center	• Business partners are not allocated costs at all *or* are allocated costs based on a predetermined rate (e.g., percent of revenues or FTEs) • Cost allocations provide little incentive for business units to change consumption

Planning and Governing for Value

Business Driver	• Technology budgets are integral to product-line fiscal plans • Business planning is tech planning
Value Partner	• The budget is based on business plans with a clear connection between innovation and service demands and their resource needs • Investment targets are evaluated to ensure alignment between portfolio needs and funding levels
Service Provider	• The budget is often set based on the amount of services to be delivered and consumed by the business, after considering headwinds (e.g., salary increases) and tailwinds (e.g., depreciation roll-offs) • Some top-down pressures on the overall budget may exist, but they are weighed against service and project funding needs • Project funds are established separately based on business requirements and IT4IT improvements
Expense Center	• The technology budget is often based on a percentage of revenues, cost per employee, or another, mostly arbitrary formula • Budgets are managed at the cost center level, and cuts are often made top down without an understanding of how services will be impacted

Appendix B:
CFO of IT Competency Model

In the first part of 2015, the Technology Business Management Council's CFO of IT workgroup recognized that both the business value and career progression of IT finance leaders was limited because too many operated as technology controllers. In other words, they were being accountants, not finance leaders.

This mattered, in part, because Technology Business Management is not an accounting discipline; it is not passive. Rather, TBM fosters the four value conversations that CIOs and other IT leaders must be having as an active part of decision-making. They help achieve better business outcomes such as efficiency, transformation and agility. The IT finance leader is not only in a good position to make these conversations possible, she should be instrumental in making them happen.

The CFO of IT workgroup's leadership, including Carl Stumpf[86] of CME Group, Drew Adam of Hillshire Brands,[87] Mareida Mackenna of Aon, Chuck Niethold of First American, Jodi Hunter of Comerica Bank, Nigel Hughes of ISG and I introduced a new model to shape the profession of IT financial management. The purpose of this model is to make IT financial managers indispensable through the clear articulation and delivery of business value by:

- Redefining the IT finance leadership role to focus on business value creation

- Giving IT finance leaders a clearer path to professional and career development

- Providing the TBM community a method to measure CFO of IT competencies and skills

---

[86] Also chairman of the CFO of IT workgroup. Has since left CME Group to join Nike.

[87] Has since left Hillshire Brands to join Marmon Group, a Berkshire Hathaway Company.

Depicted in the figure below, the CFO of IT Competency Model™ defines the four essential roles that IT finance leaders and their team members should fulfill for the business.

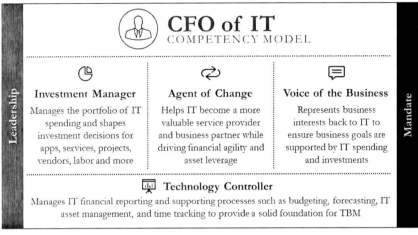

Figure B-1: The CFO of IT Competency Model™ defines the four essential roles that IT finance leaders must serve to best satisfy the needs of the business

Each role, along with the responsibilities for each, are described below.

Technology Controller

The technology or IT controller executes core IT financial accounting and management practices such as budgeting and forecasting, monthly or quarterly accruals, financial transparency, chargeback, showback, benchmarking and more. Success in this role normally depends on a strong relationship with Corporate Finance (if the role lives in the technology organization). The role may perform procurement and asset management functions as well, although those are not included in this model.

Responsibilities of this role include:

- Ensure compliance with accounting policies and manages the quality of data

- Govern and manage financial planning and forecasting

- Enforce controls over IT assets, labor, vendors and other resources

- Deliver integrated business and financial metrics to optimize technology spending as well as nonfinancial outcomes

As depicted in the visual model, this role is the foundation of the others. Without strong controllership, it is difficult to impossible to fulfill the other roles. In other words, technology controller is table stakes for the CFO of IT. However, it should not be viewed as sufficient in and of itself. Satisfying only this role limits the value and career opportunities that IT financial management can provide.

Investment Manager

The investment manager helps ensure that the level of expenditures in applications, services, projects, vendors, labor and other portfolios are best aligned to the needs of the business. In this role, the CFO of IT works with project portfolio managers and other roles, such as vendor managers (strategic vendor management), to realize the benefits of the insights gained. They also must partner with business process owners and service owners to support business cases (e.g., cost-benefit analysis) for new investments.

Responsibilities of this role include:

- Deliver and manage a portfolio-oriented framework for maximizing the overall benefits of IT spending

- Identify new ideas and opportunities to improve value

- Facilitate and review business cases for new investments and help secure funding

- Review value and returns on investments and portfolio spending over time

These responsibilities are essential to fostering the tradeoff conversations needed for a business-aligned portfolio and for properly governing investments in innovation.

Agent of Change

The agent of change supports the CIO's transformation goals, such as shifting from a technology orientation to being a service delivery organization (e.g., IT-as-a-Service transformation) or creating a digital innovation capability. In this role, the CFO of IT works closely with those who are also responsible for the transformation or whose roles were created by it. For example, the CFO of IT collaborates with service owners and service delivery management leaders on creating transparency and putting in place a decision-making framework for governing supply and demand of services in the catalog. She may also work with infrastructure & operations leaders on cloud, modernization and similar initiatives, often supporting efforts to become a better broker of services as well.

Responsibilities of this role include:

- Facilitate IT's transformation into a service provider for and value partner with the lines of business

- Empower IT be an effective broker of services by adding decision-making value for acquiring public cloud services or more traditional third-party ones

- Help improve agility through adjusting IT's cost structure, sourcing decisions and other financial levers (e.g., shifting from heavy fixed cost structure to a more variable one)

- Help the enterprise improve economies of scale and better leverage existing investments by enabling a shared services model

Meeting these responsibilities helps not only to transform the IT organization but to improve enterprise agility.

Voice of the Business

The voice of the business represents business interests back to IT during important decisions to help ensure that business goals are supported by IT spending and investments. In this role, CFOs of IT collaborate with corporate finance as well as IT's business relationship managers, who are often at the front lines with their line-of-business partners. She also incorporates non-financial metrics such as quality, satisfaction, and "tech debt" into decision-making, to ensure that tradeoffs between cost, speed, performance and risk are better understood.

Responsibilities of this role include:

- Advise business and top management on cost-effective approaches for technologies, resources, labor and vendors

- Represent business interests during major IT decisions[88]

- Clarify options and tradeoffs for business decisions about cost, consumption and quality

- Analyze the IT impact of M&A and divestitures during due diligence and after transactions are completed

In performing these functions, the CFO of IT not only helps ensure business needs are met; as a benefit for technology leaders, she helps shape demand by clarifying the tradeoffs for business leaders, oftentimes in financial terms.

---

[88] Other roles, such as business relationship managers, may also represent business interests, but the CFO of IT often brings a unique, enterprise perspective to those conversations.

Glossary

The following definitions only describe the terms in the context of Technology Business Management. Many of these terms have other meanings that are less relevant here.

ACTIVITY-BASED COSTING (ABC)

A method of costing a service, technology, project or other object by first determining the activities that drive its total cost, then costing those activities, and finally summing up those costs. Best performed with data that reflects the consumption of resources, such as hours of support labor, floor space in a data center, gigabyte of storage used, number of physical ports, and so on. As such, provides a way of tracing consumption to cost and exposes more ways to control costs through tradeoffs.

ACTUALS (ACTUAL SPENDING)

The amount of expenditures incurred during a fiscal period, such as a year, quarter or month. Reflects the real amounts for that period as opposed to the budgeted amounts. Often compared against the *budget* amounts for the same period to determine budget vs. actual variances (differences).

ALLOCATION

An assignment or apportionment of a cost or expenditure to one or more entities or objects. Often refers to the distribution of IT costs to business units based on an agreed-upon approach, such as actual or planned consumption, by percentage of total revenues or by employee counts. Also refers to the apportionment of costs from one object in the *TBM model* to another, such as from labor (a *cost pool*) to servers (a *tower*) or from storage (a tower) to an *application* or *service*.

AMORTIZATION

An accounting mechanism used to spread the cost of acquiring and/or developing an intangible asset, such as software or goodwill, over its useful life. Similar to *depreciation*, which is used for tangible assets such as hardware or a building.

APPLICATION

A software tool used by IT, the lines of business, external business customers and/or external *business partners* to accomplish a task or execute a process. Also called an app. Often the primary technology used to deliver a service to the business.

APPLICATION OWNER

Generally, the technology employee responsible for managing the entire lifecycle of an *application*, from identifying the business requirements for a software application, building the business case for acquiring and/or developing it, overseeing its implementation, training and enabling users and so on. Sometimes exists within the lines of business. More and more, is being supplanted by a *service owner*, who has similar responsibilities but for a *service,* including all applications that support that service.

APPLICATION PORTFOLIO

The collection of *applications* used by the business and/or delivered by the IT organization, including those currently in development (pipeline) and those being retired. The *portfolio* concept means that investments in one application are made at the expense of others and that investments must be balanced based on an appreciation of the tradeoffs, risks and returns.

AUTHORIZATION FOR EXPENDITURE

An accounting mechanism, usually found in a *general ledger*, that distinctly associates outlays to a capital item such as a new *application*, hardware or data center. Defined during an approval process for a capital outlay such as a new project and defines the spending limit for that outlay. Then used to create accountability for spending against the limit. In the general ledger, it appears similar to *cost centers*, which are normally used for *operating expenses* only.

BENCHMARKING

Comparing cost, cost ratios, performance or other internal metrics against those of other companies, locations, providers, consumer, time periods or other variables. Often refers to comparisons against other companies in an industry peer group, but it can be used to compare many measures against those of others (or other time periods) provided they are similar enough to make the comparison meaningful. A key method for demonstrating value-for-money and cost-efficiency.

BILL OF IT

A bill presented to a business unit, *service owner*, *application owner*, or other consumer that shows their consumption of IT services, assets or labor and the associated cost or charges for what they have consumed. Typically delivered on a monthly or quarterly basis. The cost is sometimes based on actual cost but may also be based on agreed-upon *rates* (prices). The units are defined per agreement with the consumer and may include things such as number of licensed users of an *application*, number of workstations supported, number of terabytes of storage consumed, number of hours worked on a project, and so on.

BUDGET

The financial and resource plan for an organization, such as the IT department, for a defined time period, such as a fiscal year, quarter or month. Includes the anticipated operating expenditures (OpEx) for expenses that will hit the income statement in the given period and the *capital expenditure*s (CapEx) that will be used to purchase or create assets in the given period. May also include the headcount plan (e.g., employees, contractors, consultants).

Generally created by a *budget* owner or many budget owners (e.g., cost center owners, project owners) who estimate their needs for the year and submit them for approval as part of the annual budgeting process. Generally requires approval by a senior executive within the budgeting department and then further approval by the chief financial officer (CFO) and/or the executive committee of the company.

Is used to provide authority for spending and staffing for the current year, to communicate anticipated IT spending to key stakeholder such as business unit leaders, and to negotiate investments and spending levels. Used throughout the fiscal period to provide accountability for actual spending.

BUSINESS CAPABILITY

The capacity — including people, processes, assets, data and services — to drive a business outcome such as generating revenue, reducing costs, increasing productivity, or otherwise improving corporate performance in the eyes of your firm's partners, suppliers, or customers.

Supported by IT through services that increase revenues, reduce business costs, increase productivity, or otherwise improve corporate performance in the eyes of your firm's partners, suppliers, or customers. Business transactions occur at this level.

Order-to-cash and procure-to-pay are simple, generic examples of business capabilities.

BUSINESS DRIVER

One of the four *technology business model archetypes*. Characterized by organizations where the products or services delivered to external customers are technology-centric, such as when it delivers Software- (*SaaS*), Platform- (*PaaS*), or *Infrastructure-as-a-Service* (*IaaS*) to generate revenue. Also applies to organizations not in the "as-a-service" business as long as they provide technology-based services to the company's customers. Examples may include the technology department of a SaaS company, the online store division of a brick-and-mortar retailer, and the digital department of a fashion company.

BUSINESS PARTNER

Internal customers of the technology department (such as line-of-business leaders) and other executive stakeholders (e.g., the CEO, CFO and COO). Generically refers to those executives outside of the technology department who need to be part of *value conversations* that drive improve business outcomes. In the context of this book, does not mean partners of the corporation.

BUSINESS RELATIONSHIP MANAGER (BRM)

An employee of the technology department who is responsible for ensuring *business partners* are successful and satisfied with what the technology department is providing them.

Sometimes called account manager or client relationship manager, they liaise with business partners to understand their needs and their business plans; work with *service owners*, enterprise architects, business process owners, and others to define and propose solutions for new business problems; communicate the business value, business consumption, and cost of the services in the *portfolio* (or, more specifically, the catalog) to business partners; assess and negotiate the business *demand* for IT services; and identify and address service-related issues by working with service owners, service managers, enterprise architects, and others.

Responsible for listening to business partners, understanding their plans and pains, and proposing solutions. Also wield the *service catalog* and identify the need for new services in the pipeline. In this regard, the BRMs influence the technology supply.

BUSINESS-ALIGNED PORTFOLIO

One of the four *value conversations* that CIOs have with their people, providers and *business partners*; ensures that the *portfolios* of services, projects, vendors, technologies, data centers and other types are optimized to deliver the most value for the level of spending or investment. Enables IT to focus its time and resources on the right services, technologies, and providers for the business. Involves tradeoffs, namely, the shifting of resources or time between items in each portfolio.

Driven by initiatives such as rationalization (e.g., *application rationalization*) and consolidation (e.g., data center consolidation), which help simplify a portfolio.

CAPITAL EXPENDITURE (CAPEX)

Funds used by a company to acquire, build, develop, enhance or upgrade assets such as buildings, leaseholds, equipment, software, and data. Also made by companies to maintain or increase the scope of their operations. Must result in a new asset, improve the useful life of an existing asset, and/or significantly enhance an existing asset. Realized as an *operating expense* through *depreciation* (for tangible assets) or *amortization* (for intangible assets) over the accounting life of the asset.

CHANGE-THE-BUSINESS (CTB)

Refers to spending and investments used to grow or transform the business. May include both operating and *capital expenditure*s. Operating expenditures that qualify often include project spending that occurs before capitalization begins and operational resources on services that are categorized as change-the-business.

Capital expenditures that qualify include the purchases and/or development of new assets that directly enable business growth or transformation. Is a superset of both *grow-the-business* and *transform-the-business* classifications. Is usually comprised of discretionary spending.

The opposite of *run-the-business*.

CHARGEBACK

The internal accounting process of funding a technology *service provider* by transferring funds from one or more business units (e.g., the consumers of technology) to the provider organization (e.g., Corporate IT, shared services). The units charged may be based on the actual or planned consumption of shared or dedicated technology services, projects and resources. The costs charged may be based on actual costs, planned costs and/or defined *rates*. May be paired with *showback* to give consumers a clear perspective of how their consumption drives costs.

CHIEF FINANCIAL OFFICER (CFO) OF IT

The head of the *IT finance* department, which usually exists within the IT or technology department but may also exist in corporate finance. Often serves a variety of roles, including *technology controller*, *investment manager*, *agent of change* and *voice of the business*. See *CFO of IT* Competency Model in Appendix B.

COST CENTER

An accounting mechanism, usually found in a *general ledger*, that distinctly identifies a department, division, or other organizational unit whose managers are responsible for its budgeted and actual costs. Normally associated with *operating expenses*, whereas *authorization for expenditure*s (AFEs) are a similar accounting mechanism normally used for *capital expenditures*.

COST POOL

A category of costs that resides at the bottom layer of the hierarchical *TBM taxonomy* (and corresponding *TBM model*). A high-level group of similar costs such as hardware, software, labor (internal and external), outside services, facilities, and telecom. Makes cost allocations easier because they can be allocated upwards through the TBM model based on fewer, more generalized rules. Used to enhance reporting because they can be traced through the TBM model to reveal the composition of *tower*s, services, capabilities, and more.

COST FOR PERFORMANCE

One of the four *value conversation*s that CIOs have with their people, providers and *business partner*s; ensures that technology is being delivered efficiently to the business. Enables IT to focus its time and resources on the right services, technologies, and providers for the business. Involves tradeoffs, namely, the shifting of resources or time between items in each *portfolio*. Driven by initiatives such as rationalization (e.g., *application* rationalization) and consolidation (e.g., data center consolidation), which help simplify a portfolio.

DEMAND

The anticipated and/or actual consumption of services, applications, *towers* and other resources driven by the needs of the business. Can be translated into resource needs, such as tower-level spending, people, third-party services and even the financial *budget*.

DEPRECIATION

An accounting mechanism used to spread the cost of acquiring and/or building a tangible asset, such as hardware or a building, over its useful life. Similar to *amortization*, which is used for intangible assets such as software or goodwill.

DIRECT COST

A cost that is completely attributable to a business unit, *business capability*, service, *tower* or other object within the *TBM model* or a cost model. Implies that the resource(s) for which the cost represents is dedicated as opposed to shared. Opposite of *indirect cost*.

ECONOMIC VALUE ADDED (EVA)

A method of measuring the benefit of an investment in terms of shareholder returns. Considers only the current time period (e.g., current fiscal year) of the investment and its benefits and therefore provides an accurate measure of profit contribution for a period of activity. Calculated by deducting the cost of capital from the net operating profit (after taxes) of an investment. For example, if you spend $1 million on a new technology that drives a net operating profit after taxes of $400,000 per year, and your average cost of capital is 12 percent, the economic value added is $280,000, or $400,000 – ($1,000,000 x 12%).

END-USER SERVICE

Delivering, supporting and maintaining desktops, laptops, workstations, tablets and other mobile devices (including cell phones) that enable workplace productivity by employees or other personnel (e.g., contractors). Often includes remote connectivity, productivity applications such as an office suite, and messaging services like email.

ENTERPRISE AGILITY

One of the four *value conversations* that CIOs have with their people, providers and *business partners*; ensures that the technology organization can respond quickly to changing needs of the business and also helps the business to respond to market opportunities or threats. Enables changes to the existing cost and investment structures to more flexible models, leveraging the cloud, exploiting decentralized IT decisions, and using data to make better decisions faster.

EXPENSE CENTER

One of the four *technology business model archetypes*. Characterized by a lack of service orientation, this type of technology organization is the least connected to business *demand* because it is usually funded as a percentage of revenues, based on headcount, or through a baseline *budget* adjustment, methods which inadequately reflect business needs. Is not appropriate for any corporate strategy today and is a vestige of an era when technology was an unimportant component of corporate strategy. All CIOs should seek to move beyond this archetypical business model.

FIXED COST

A cost that does not vary materially or in concert with the level of output, i.e., is not strongly correlated with the units of services delivered. Inhibits financial agility because it does not go down when business volumes decline. *Service providers*, such as *IaaS* or *SaaS* companies, often convert their *fixed costs* into *variable costs* for their customers by assuming the risk of *demand* fluctuations.

FORECAST (FORECASTED SPENDING)

The amount of expenditures expected to be incurred during the remainder fiscal period, such as a year or quarter, plus the *actuals* incurred up to the current cutoff date. For example, the annual *forecast* at June 30 for a calendar year end would include the actual spending through the month of June plus the anticipated spending through the end of the year. Similar to an updated *budget*, except the process is usually far less complex and requires fewer or no approvals.

*Forecast*s are used to anticipate *budget* variances for a fiscal period that has not completed, such as the year. By calculating the expected amounts, budget owners and other stakeholders can compare forecasts against budgets and make necessary corrections to reduce or eliminated anticipated variances.

GENERAL LEDGER (GL)

System for recording, classifying, summarizing and reporting an organization's accounting transactions. Includes accounts for the company's assets, liabilities, owner's equity (including retained earnings), revenue and expenses. A *general ledger* is often supported by many sub-ledgers such as accounts payable, accounts receivable and fixed assets, which maintain more detailed records for each area of concern.

Usually structured by GL accounts and *cost center*s, and may also include other fields or characteristics such as requests for expenditure and company codes. May be used to capture *actuals*, *budget* amounts and sometimes *forecast* amounts.

Supports external and internal financial reporting for the organization. Normally audited by the organization's external auditors as part of an annual financial audit to ensure that internal controls exist and are effective and that the period's financial statements present fairly, in all material respects, the financial position and the results of operations and cash flows.

GENERALLY ACCEPTED ACCOUNTING PRINCIPLES (GAAP)

Standards for recording, classifying, processing and reporting the financial transactions of an enterprise. Established through a standards setting process by an accounting standards board, such as the Financial Accounting Standards Board (FASB) for the United States or the

International Accounting Standards Board for Europe and other regions (which call them International Financial Reporting Standards).

GROW-THE-BUSINESS (GTB)

Refers to spending and investments used to increase business volumes and/or revenues and/or profits in existing or complementary markets and product lines. May include both operating and *capital expenditures*. Operating expenditures that qualify often include project spending that occurs before capitalization begins and additional operational resources employed to increase capacity. Capital expenditures that qualify include the purchases and/or development of new assets, such as increased capacity, that directly enable business growth.

Is a subset within *change-the-business* spending.

INDIRECT COST

A cost that is allocated to a business unit, *business capability*, service, *tower* or other object within the *TBM model* or a cost model based on an assumption or some measure (such as consumption). Implies that the resource(s) for which the cost represents is shared as opposed to dedicated. Opposite of *direct cost*.

INFRASTRUCTURE

Refers to the underlying servers, storage, networking, data center facilities, and other assets and services that allow the business to deliver, support, interact with and benefit from applications and services. May be delivered as a service (i.e., Infrastructure as a Service, or IaaS).

INFRASTRUCTURE AS A SERVICE (IAAS)

Generally considered one of three cloud service models (along with *Software as a Service* and *Platform as a Service*), includes *infrastructure* delivered to consumers whereby the features and benefits of the *infrastructure* are well defined along with warranty attributes and other service levels (e.g., availability, reliability). Used by consumers to build, deploy and support software platforms and applications and/or host data.

INVESTMENT IN INNOVATION

One of the four *value conversations* that CIOs have with their people, providers and *business partners*; ensures that the technology organization spends adequate resources on new and enhanced services and on business innovation and governs those investments wisely. Provides more comprehensive oversight of project costs, helps shift to a service-oriented approach to managing investments, funds the innovation program and drives (justifies) shared investments.

IT FINANCE

Team, department or function dedicated to the financial management of the IT or technology organization. Often headed by a VP of *IT finance* or *CFO of IT* or *IT finance* director. Usually responsible for the annual *budget*, monthly and/or quarterly *forecast*s, *budget*-to-actual variance reviews, accounting for IT expenses and *capital expenditure*s, and *chargeback*, if performed. May house the *TBM office*, and may own other functions or duties such as the management of IT assets, software licenses, time tracking, IT purchasing, IT *benchmarking*, and performance metrics. Usually resides within the technology organization but may reside in corporate finance.

IT SPEND RATIO

May refer to a variety of expense ratios for the IT or technology organization, but often means the total IT *budget* divided by corporate revenues. Is used, usually erroneously, to assess spending on IT. If used, should only be used as a rough measure and should be put into context with many other measures and considerations.

IT AS A SERVICE

Mostly synonymous with the *service provider* technology business model archetype. Refers to an IT model whereby everything (or nearly everything) that is delivered to the business is structured and managed as a service.

KEY PERFORMANCE INDICATOR (KPI)

A metric or fact used to evaluate an important aspect of business or technical performance such as revenue contribution, cost efficiency, agility, or risk. Allows an executive or manager to set a meaningful and measurable target and then evaluate and track execution against that target over time.

OPERATING EXPENSE (OpEx)

A cost of running the business such as payroll costs, utilities, insurance, taxes, lease payments and more. Includes the *depreciation* of tangible assets and the *amortization* of intangible assets over their useful lives. Does not include expenditures that are capitalized, including salaries and benefits associated with software development for applications that meet capitalization requirements or construction labor for new buildings or building enhancements.

OUTSOURCING

Contracting with third party providers for services consumed by either IT or the lines-of-business in place of an internal source.

PLATFORM AS A SERVICE (PaaS)

Generally considered one of three cloud service models (along with *Software as a Service* and *Infrastructure as a Service*), provides a technology stack and software environment that is needed by *application owners* to build, deploy and support software applications over the internet. Generally includes programming languages, libraries, and other tools along with the underlying *infrastructure* and can be provisioned on *demand*.

PORTFOLIO

A collection of services, applications, technologies (i.e., platforms, standard technologies), data centers, vendors, suppliers, and other assets or resources owned, delivered and/or supported by the technology organization. The *portfolio* concept means that investments or expenditures in one asset or resource are made at the expense of others and that investments must be balanced based on an appreciation of the tradeoffs, risks and returns. Portfolio management is central to *business-aligned portfolio* value conversations.

PROFIT MARGIN

The percentage of a company's sales that is retained as net income. For example, a company that earns $20 in net income for every $100 in net sales (gross sales minus returns and allowances) achieves a *profit margin* of 20 percent. Is sometimes used to generically describe the difference between the price of a service, including an IT service delivered to business consumers, and the fully-burdened cost of delivering that service.

RATE

The *unit cost* or set price for delivering a given technology or service. May be used internally to the technology organization to understand the unit cost, such as monitoring changes over time. May be used externally to the technology organization to advertise the cost of technologies or services to the business. On rare occasions, called a price.

RATES MANAGEMENT

The process of measuring, or setting, and then communicating the *rates* for technologies, services and/or other resources. Often includes setting chargeable rates on a periodic basis (e.g., annually) by understanding *unit costs* and establishing prices that sufficiently recover the average unit cost and costs in total of technologies and services. May include incentivized pricing, whereby discounts are included in rates to encourage consumption, or, conversely, premiums are applied to rates to discourage consumption of a technology, service and/or resource. May include the work to measure and then influence or improve the unit costs (rates). Also used to support *benchmarking*.

RETURN ON INVESTMENT (ROI)

A performance measure used to evaluate the efficiency of an expenditure in generating a business benefit, such as increased revenues or improved profitability. Normally calculated as follows, expressed as a percentage:

$$ROI = \frac{Benefit - Expenditure}{Expenditure}$$

Often difficult to measure for expenditures that are specific to IT or technology because the benefit is derived from a *business capability* or process, not merely a technical one. Especially difficult to measure for shared IT expenditures that benefit multiple lines of business or capabilities. Some technology expenditures reduce an IT or technology cost and therefore convey a clear and often measurable (dollar-denominated) technology benefit; in those cases, ROI can be measured directly. In most cases, however, ROI can only be measured in combination with the non-technology (non-IT) expenditures as well, such as the business process costs that are associated with the revenue generated (or improved).

Often replaced with Net Present Value. Used as a more generic concept in this book to imply the benefits of technology expenditures that exceed the cost.

RETURN ON IT ASSETS (ROITA)

A performance measure calculated by dividing annual (or trailing twelve months) of operating income by average annual IT assets (capitalized hardware, software, and other costs). The higher the return (as a percentage), the better a technology organization is doing to derive service value (e.g., IT billings) from assets. Varies considerably from one company to the next, so CIOs should focus on improving this metric over time. With this measure, a dollar earned (added to operating income) is generally better than a dollar saved (removed from IT assets).

RUN/GROW/TRANSFORM

A common set of classifications used to assess overall spending, usually through a ratio of the three types of spending. Introduced by Meta Group (acquired by Gartner in 2005) in the early 2000s. *Run-the-business* spending often consumes 60 to 70 percent of overall spending for the year. *Grow-the-business* spending and *transform-the-business* spending account for the rest. Many CIOs try to optimize their *run-the-business* spending to bring it down as a percentage of the overall spending, thereby increasing the relative ratio of grow- and *transform-the-business* spending.

Can be benchmarked and compared over time and against industry peers, although organizations often define and apply the categories somewhat uniquely (making meaningful industry benchmark comparisons difficult).

See also the definitions for *run-the-business*, *grow-the-business* and *change-the-business*.

RUN-THE-BUSINESS (RTB)

Refers to spending and investments used for ongoing operations of the business. May include both operating and *capital expenditure*s. Operating expenditures that qualify often include internal and external labor, *depreciation* and *amortization* of assets, facilities expenses, utilities, and telecommunication services. Capital expenditures that qualify hardware refreshes or upgrades that do not qualify as grow- or *transform-the-business*.

Mostly includes non-discretionary expenditures, although some discretionary expenses such as training and travel may also be run-the-business. Most mandatory expenditures such as compliance, safety or risk investments are also run-the-business.

The opposite of *change-the-business*.

SERVICE

Work performed through a combination of internal labor, automation, and/or third-parties to execute a process or otherwise facilitate an outcome on behalf of a business or technology consumer. Its delivery can be measured, costed and priced.

SERVICE CATALOG

The list of services that an organization offers to its employees or customers that includes a description of each service and, in many cases, the cost or price of consuming or subscribing to the service.

SERVICE OWNER

Generally, the technology employee responsible for managing the entire lifecycle of a service, from identifying the business requirements, building the business case for subscribing to and/or creating the service, overseeing its delivery, training and enabling users and so on. Sometimes exists within the lines of business. An essential role for creating and delivering the business value of services, especially focused on translating and prioritizing business requirements and optimizing cost-effectiveness of delivery.

SERVICE PORTFOLIO

The collection of all services used by the business and/or delivered by the technology organization, those currently in development (pipeline) and those being retired. Includes the services in the *service catalog* (i.e., those available for consumption) as well as those that will be introduced later. The *portfolio* concept means that investments in one service are made at the expense of others and that investments must be balanced based on an appreciation of the tradeoffs, risks and returns.

SERVICE PROVIDER

One of the four *technology business model archetypes*. Characterized by organizations that have introduced a *service portfolio* and created or assigned *service owners* and *business relationship managers* (BRMs). This type of technology organization focuses on the maturity of service management processes (e.g., ITIL or Microsoft Operations Framework) in order to define and deliver services efficiently at the promised level of quality.

SHOWBACK

The process of providing business unit leaders or other consumers of technology the amount and cost of what they have consumed. Often accomplished through a formal *bill of IT*, but may be less formal. May be paired with *chargeback* to provide greater accountability for the cost of what is consumed.

SOFTWARE AS A SERVICE (SAAS)

Generally considered one of three cloud service models (along with *Platform as a Service* and *Infrastructure as a Service*). Includes software applications that are delivered on demand over the internet.

TBM ANALYST

Sometimes called a TBM architect, this professional understands the data and reports, works with data owners and report consumers to improve reporting, analyze output and guide decisions. Often has served in various IT roles prior to becoming the TBM analyst and has learned many of the core disciplines of IT, such as systems administration, project management, service delivery, support, architecture, and application development. Often understands both finance and enterprise technology and works closely with the TBM administrator to create meaningful reports, help users understand those reports, and facilitate deeper dives into the data.

In some organizations, the TBM analyst is also the *TBM system administrator*.

TBM FRAMEWORK

The core elements — organization/culture, financial management disciplines, and *value conversation*s — that make up a mature TBM program. Defined through interviews with board members and principal members of the TBM Council and a series of workshops run in 2013 and 2014. Depicted in a graphical model in this book.

TBM METRICS

KPIs that allow CIOs and other technology leaders and stakeholders to measure, manage, and communicate business value.

TBM MODEL

A tool for mapping and allocating costs and other resources from one layer of the *TBM taxonomy* to another. Includes the TBM taxonomy objects and layers plus the data requirements, *allocation* rules, and metrics needed to create *transparency* and enable the reporting that is needed for the *value conversations* of TBM. Creates the financial, technical, and business views that are meaningful to various decision makers and stakeholders. Normally built and processed using software (see *TBM system*).

TBM OFFICE (TBMO)

Normally a small team within the technology organization comprised of the *TBM program director*, *TBM system administrator*, and *TBM analyst*(s). Responsible for maintaining and administering the *TBM system*, sourcing and integrating data, developing and delivering reports, liaising with data owners, advising and supporting decision makers, and other duties necessary to enable *value conversations* between and among IT leaders and their *business partners*.

TBM PROGRAM DIRECTOR

The head of your *TBM office* or TBM team. May be the *IT finance* leader, such as the *CFO of IT*, but is often distinct from this role, such as when the IT finance leader reports into the IT organization. Should be influential, able to drive organizational change and address resistance to *transparency*. Should be included in the office of the CIO or be part of the IT governance organization. Sometimes a vice president (VP) or, less commonly, a manager-level employee.

TBM SYSTEM

The enterprise software solution for: creating, supporting, and processing your *TBM model* (or models); extracting, transforming, and loading data; processing and delivering reports, metrics, dashboards, and analyses; enabling decision makers to interact with the data and reports; and providing security, including user authentication, role-based access controls, and the ability to redact sensitive information from reports.

TBM SYSTEM ADMINISTRATOR

Employee, contractor or *service provider* who manages the *TBM models* and data, builds reports, administers *TBM system* user accounts, and trains users. For most organizations, even large ones, it is not a full time job. Sometimes outsourced to the third-party provider who delivers the TBM system as a managed service. In some organizations, the same person as the *TBM analyst*.

TBM TAXONOMY

Classifies and organizes IT costs, units, and other metrics from disparate sources, assets, and services in a hierarchical manner and provides a common set of terms to describe them. Its hierarchy includes three views — finance, IT and business — supported by four main layers of objects: *cost pools* & sub-pools, *towers* & sub-towers, applications & services, and business units.

TECHNOLOGY BUSINESS MANAGEMENT (TBM)

A practical, applied set of disciplines and *value conversations* for improving the business outcomes enabled by the technology *portfolio*. Enables technology leaders and their *business partners* to collaborate on business-aligned decisions. Relies on *transparency* to provide a foundation for managing the supply of and *demand* for technology services and projects. Supports financial and performance tradeoffs for optimizing *run-the-business* spending and improving *change-the-business* investments.

TCO

See *total cost of ownership*.

TECHNOLOGY BUSINESS MODEL

The business management characteristics of a technology organization such as how it is funded, the nature of *transparency* it provides to its *business partner*s, what roles it relies upon for business alignment, and what its *service portfolio* looks like (if it has one). Four archetypical *technology business model*s are described in this book: *expense center*, *service provider*, *value partner*, and *business driver*.

TOTAL COST

See *total cost of ownership (TCO)*.

TOTAL COST OF OWNERSHIP (TCO)

All expenditures and expenses to acquire, build and/or develop a technology, facility, service or other asset, plus those to support, maintain and operate it over time. Includes both *capital expenditures* and *operating expenses*. Often used synonymously with *total cost*.

TOWER

Categories that reside at the middle layer of the hierarchical *TBM taxonomy* (and corresponding *TBM model*), above *cost pools* in the Finance layer. Includes the technology functions acquired, supported and/or delivered by IT in order to deliver and support services. Includes applications (including *application* development, support & operations, quality assurance, etc.), data centers, distributed computing, mainframe, storage, network, databases, communication, and end user technologies. Also includes elements like IT management, security and compliance, service desk, project management (PMO), and other categories of overhead.

TRANSFORM-THE-BUSINESS (TTB)

Refers to spending and investments used to improve the long-term competitiveness and growth opportunities of the company. Often implies game-changing investments, in that they often allow the business to employ revolutionary sourcing models, tap into new markets, dramatically improve efficiency or rapidly launch new and significantly different products and services.

May include both operating and *capital expenditures*. Operating expenditures that qualify often include project spending that occurs before capitalization begins and additional operational resources that are categorized as *transform-the-business*. Capital expenditures that qualify include the purchases and/or development of new assets that directly enable business transformation.

A subset within *change-the-business* spending.

TRANSPARENCY

The essential discipline of putting facts about cost, consumption, utilization, capacity and other aspects of your services and resources into meaningful contexts for decision makers. Its exact nature depends on each decision maker because their decision-making needs vary. Allows CIOs and IT leaders to exploit the forces of supply and *demand*, empower their people to make value-based decisions, and accelerate initiatives that are important to the business.

UNIT COST

The *total cost* of a technology, service or other asset divided by the number of units provided, supported or delivered. May be based on budgeted, planned or actual costs and planned or actual units. Useful as a measure to evaluate cost fluctuations over time and the relationship between volumes and total cost.

VALUE CONSERVATION

An interaction between technology decision makers internally and/or with *business partner*s that focuses on the tradeoffs between cost, consumption, capacity, performance, features, benefits, and risk, in the pursuit of better business outcomes. Four types of value conversations enabled by TBM are described in the book: *cost for performance, business-aligned portfolio, investment in innovation* and *enterprise agility*.

VALUE PARTNER

One of the four *technology business model archetypes*. Responsible for delivering bespoke business applications or integrated solutions. Must know not only how to serve their *business partners*, but also know how to collaborate closely with them on innovating business capabilities, distinguishing the business from the competition, lowering business costs, and so on.

VARIABLE COSTS

A cost that varies in concert with the level of output, i.e., is strongly correlated with the units of services delivered. Supports financial agility because it goes down when business volumes decline, so business leaders can change their costs by changing their consumption. *Service providers*, such as *IaaS* or *SaaS* companies, often convert their *fixed costs* into *variable costs* for their customers by assuming the risk of *demand* fluctuations.